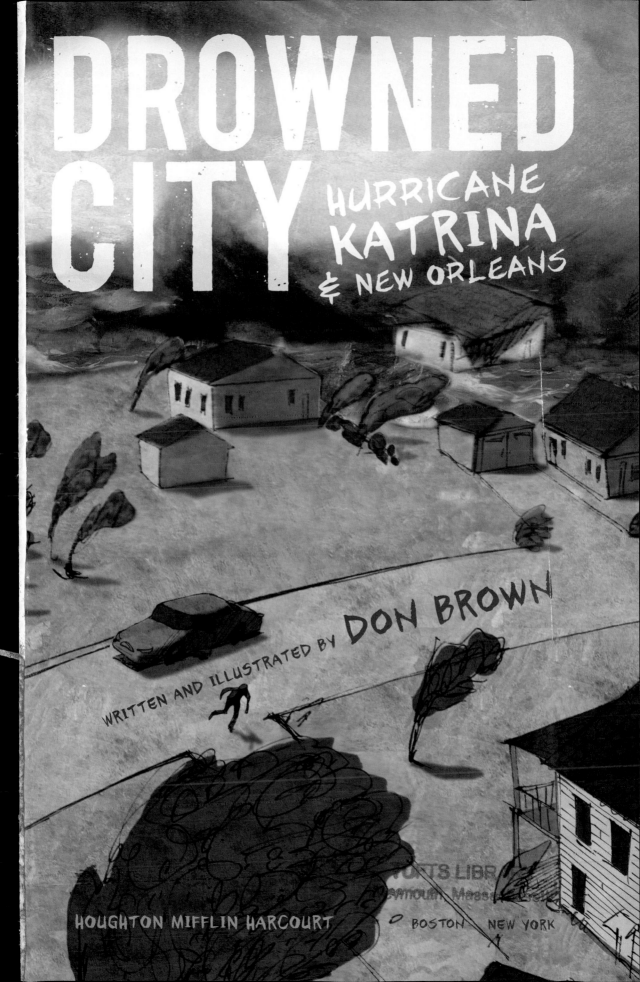

DROWNED CITY

CITY HURRICANE KATRINA & NEW ORLEANS

WRITTEN AND ILLUSTRATED BY DON BROWN

HOUGHTON MIFFLIN HARCOURT   BOSTON   NEW YORK

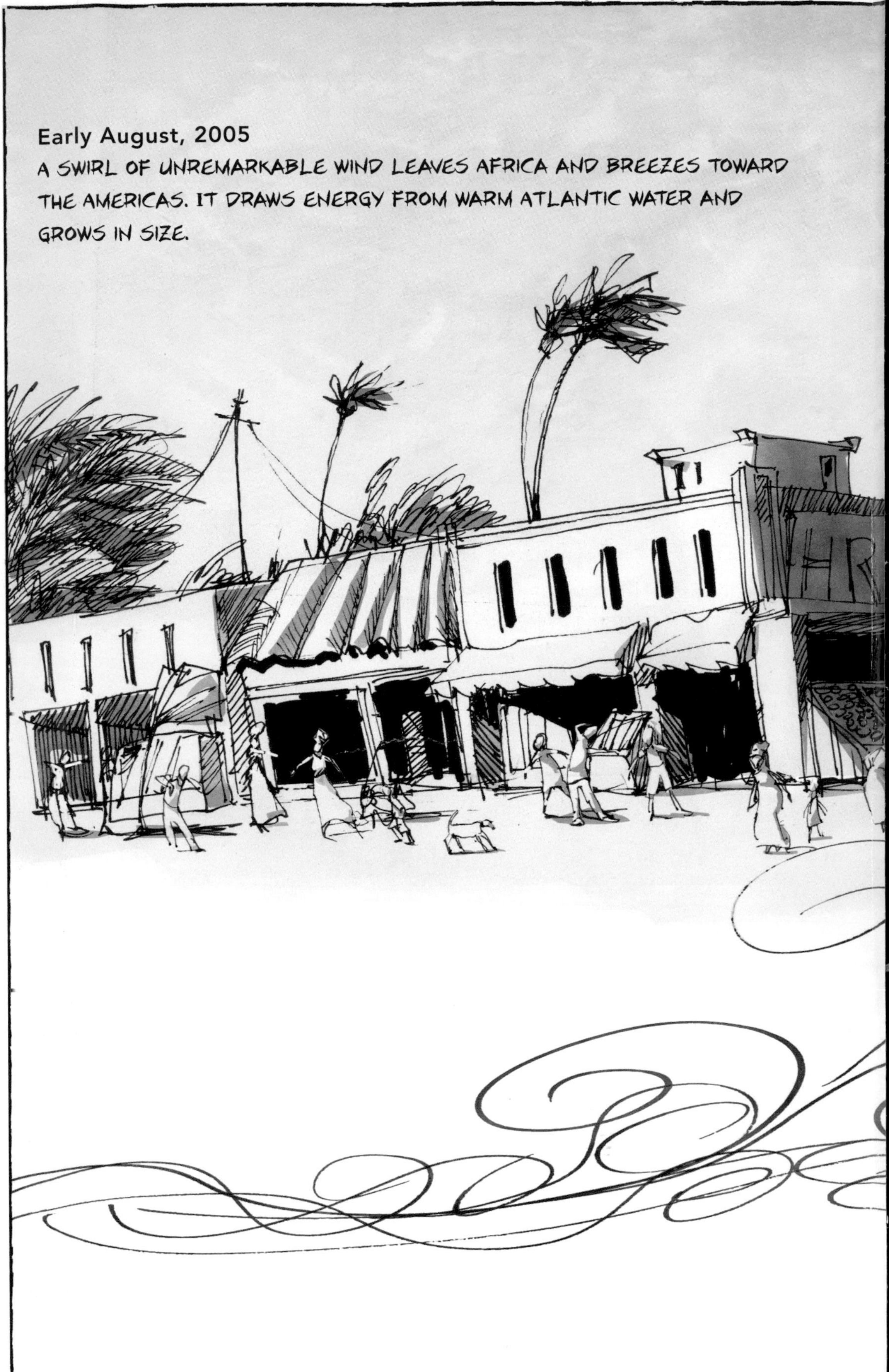
Early August, 2005
A SWIRL OF UNREMARKABLE WIND LEAVES AFRICA AND BREEZES TOWARD THE AMERICAS. IT DRAWS ENERGY FROM WARM ATLANTIC WATER AND GROWS IN SIZE.

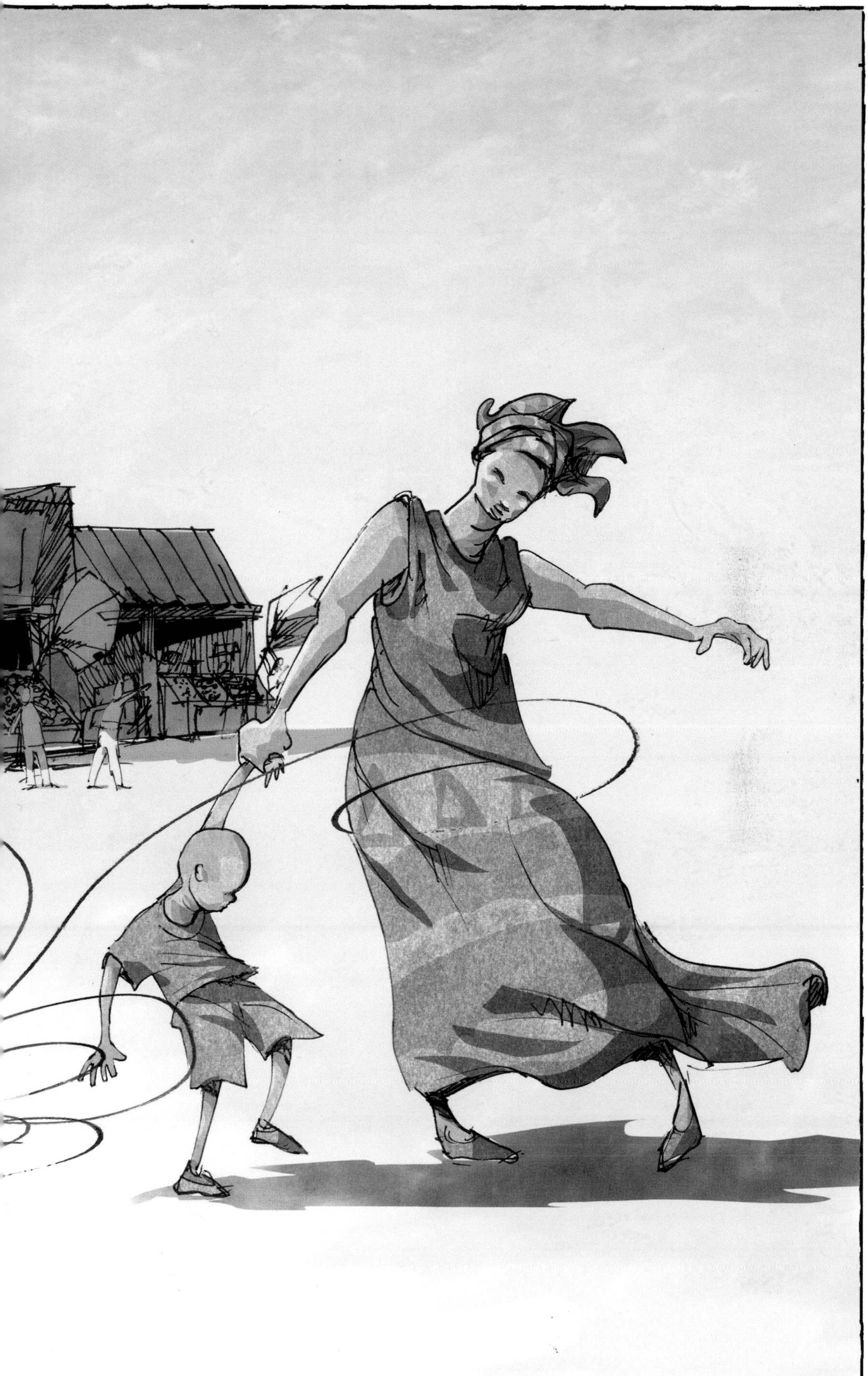

FROM A SMUDGE OF FOUL WEATHER IT BECOMES A NASTY TROPICAL STORM, AND THEN ERUPTS INTO A VICIOUS HURRICANE WITH HOWLING WINDS, PIN-WHEELING COUNTERCLOCKWISE. AS IT DOES WITH ALL BIG STORMS, THE NATIONAL HURRICANE CENTER IN MIAMI, FLORIDA, ASSIGNS IT A NAME: KATRINA.

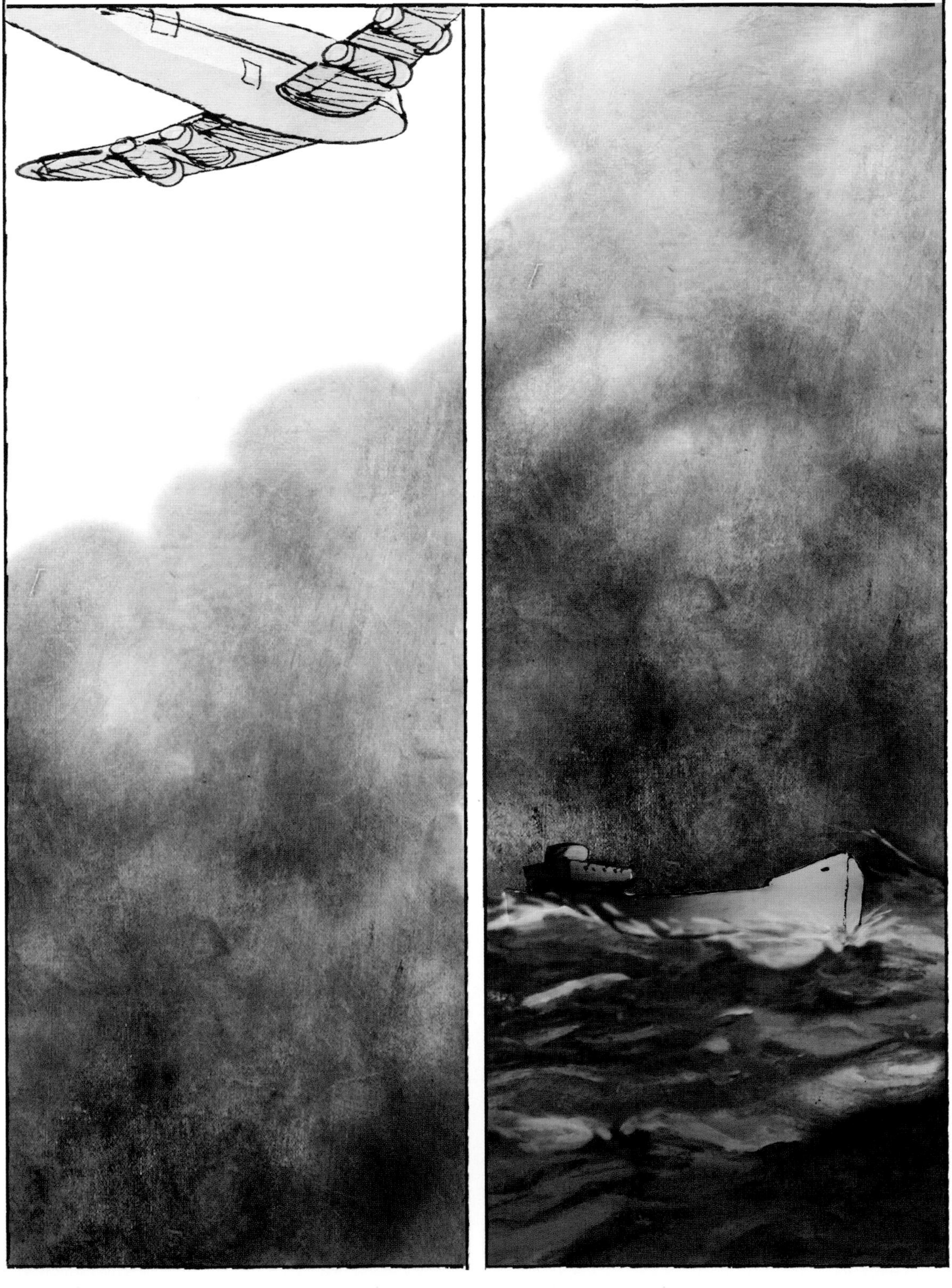

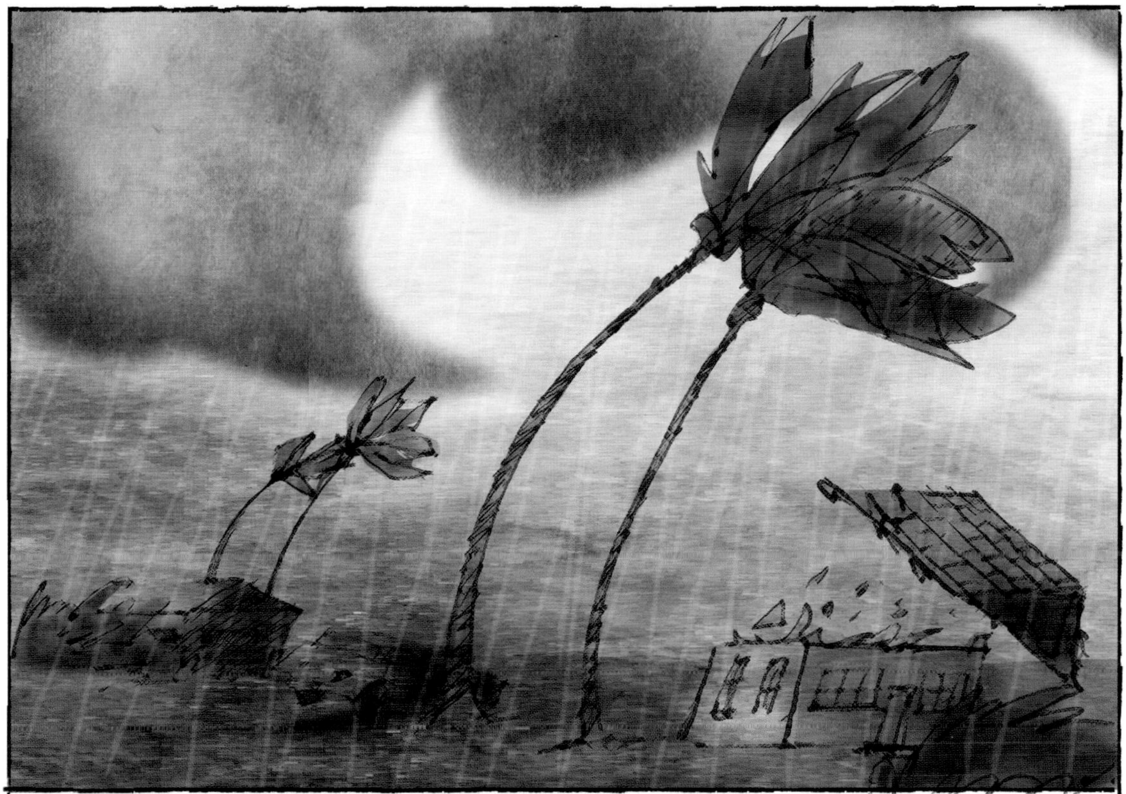

HURRICANE KATRINA SLICES ACROSS FLORIDA. ALTHOUGH IT IS ONLY A CATEGORY 1 HURRICANE—THE LEAST STRONG—KATRINA KILLS SIX PEOPLE, LEAVES A HALF MILLION WITHOUT POWER, AND DRENCHES ITS PATH WITH A FOOT AND A HALF OF WATER.

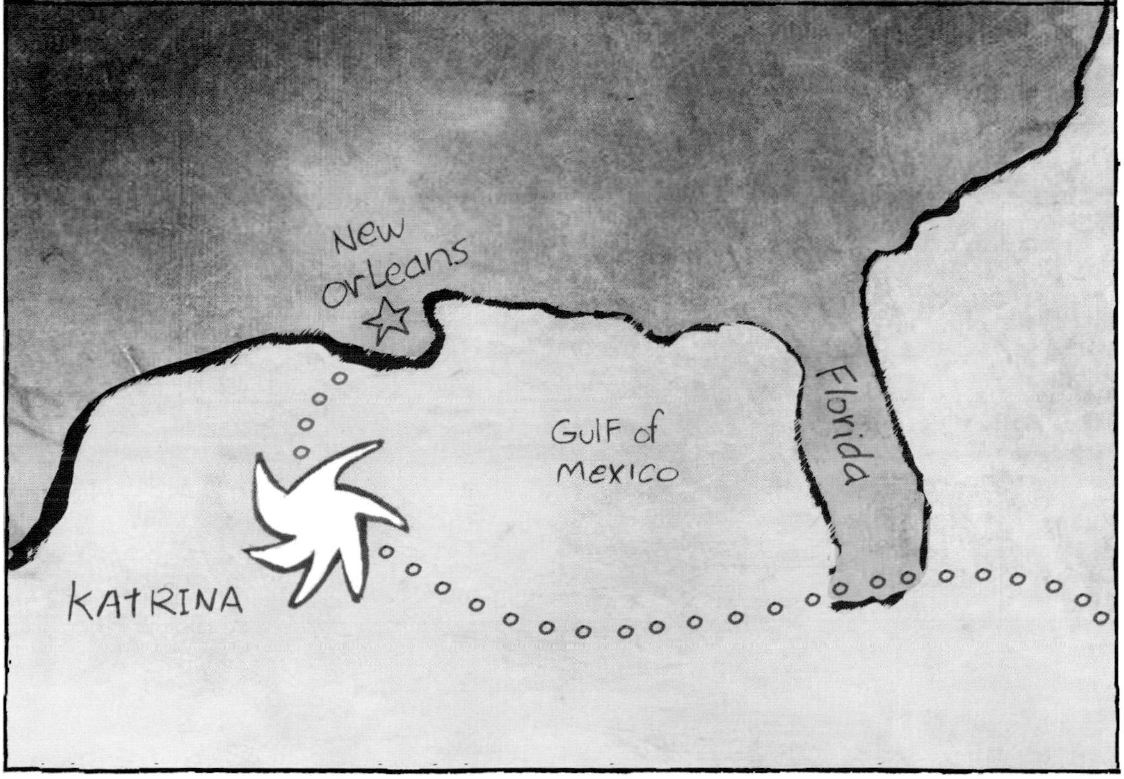
New Orleans
Gulf of Mexico
Florida
KATRINA

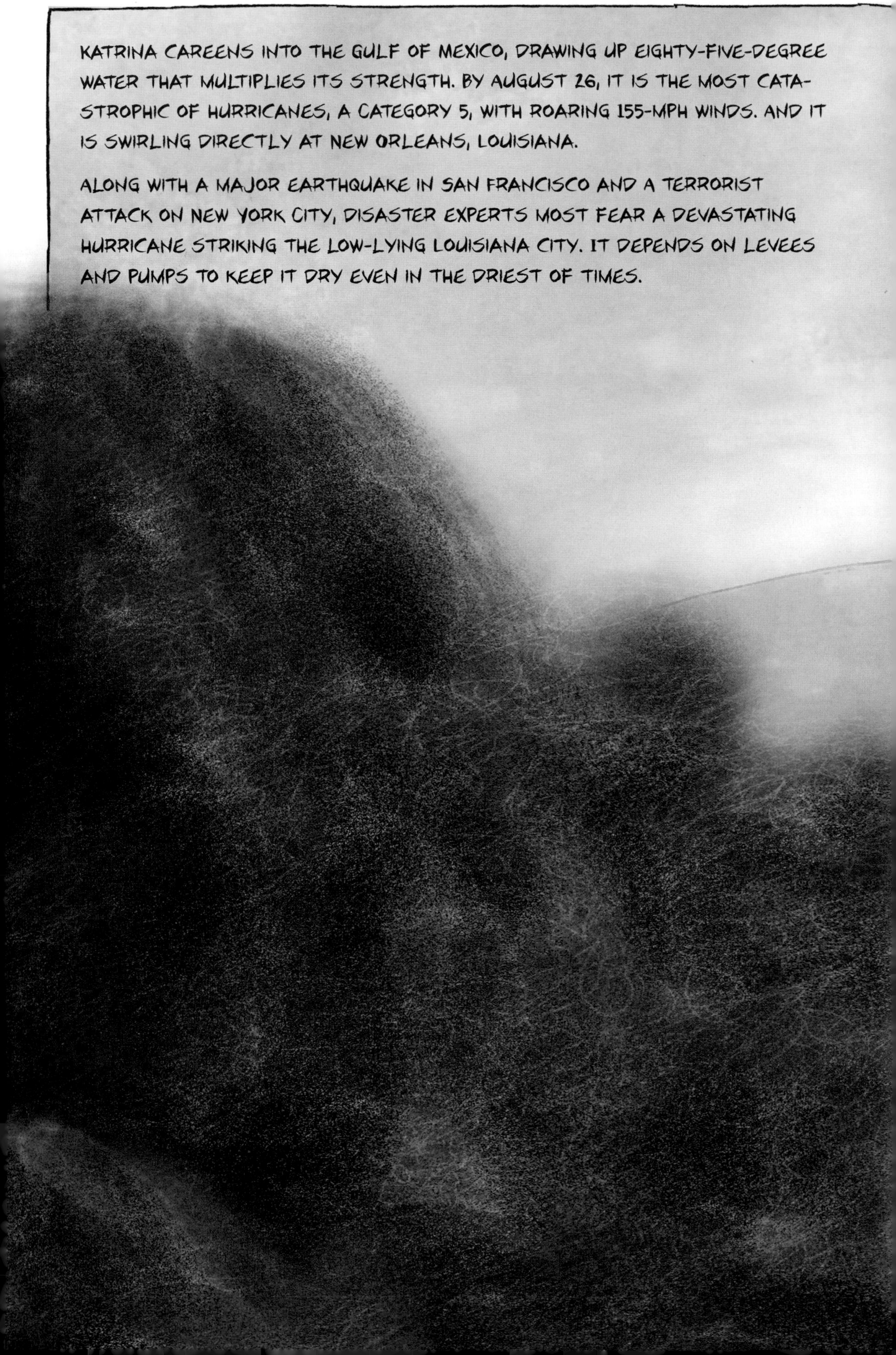
KATRINA CAREENS INTO THE GULF OF MEXICO, DRAWING UP EIGHTY-FIVE-DEGREE WATER THAT MULTIPLIES ITS STRENGTH. BY AUGUST 26, IT IS THE MOST CATASTROPHIC OF HURRICANES, A CATEGORY 5, WITH ROARING 155-MPH WINDS. AND IT IS SWIRLING DIRECTLY AT NEW ORLEANS, LOUISIANA.
ALONG WITH A MAJOR EARTHQUAKE IN SAN FRANCISCO AND A TERRORIST ATTACK ON NEW YORK CITY, DISASTER EXPERTS MOST FEAR A DEVASTATING HURRICANE STRIKING THE LOW-LYING LOUISIANA CITY. IT DEPENDS ON LEVEES AND PUMPS TO KEEP IT DRY EVEN IN THE DRIEST OF TIMES.

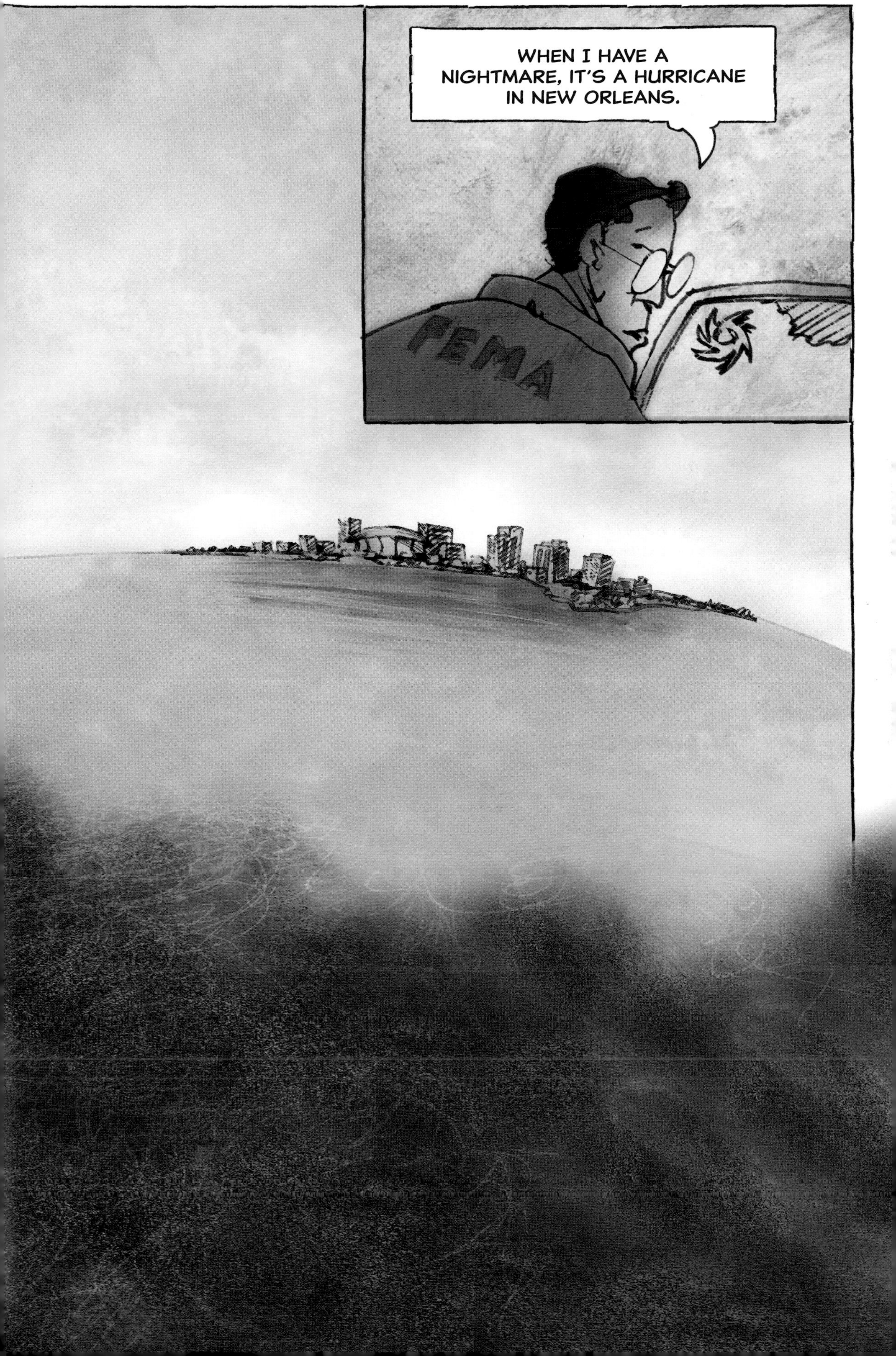
WHEN I HAVE A NIGHTMARE, IT'S A HURRICANE IN NEW ORLEANS.
FEMA

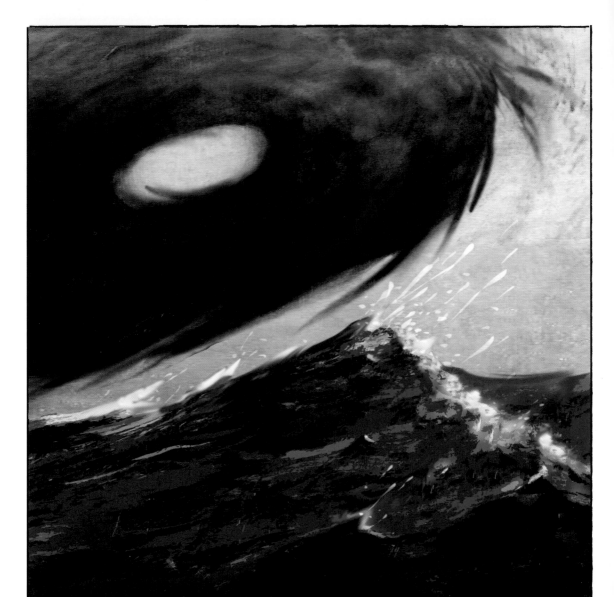

ON THE MORNING OF AUGUST 26, THE NATIONAL WEATHER SERVICE
ANNOUNCES THAT KATRINA WILL HIT NEW ORLEANS IN TWENTY-FOUR
HOURS.

AS IT CROSSES THE GULF OF MEXICO, THE WHIRLING STORM CREATES
AN AIR PRESSURE IN ITS CENTER, OR EYE, THAT LIFTS THE OCEAN'S
SURFACE INTO A KIND OF MASSIVE BUBBLE. WHEN THIS BUBBLE IS
COUPLED WITH THE WATER DRIVEN AHEAD OF IT BY KATRINA'S HIGH
WINDS, NEW ORLEANS FACES A SURGE OF HIGH WATER THAT WILL
BE TWENTY-FIVE FEET ABOVE NORMAL.

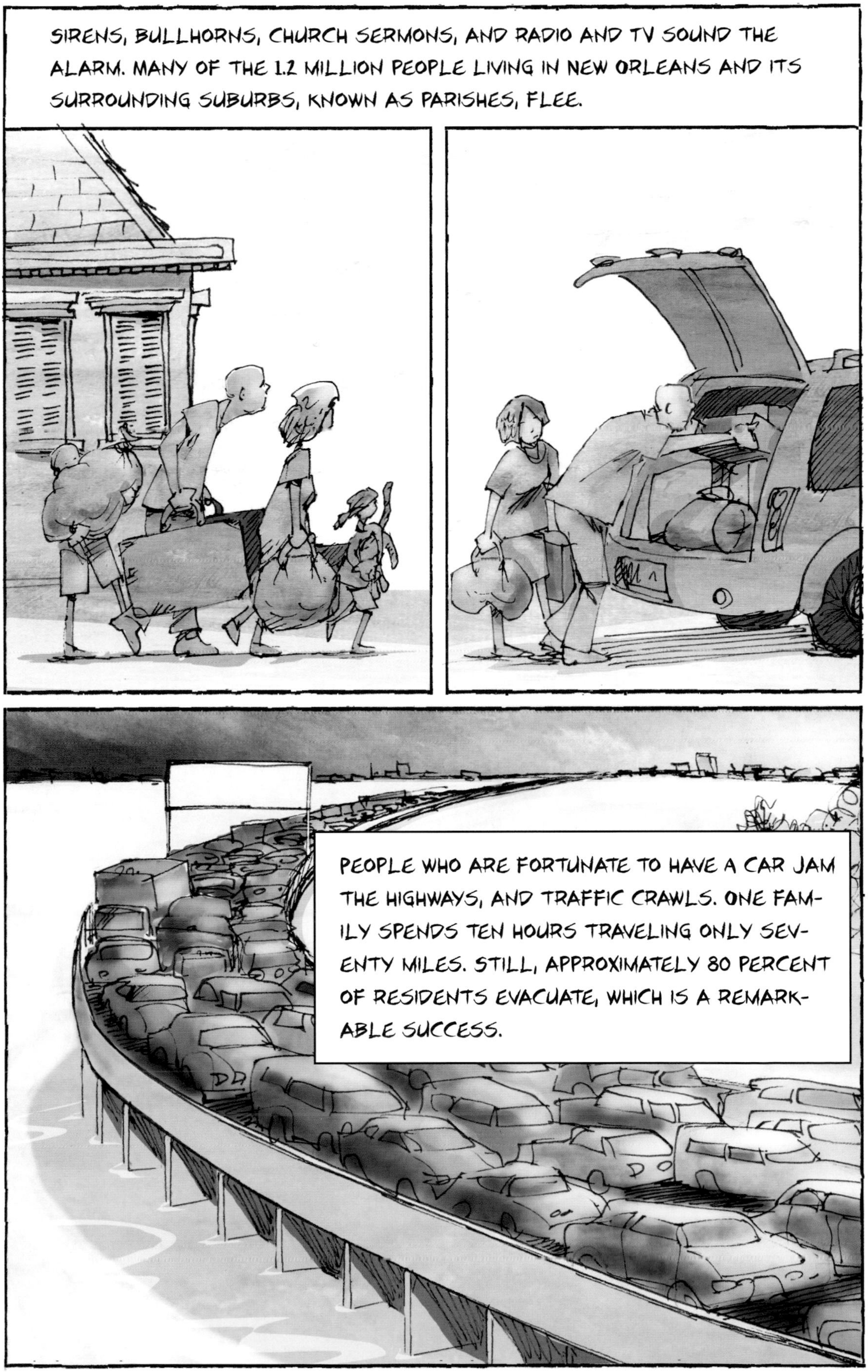
SIRENS, BULLHORNS, CHURCH SERMONS, AND RADIO AND TV SOUND THE ALARM. MANY OF THE 1.2 MILLION PEOPLE LIVING IN NEW ORLEANS AND ITS SURROUNDING SUBURBS, KNOWN AS PARISHES, FLEE.
PEOPLE WHO ARE FORTUNATE TO HAVE A CAR JAM THE HIGHWAYS, AND TRAFFIC CRAWLS. ONE FAMILY SPENDS TEN HOURS TRAVELING ONLY SEVENTY MILES. STILL, APPROXIMATELY 80 PERCENT OF RESIDENTS EVACUATE, WHICH IS A REMARKABLE SUCCESS.

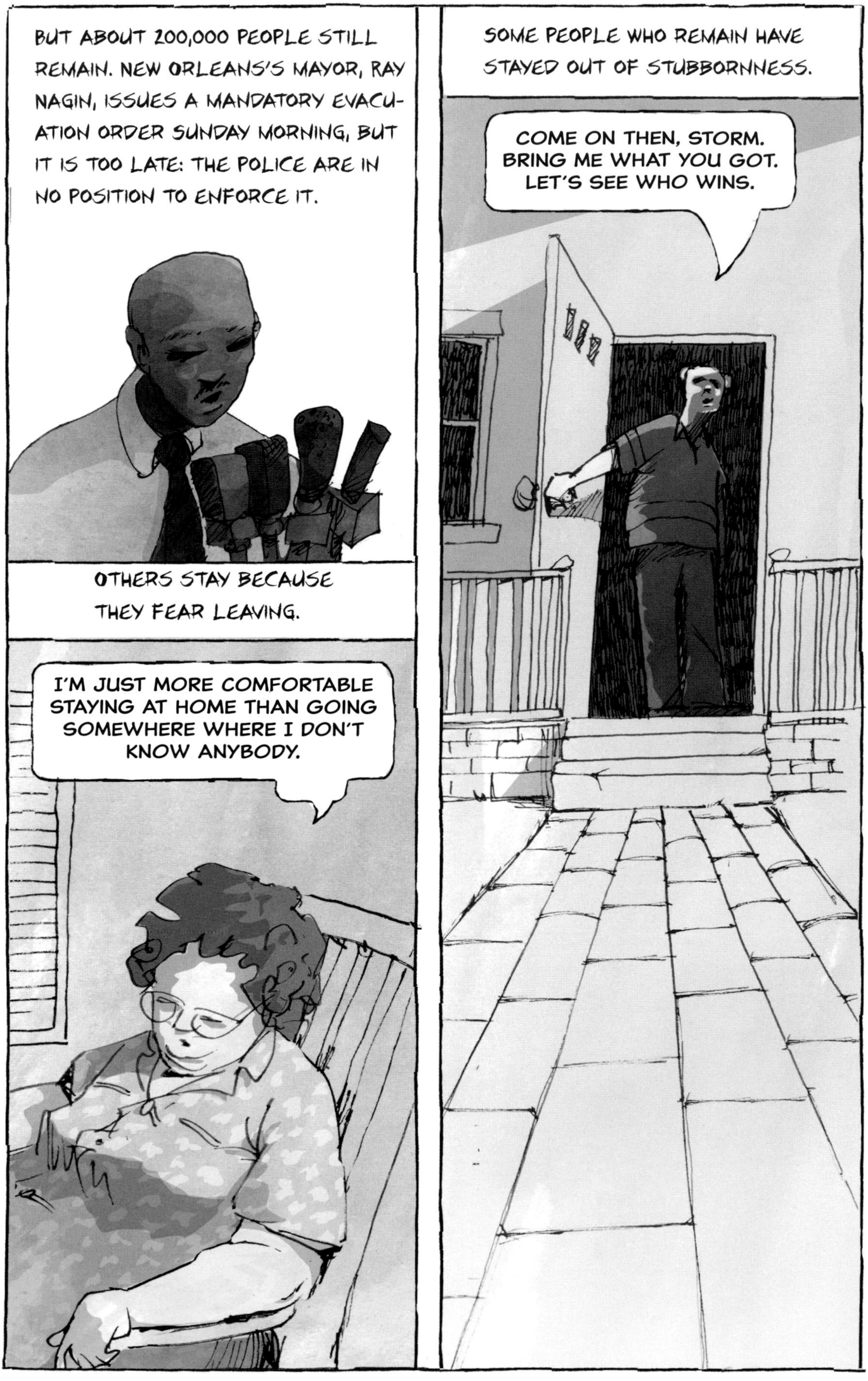
BUT ABOUT 200,000 PEOPLE STILL REMAIN. NEW ORLEANS'S MAYOR, RAY NAGIN, ISSUES A MANDATORY EVACUATION ORDER SUNDAY MORNING, BUT IT IS TOO LATE: THE POLICE ARE IN NO POSITION TO ENFORCE IT.
OTHERS STAY BECAUSE THEY FEAR LEAVING.
I'M JUST MORE COMFORTABLE STAYING AT HOME THAN GOING SOMEWHERE WHERE I DON'T KNOW ANYBODY.
SOME PEOPLE WHO REMAIN HAVE STAYED OUT OF STUBBORNNESS.
COME ON THEN, STORM. BRING ME WHAT YOU GOT. LET'S SEE WHO WINS.

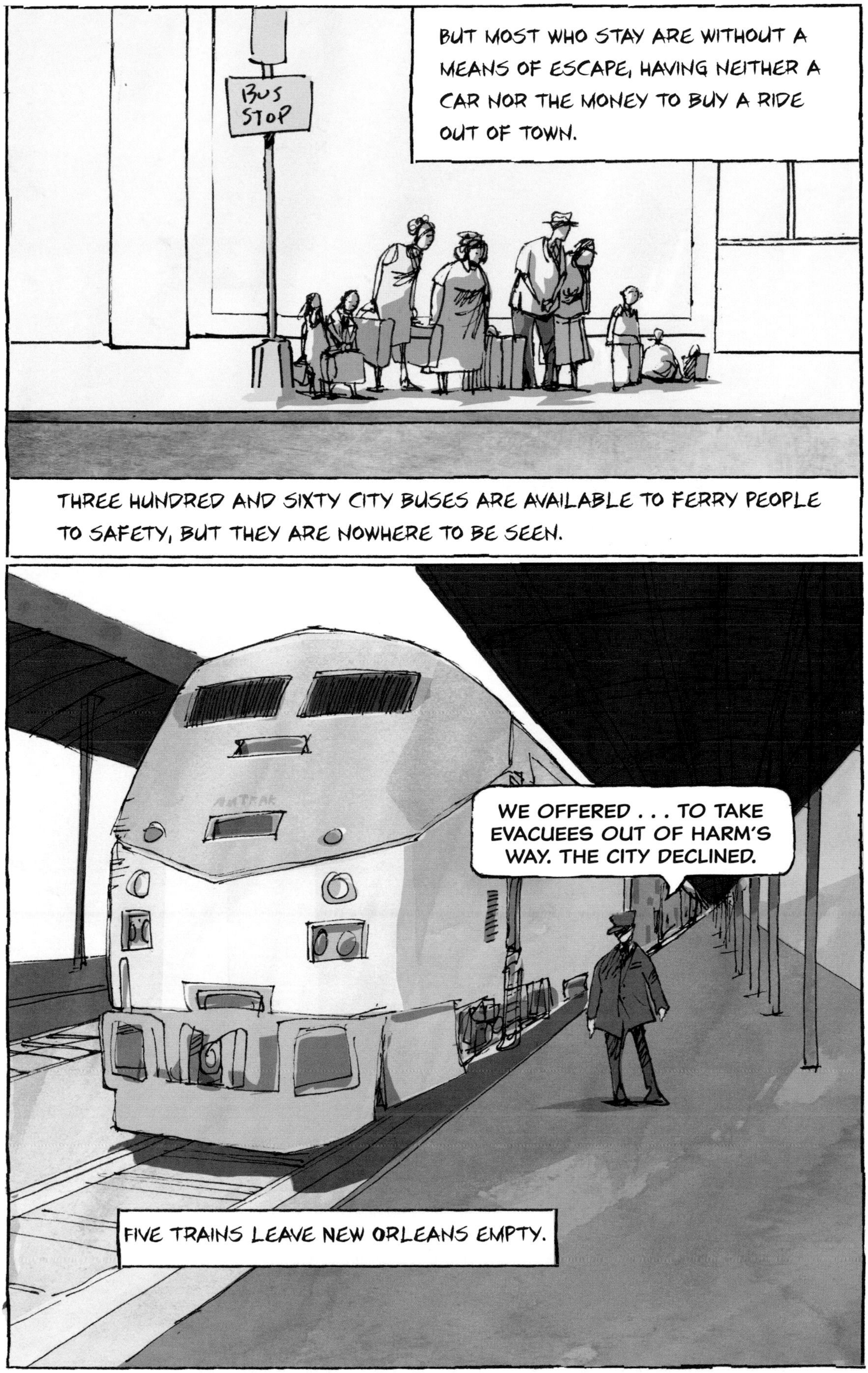
BUT MOST WHO STAY ARE WITHOUT A MEANS OF ESCAPE, HAVING NEITHER A CAR NOR THE MONEY TO BUY A RIDE OUT OF TOWN.
BUS STOP
THREE HUNDRED AND SIXTY CITY BUSES ARE AVAILABLE TO FERRY PEOPLE TO SAFETY, BUT THEY ARE NOWHERE TO BE SEEN.
WE OFFERED . . . TO TAKE EVACUEES OUT OF HARM'S WAY. THE CITY DECLINED.
FIVE TRAINS LEAVE NEW ORLEANS EMPTY.

Monday, August 29

THE HURRICANE'S STRENGTH SLIPS FROM CATEGORY 5 TO CATEGORY 3. BUT IT IS STILL A MONSTER, MEASURING FOUR HUNDRED MILES ACROSS, WITH 121-MPH WINDS. AT THE LAST MOMENT, KATRINA "WOBBLES" AND STEERS A BIT EAST OF NEW ORLEANS, SPARING THE CITY A DIRECT HIT.

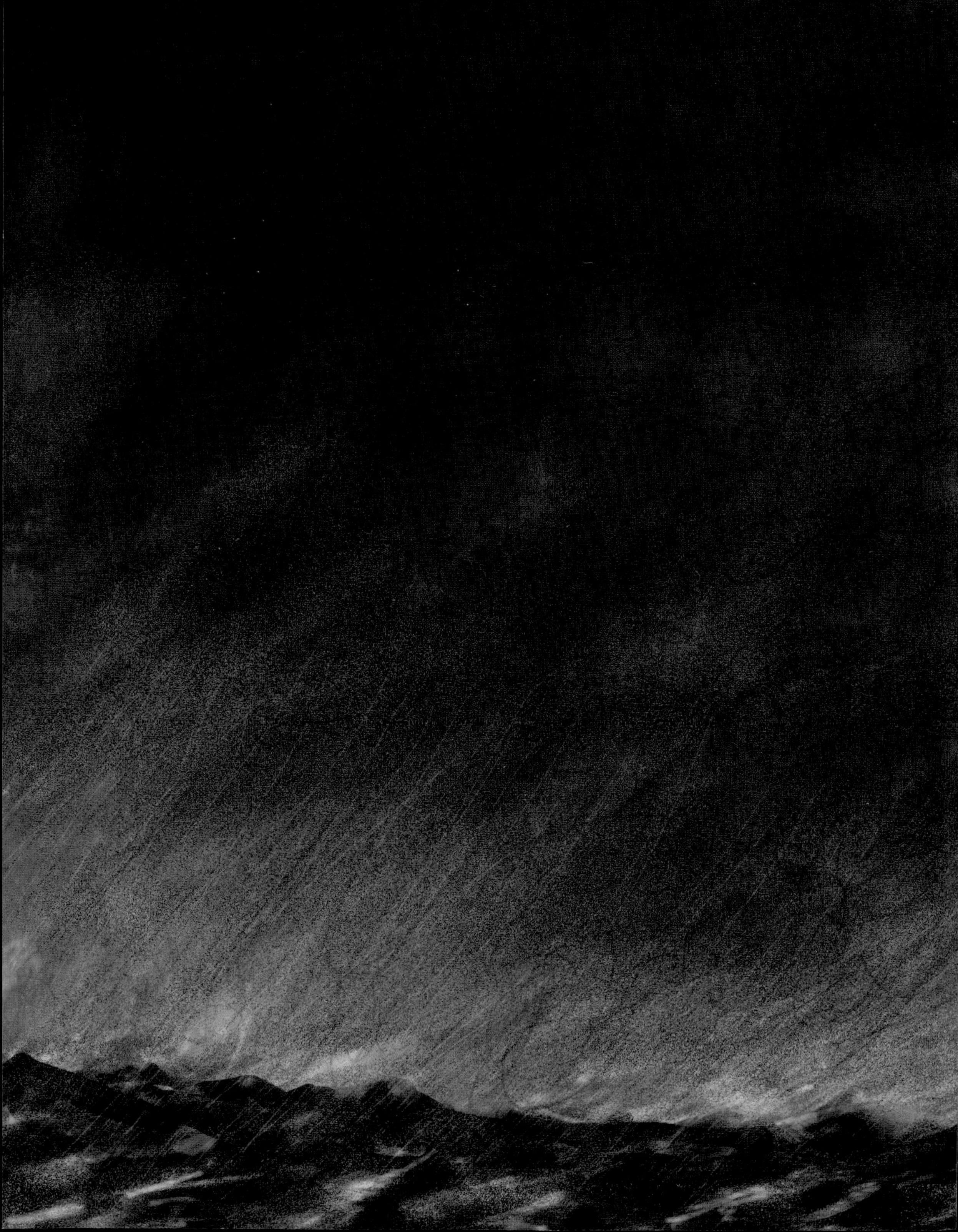

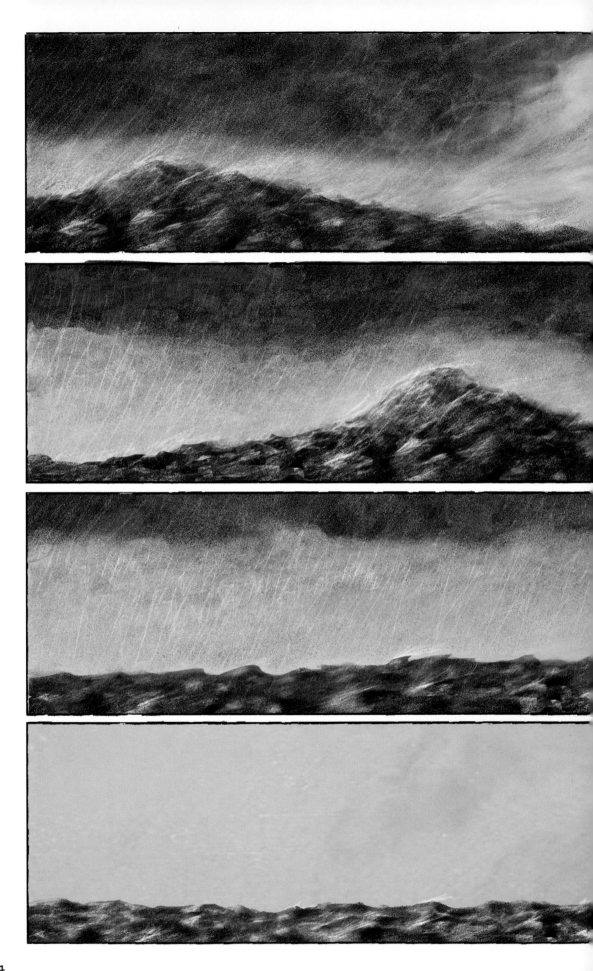

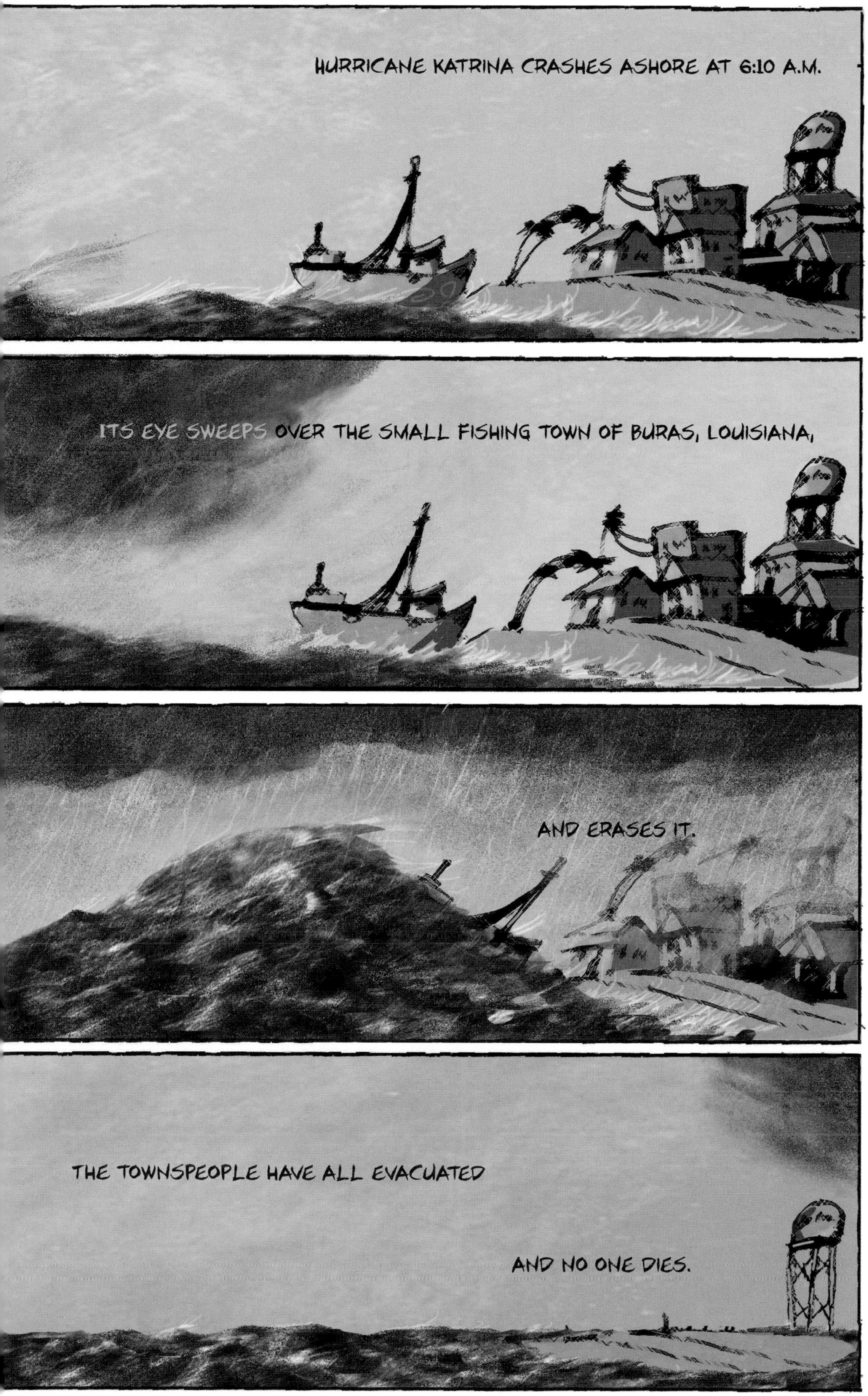
HURRICANE KATRINA CRASHES ASHORE AT 6:10 A.M.
ITS EYE SWEEPS OVER THE SMALL FISHING TOWN OF BURAS, LOUISIANA,
AND ERASES IT.
THE TOWNSPEOPLE HAVE ALL EVACUATED
AND NO ONE DIES.

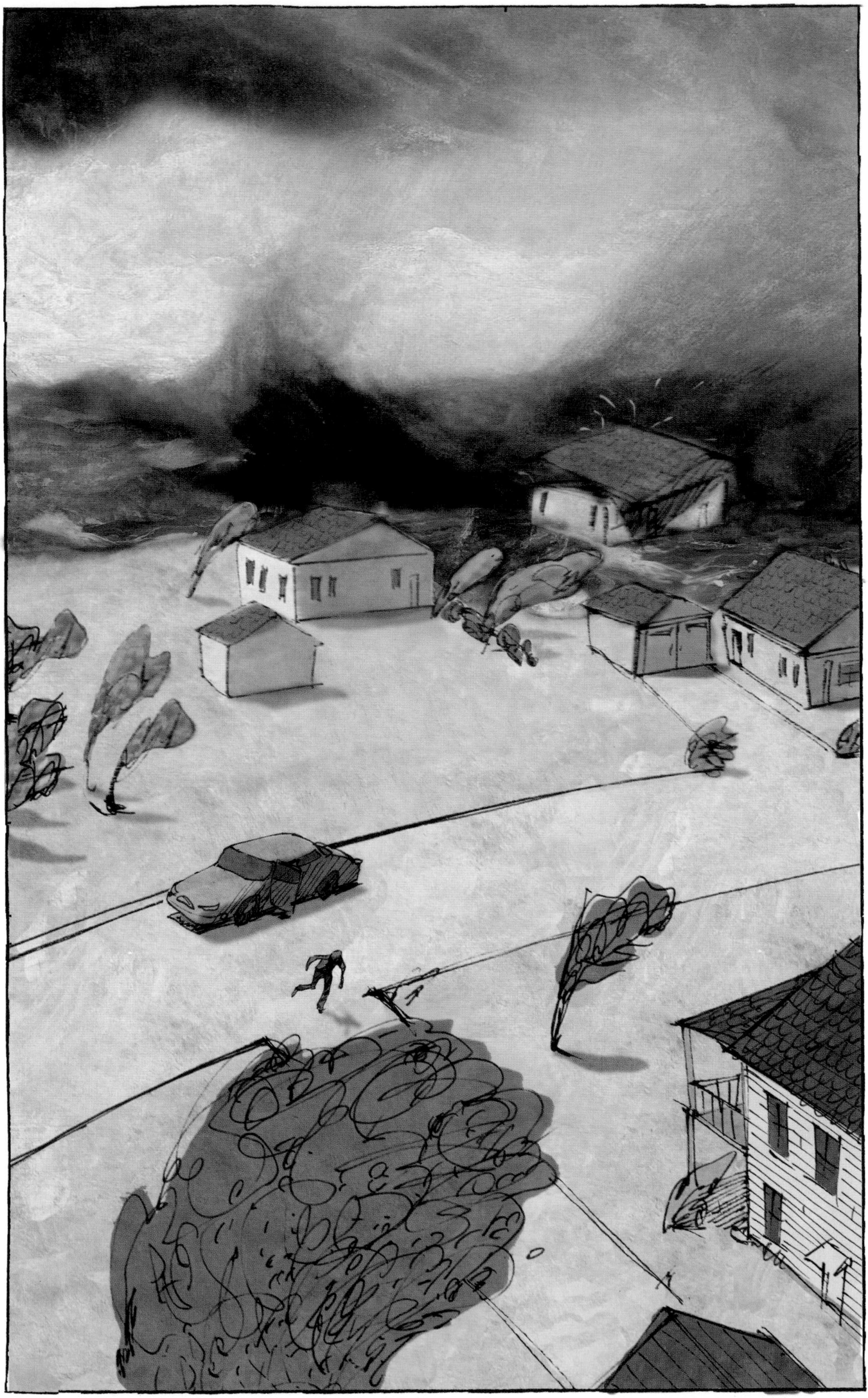

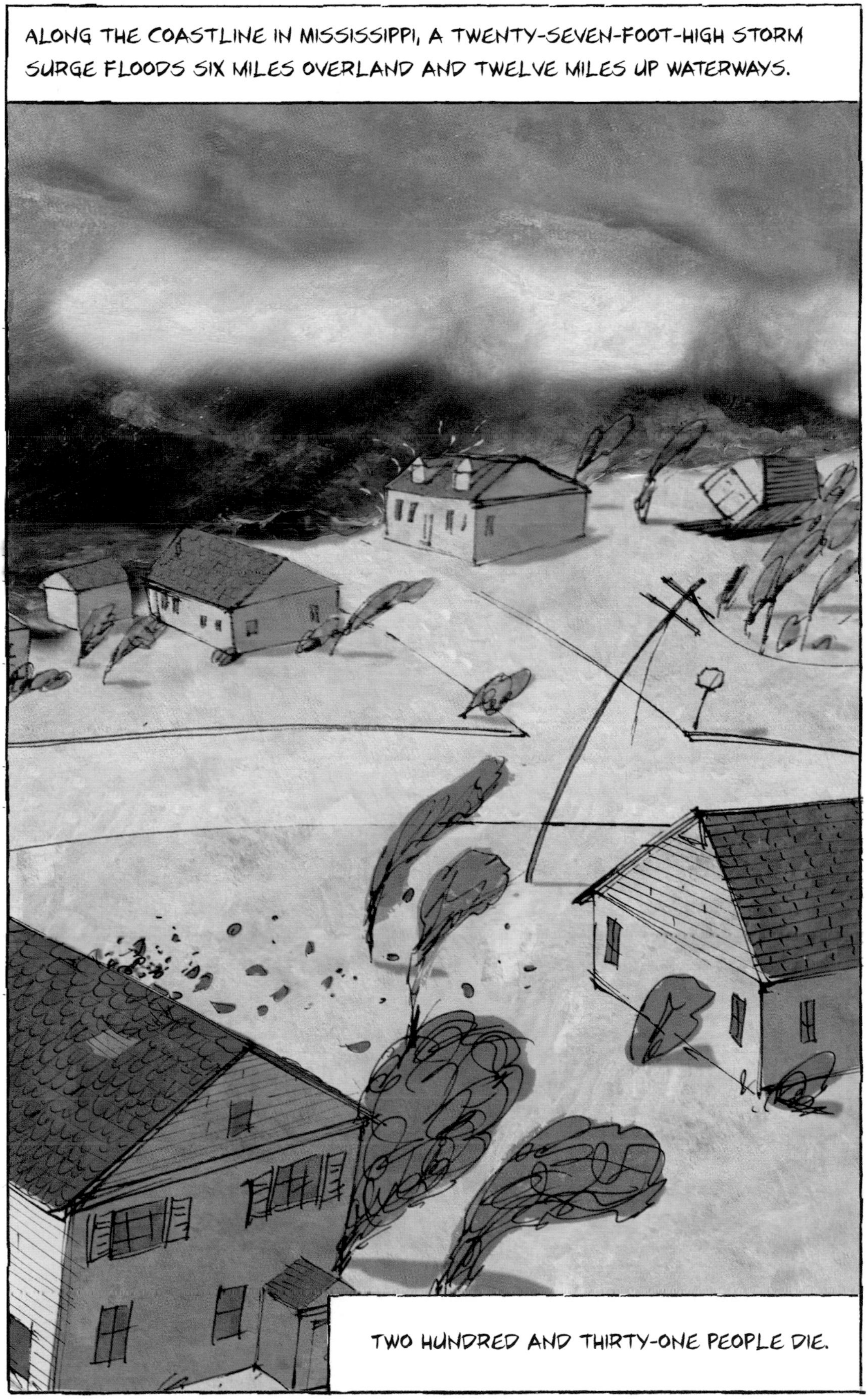
ALONG THE COASTLINE IN MISSISSIPPI, A TWENTY-SEVEN-FOOT-HIGH STORM SURGE FLOODS SIX MILES OVERLAND AND TWELVE MILES UP WATERWAYS.
TWO HUNDRED AND THIRTY-ONE PEOPLE DIE.

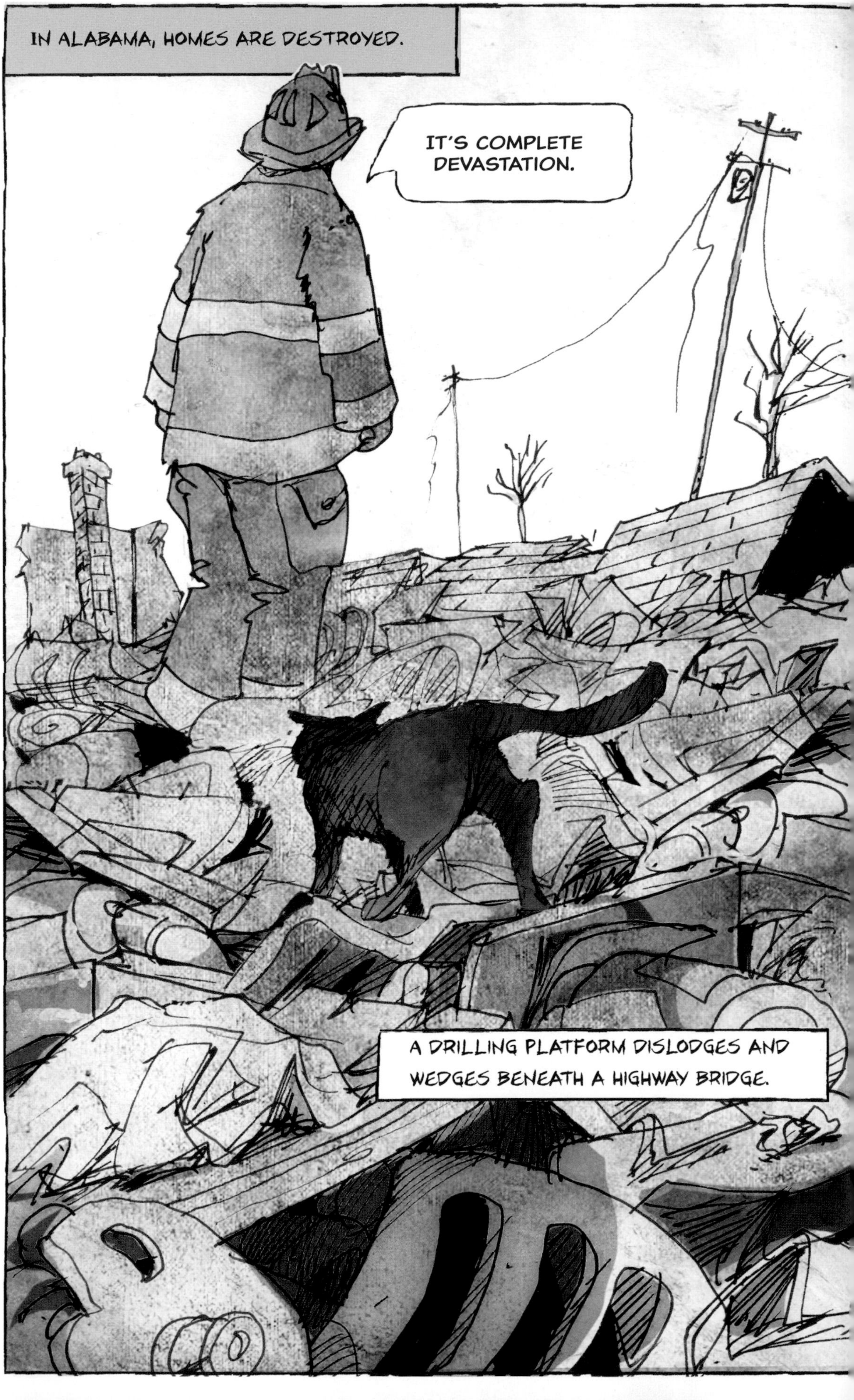
IN ALABAMA, HOMES ARE DESTROYED.
IT'S COMPLETE DEVASTATION.
A DRILLING PLATFORM DISLODGES AND WEDGES BENEATH A HIGHWAY BRIDGE.

IN NEW ORLEANS, FEROCIOUS WINDS BLOW THE GLASS OUT OF SKYSCRAPER WINDOWS, SUCKING THE CONTENTS OF THEIR ROOMS INTO THE SKY.

THE HURRICANE'S STORM SURGE FORCES WATER UP THE MISSISSIPPI RIVER, THROUGH CANALS AND WATERWAYS, AND INTO LAKE PONTCHARTRAIN.

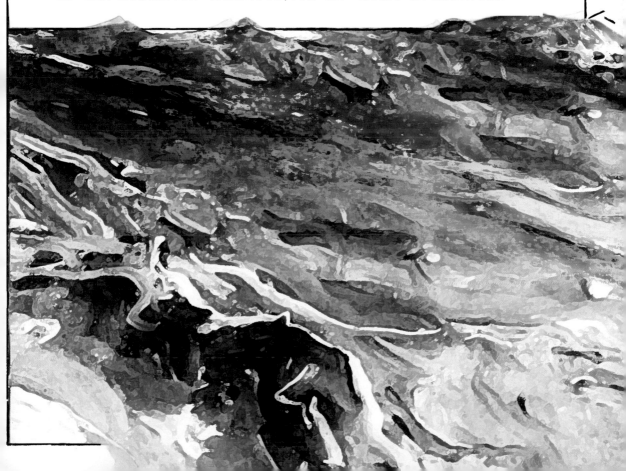

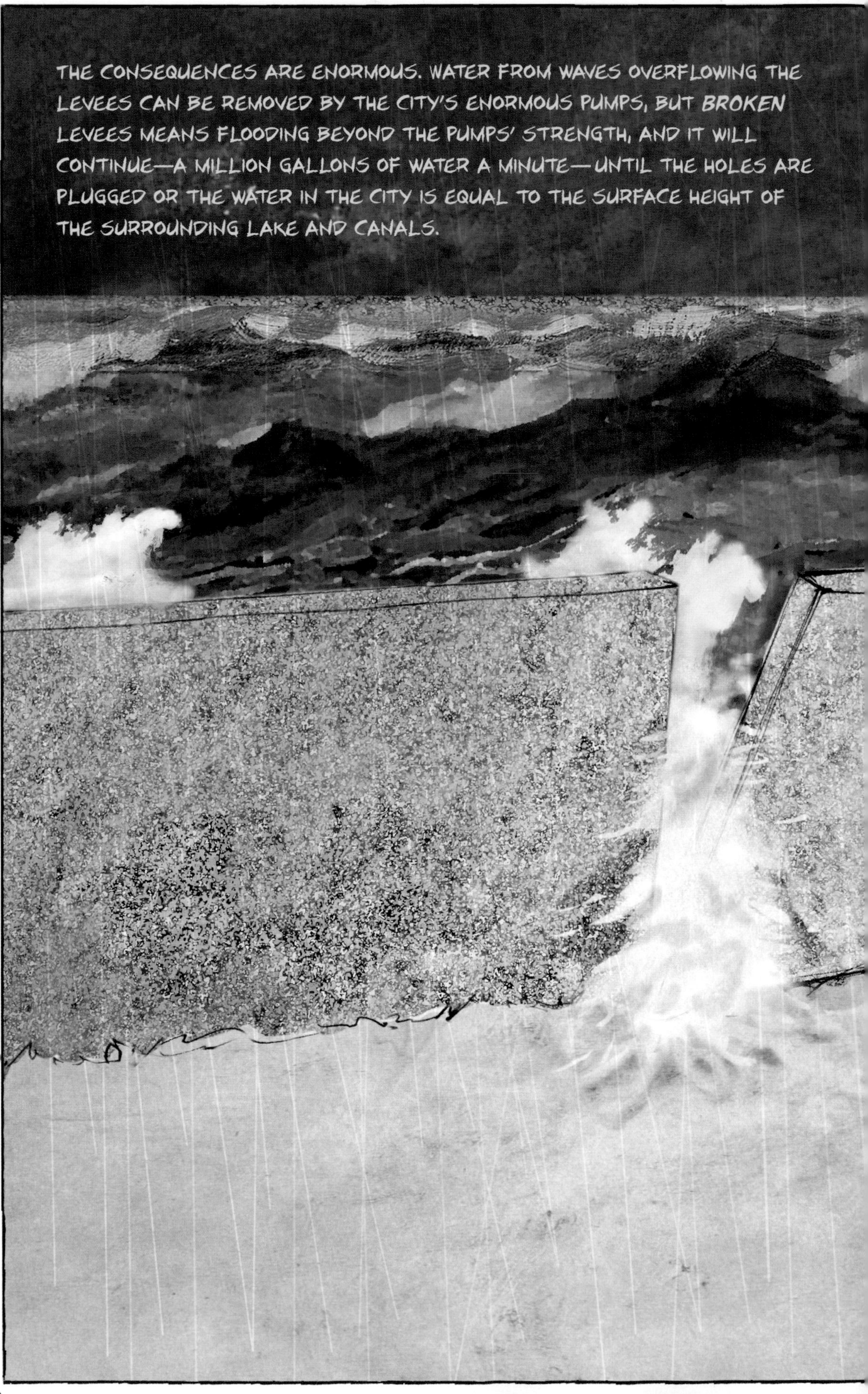
THE CONSEQUENCES ARE ENORMOUS. WATER FROM WAVES OVERFLOWING THE LEVEES CAN BE REMOVED BY THE CITY'S ENORMOUS PUMPS, BUT *BROKEN* LEVEES MEANS FLOODING BEYOND THE PUMPS' STRENGTH, AND IT WILL CONTINUE—A MILLION GALLONS OF WATER A MINUTE—UNTIL THE HOLES ARE PLUGGED OR THE WATER IN THE CITY IS EQUAL TO THE SURFACE HEIGHT OF THE SURROUNDING LAKE AND CANALS.

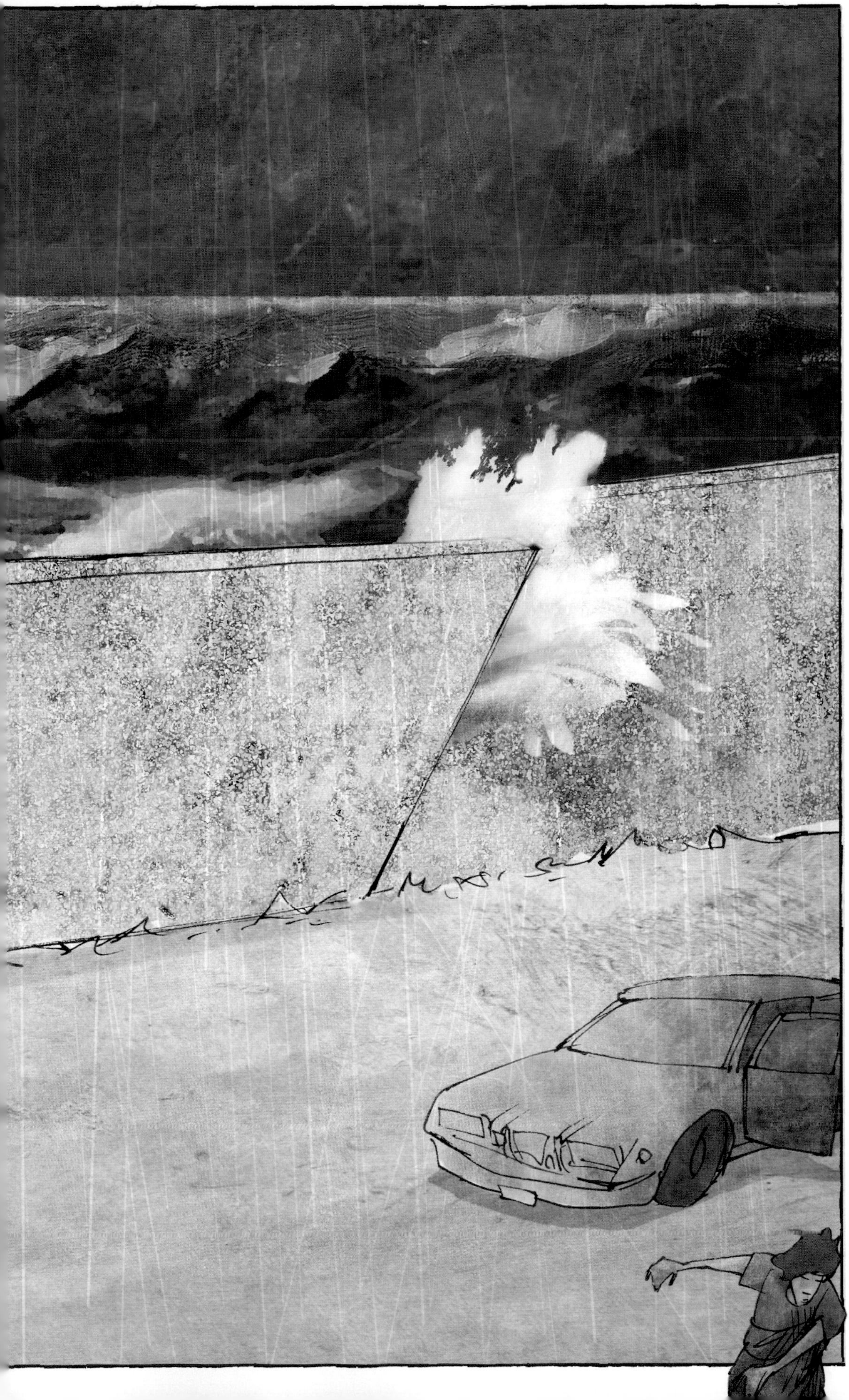

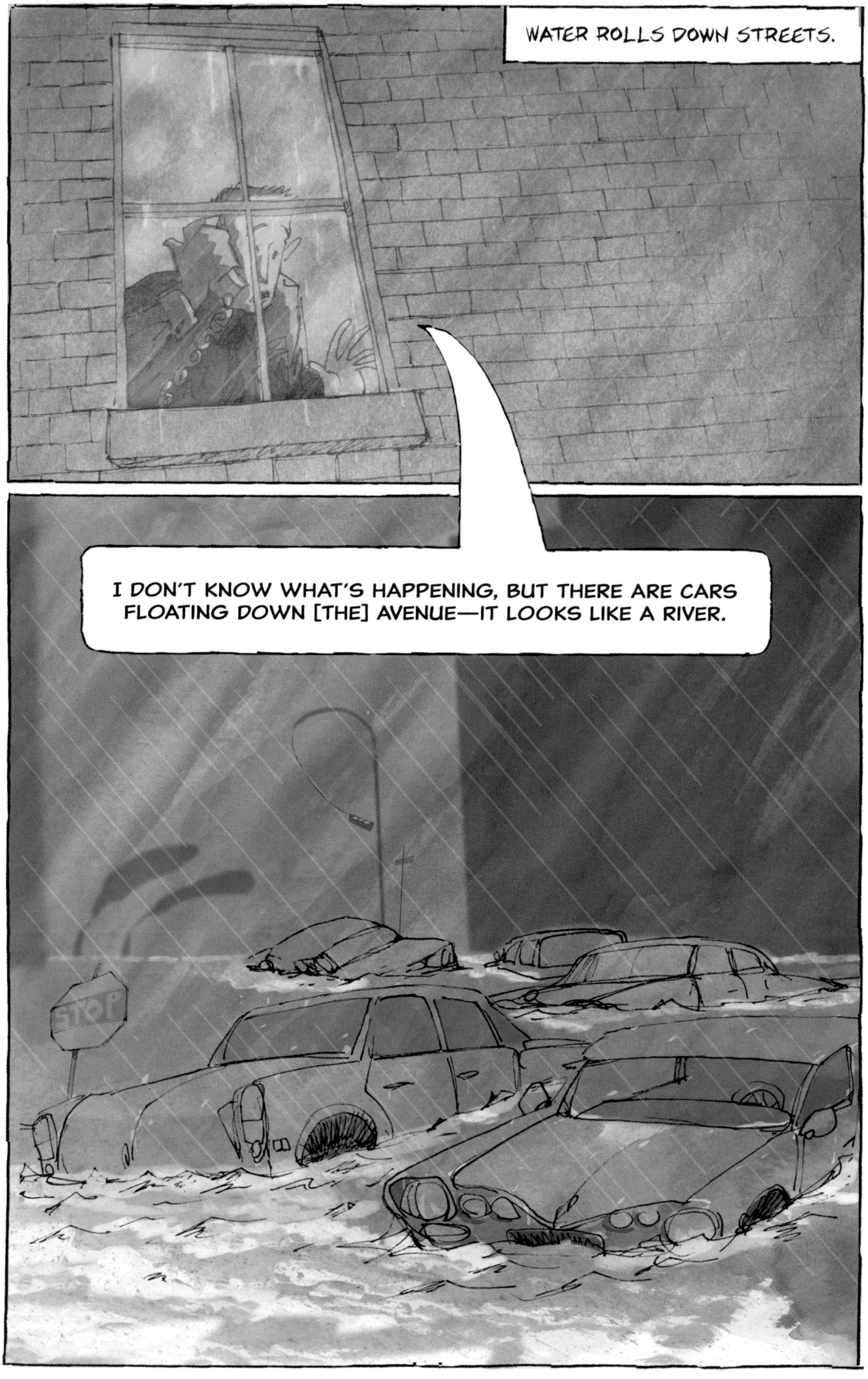
WATER ROLLS DOWN STREETS.
I DON'T KNOW WHAT'S HAPPENING, BUT THERE ARE CARS FLOATING DOWN [THE] AVENUE—IT LOOKS LIKE A RIVER.
STOP

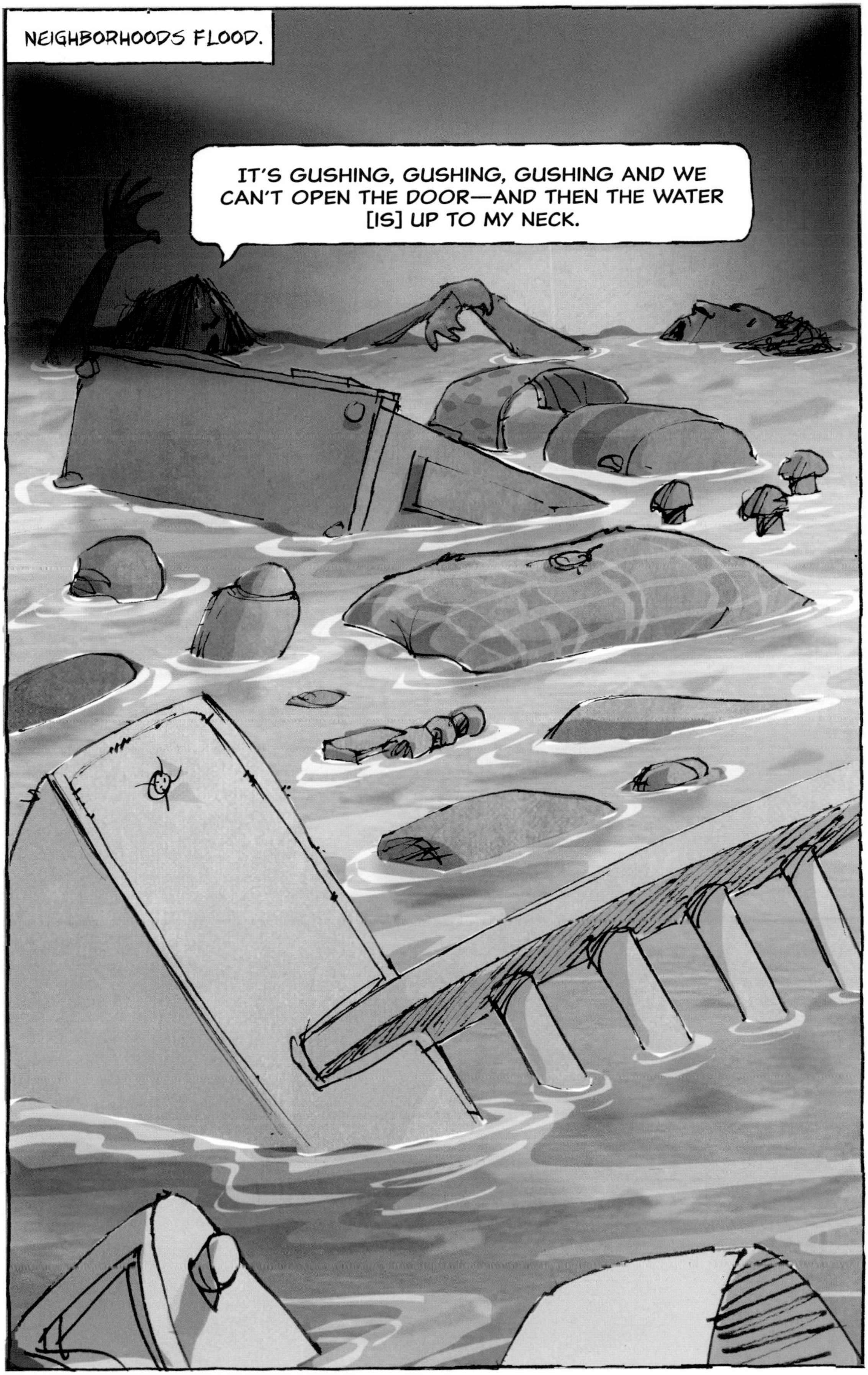
NEIGHBORHOODS FLOOD.
IT'S GUSHING, GUSHING, GUSHING AND WE CAN'T OPEN THE DOOR—AND THEN THE WATER [IS] UP TO MY NECK.

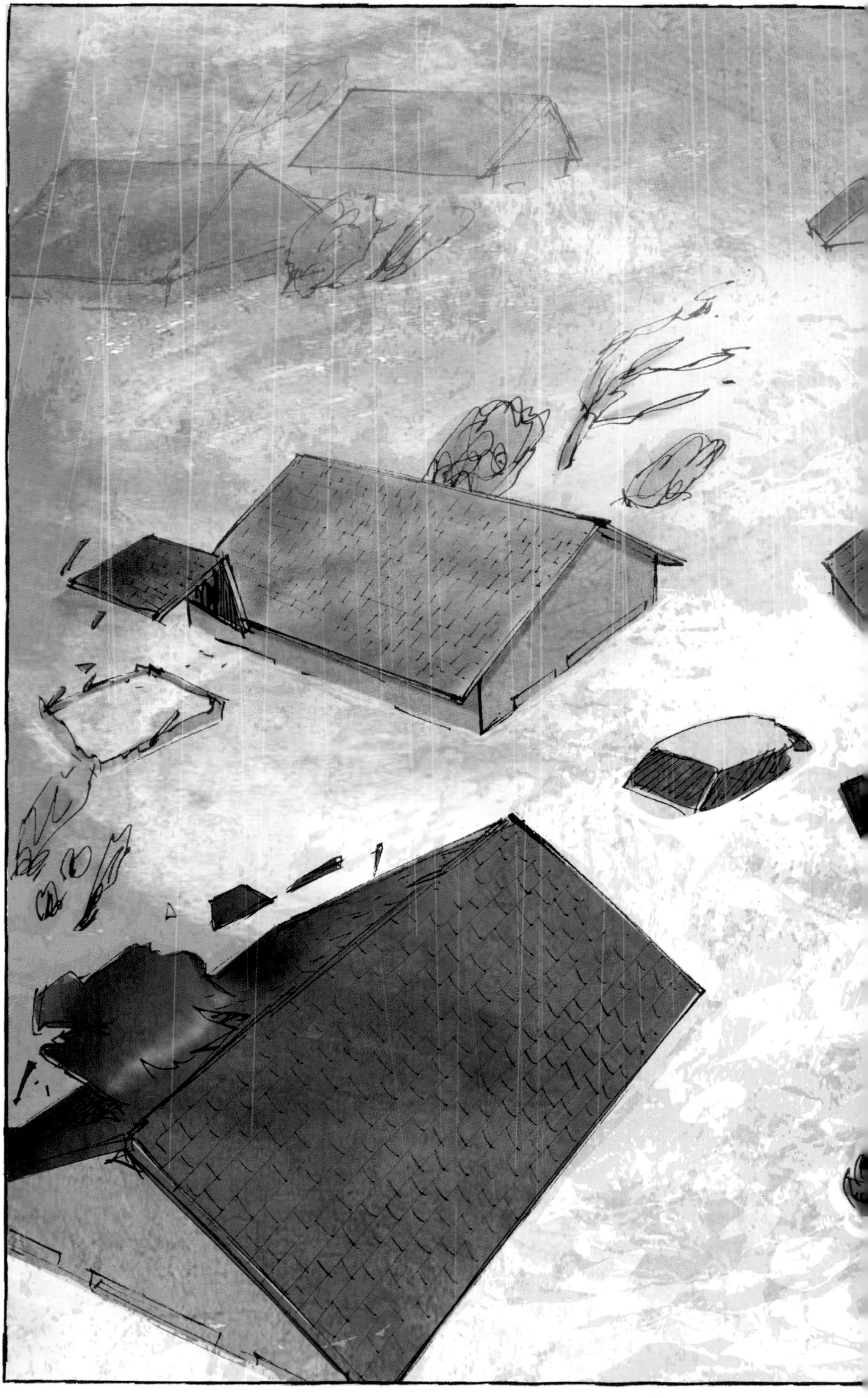

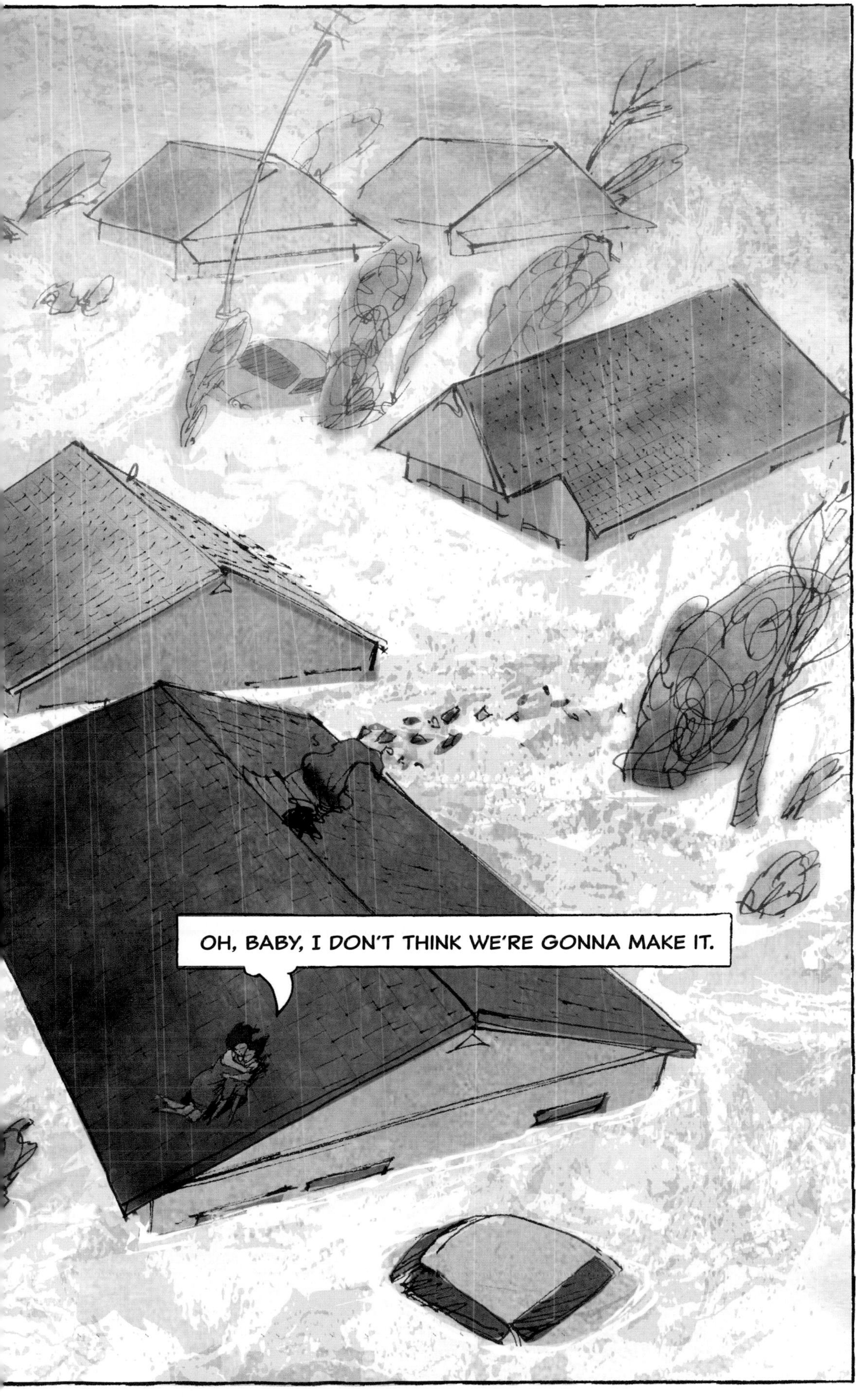
OH, BABY, I DON'T THINK WE'RE GONNA MAKE IT.

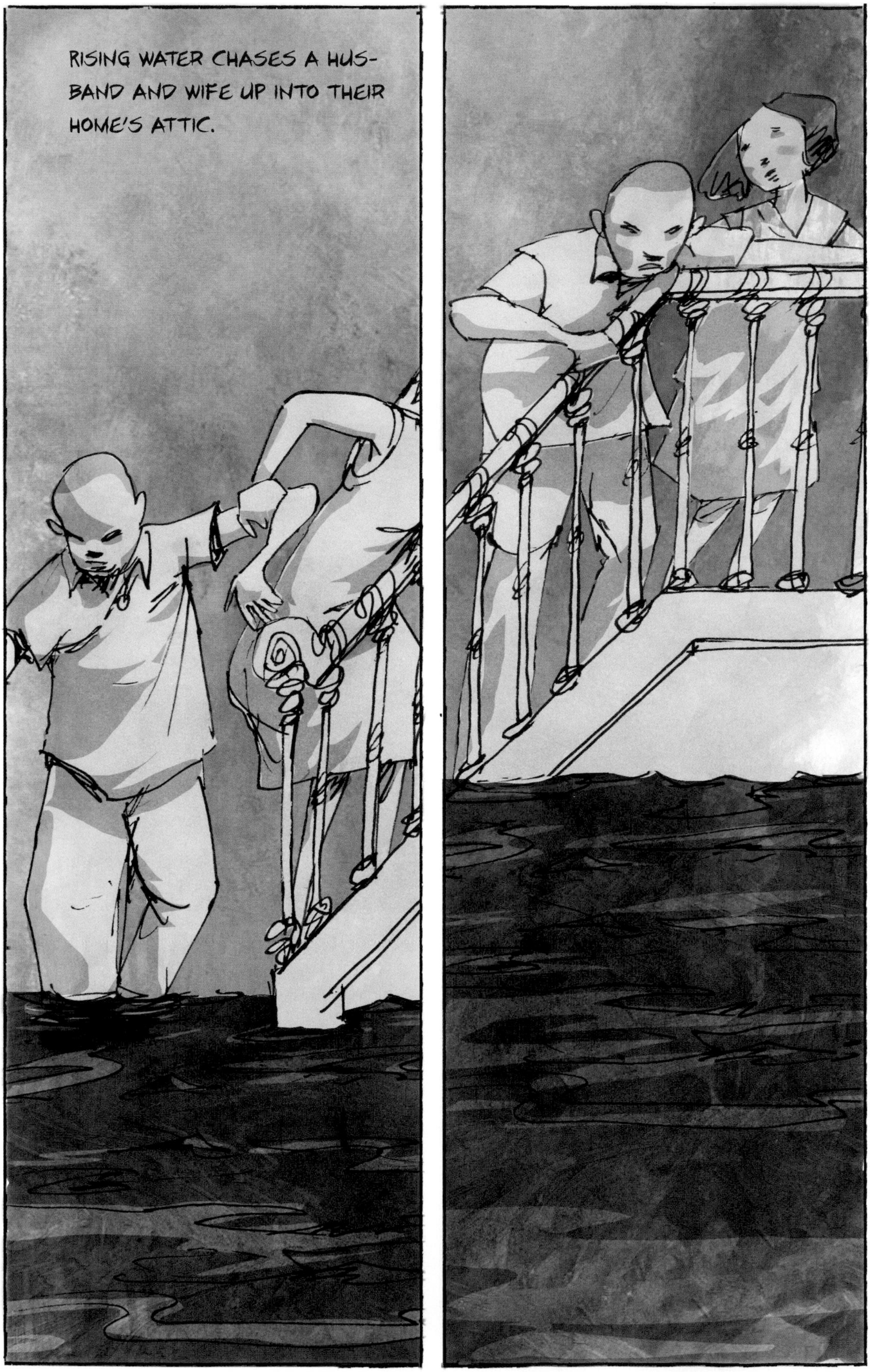
RISING WATER CHASES A HUSBAND AND WIFE UP INTO THEIR HOME'S ATTIC.

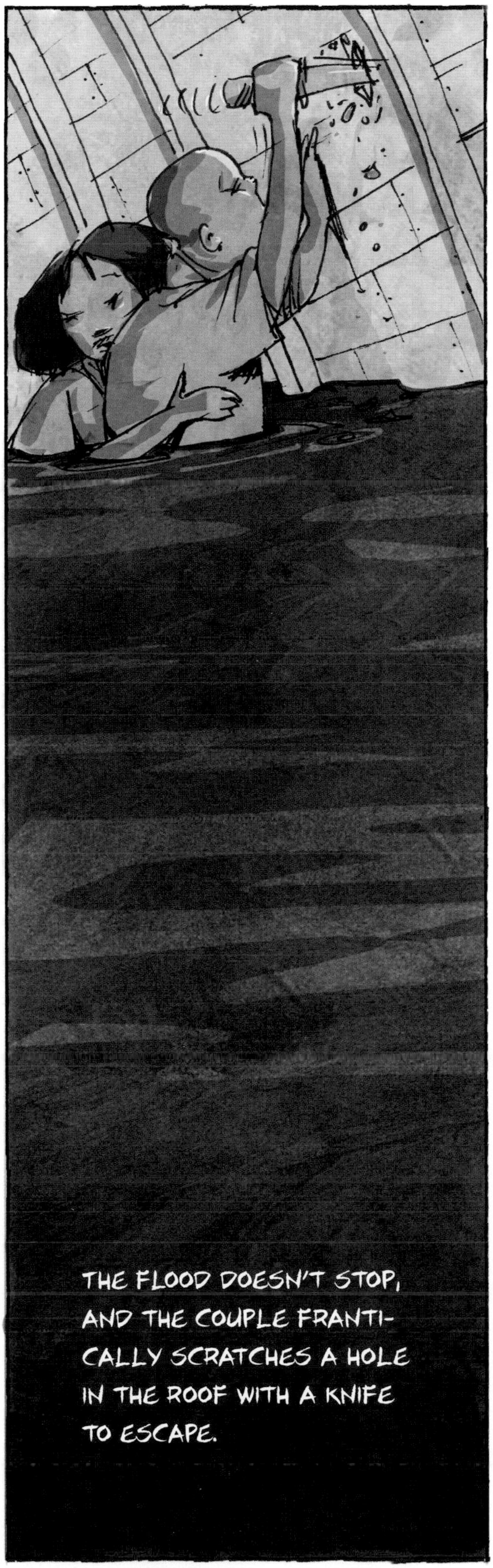
THE FLOOD DOESN'T STOP, AND THE COUPLE FRANTI-CALLY SCRATCHES A HOLE IN THE ROOF WITH A KNIFE TO ESCAPE.

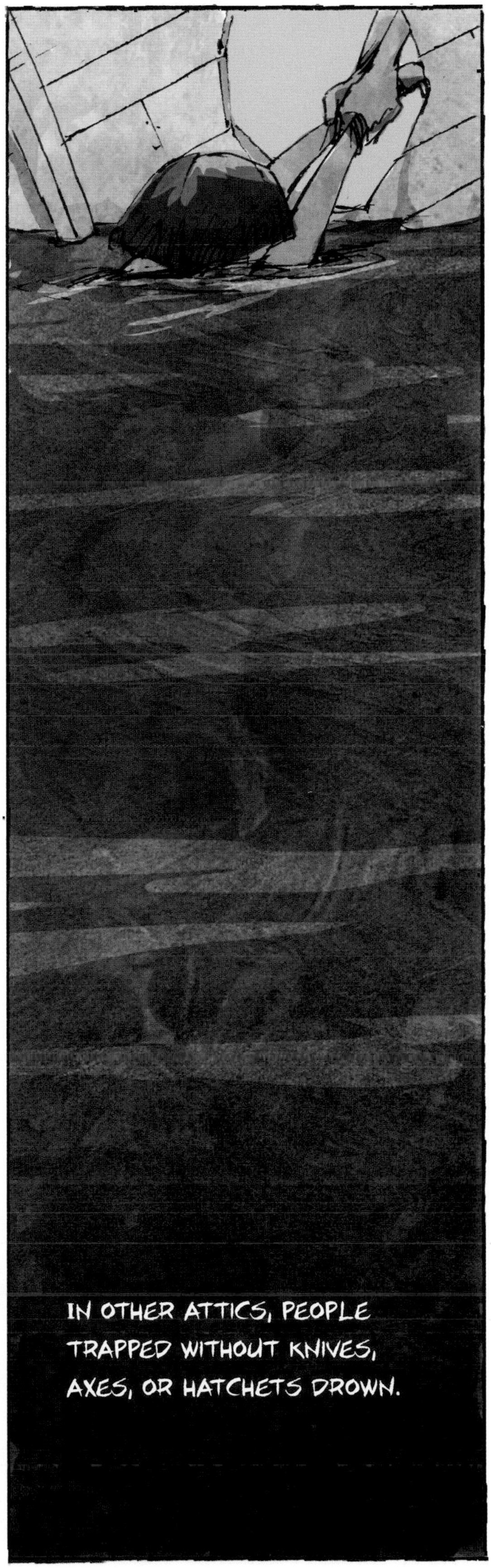
IN OTHER ATTICS, PEOPLE TRAPPED WITHOUT KNIVES, AXES, OR HATCHETS DROWN.

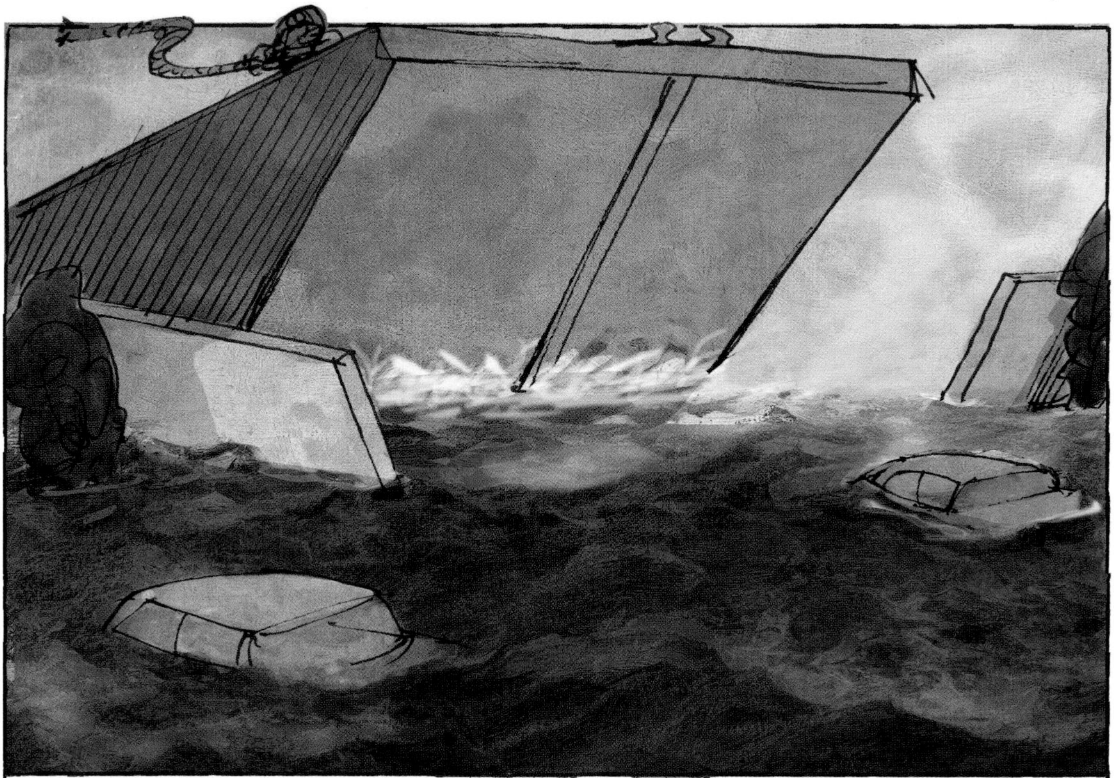

A FIVE-HUNDRED-FOOT BARGE RIDES THROUGH A GAP IN THE LEVEES AND FLOATS AMONG HOUSES.

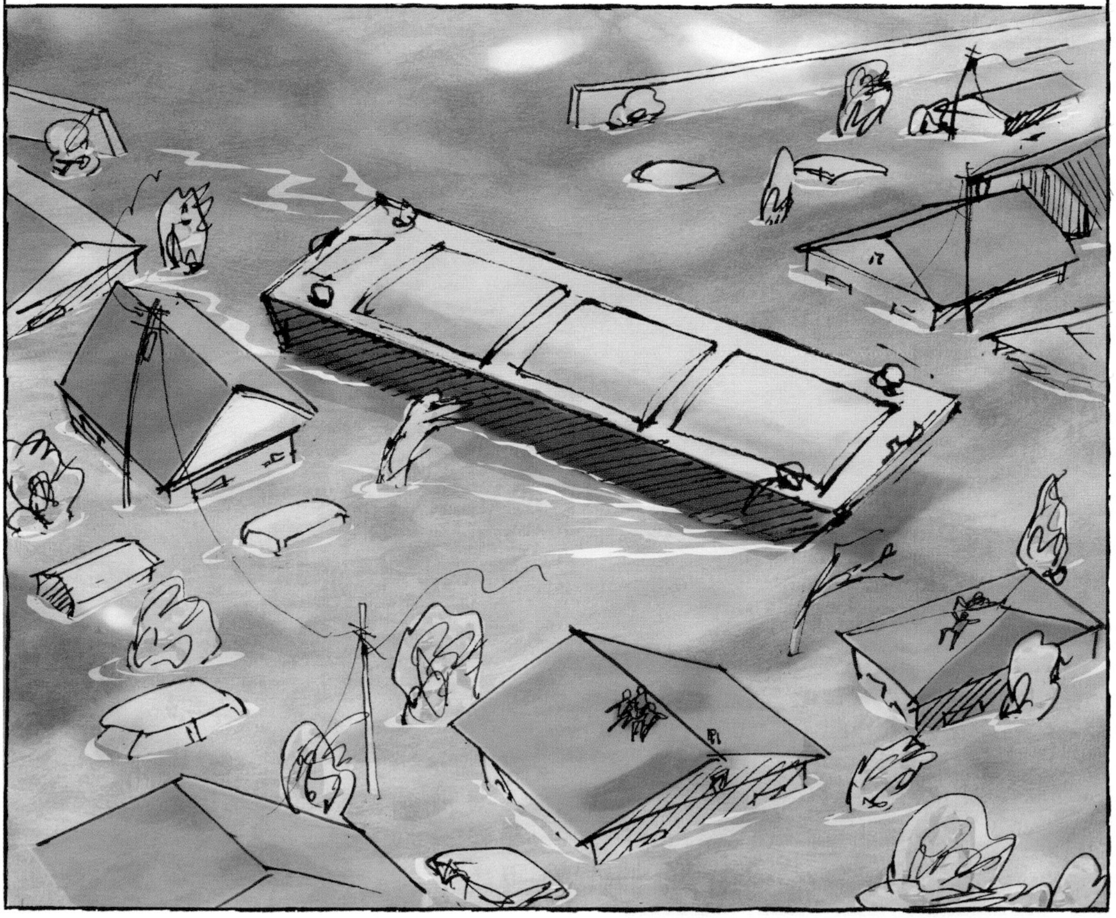

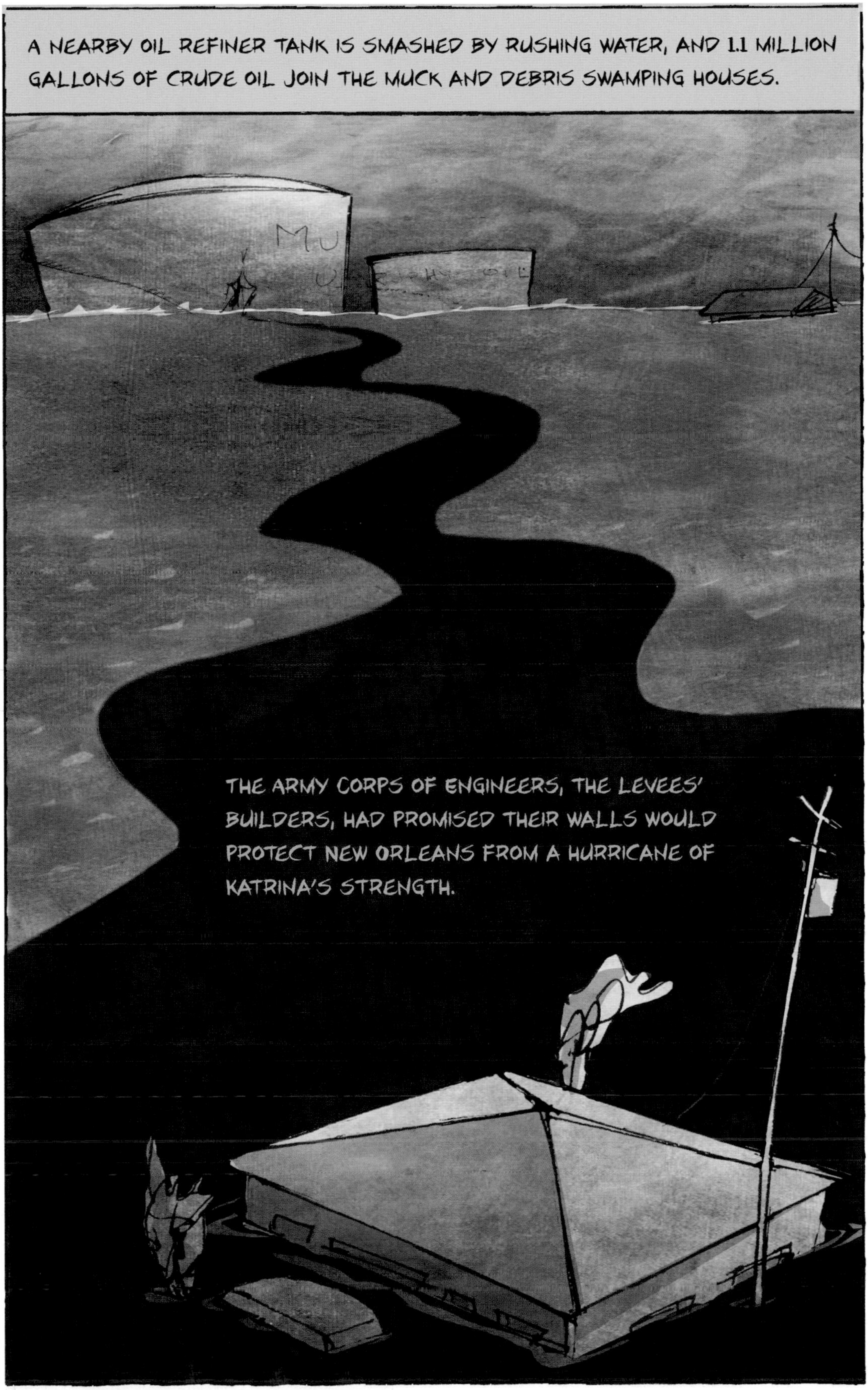
A NEARBY OIL REFINER TANK IS SMASHED BY RUSHING WATER, AND 1.1 MILLION GALLONS OF CRUDE OIL JOIN THE MUCK AND DEBRIS SWAMPING HOUSES.
THE ARMY CORPS OF ENGINEERS, THE LEVEES' BUILDERS, HAD PROMISED THEIR WALLS WOULD PROTECT NEW ORLEANS FROM A HURRICANE OF KATRINA'S STRENGTH.

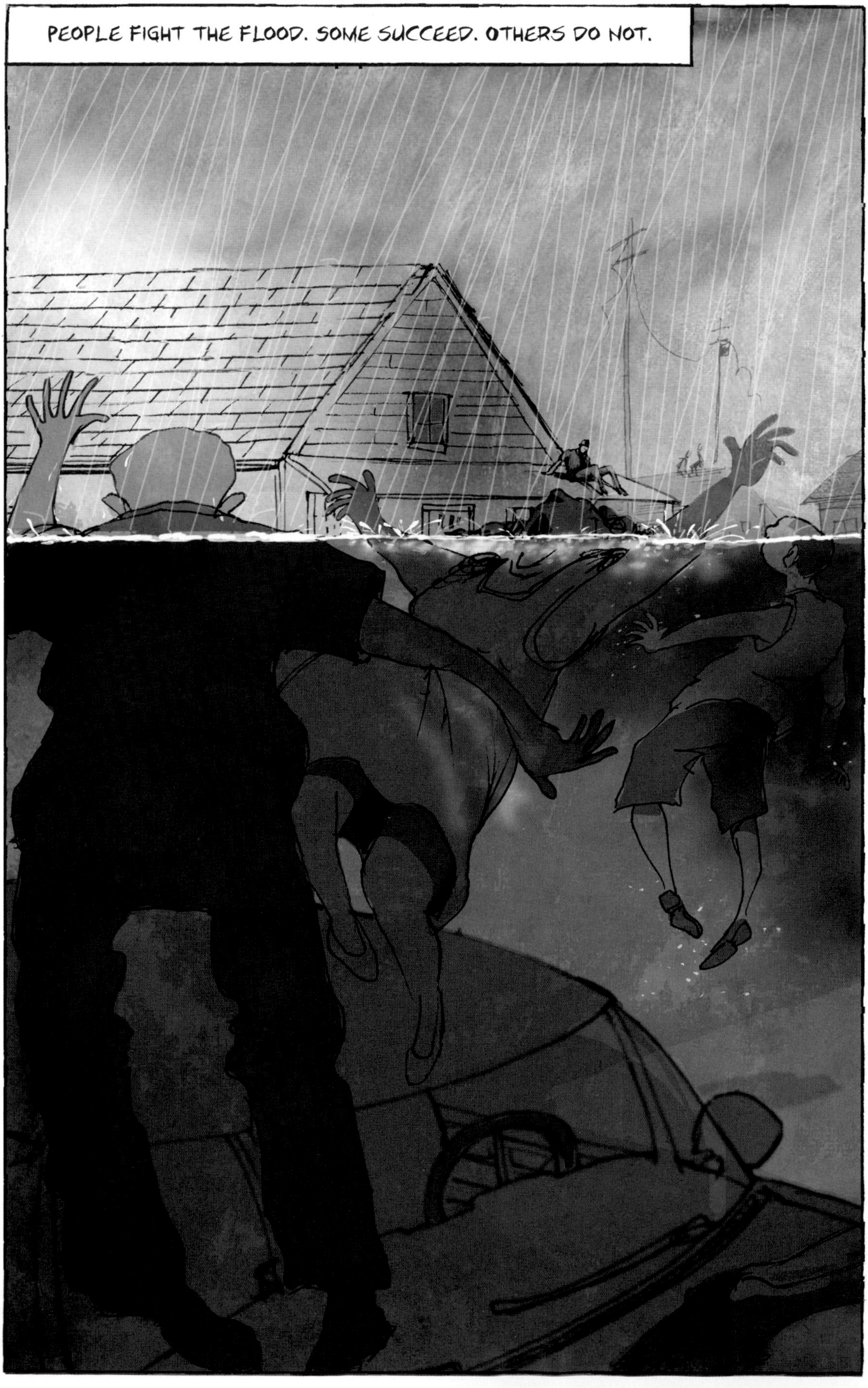
PEOPLE FIGHT THE FLOOD. SOME SUCCEED. OTHERS DO NOT.

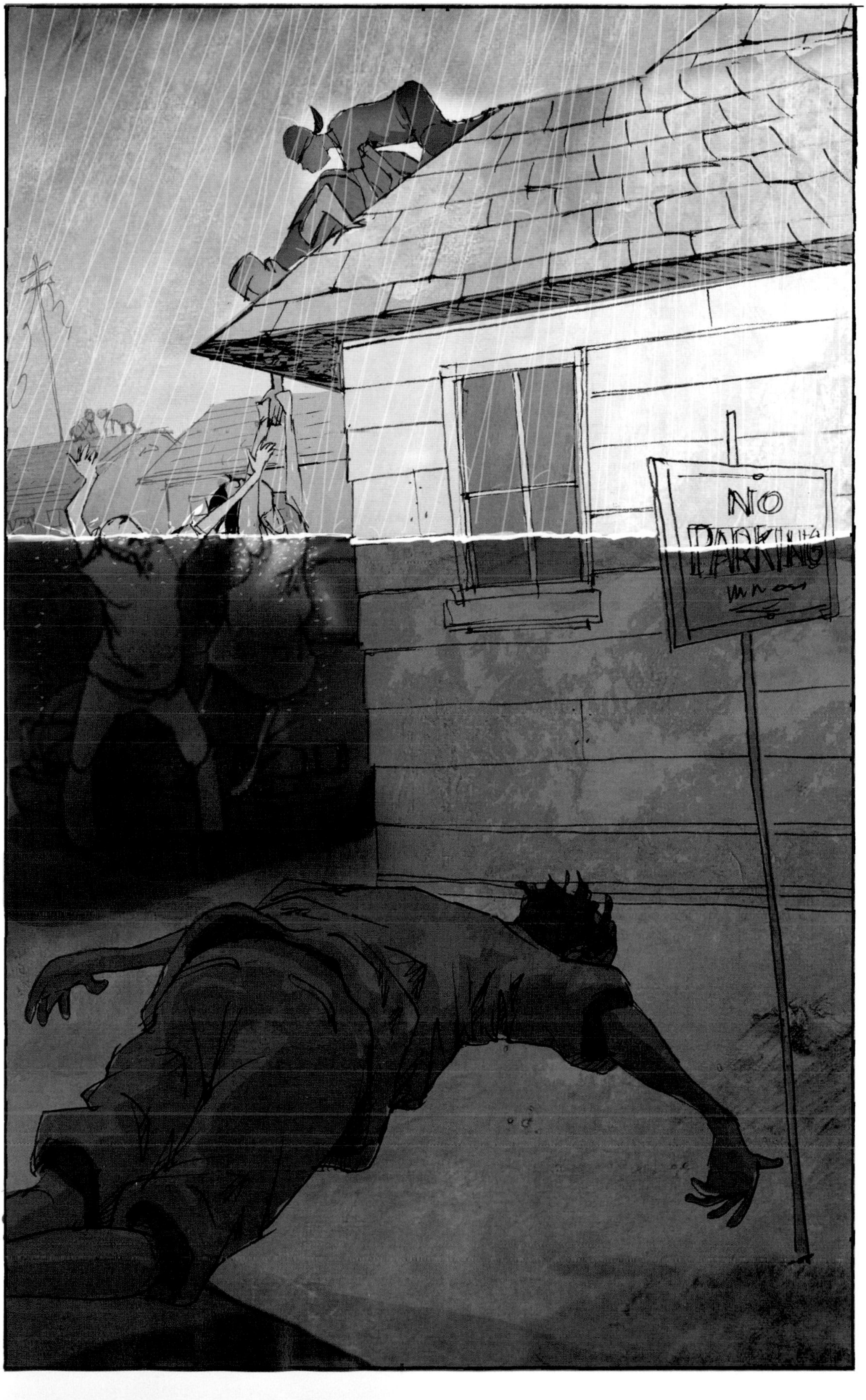
NO PARKING

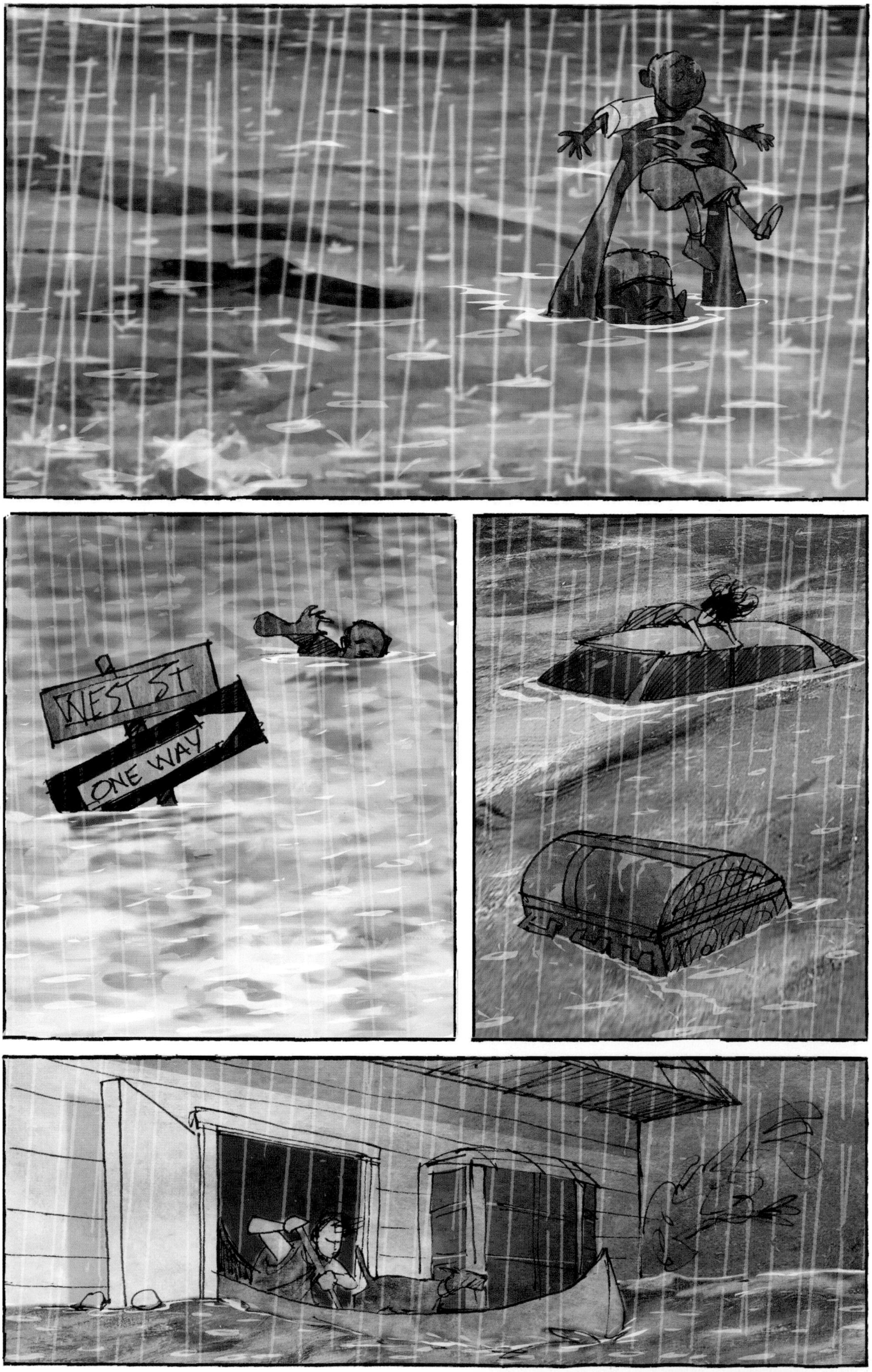
WEST ST
ONE WAY

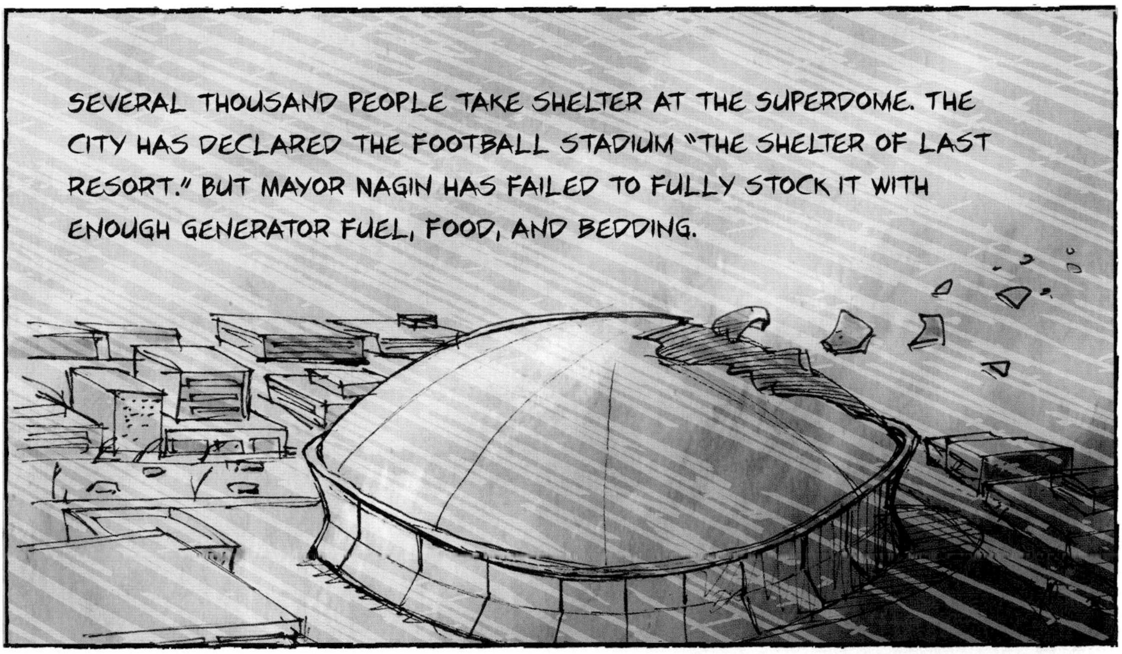
SEVERAL THOUSAND PEOPLE TAKE SHELTER AT THE SUPERDOME. THE CITY HAS DECLARED THE FOOTBALL STADIUM "THE SHELTER OF LAST RESORT." BUT MAYOR NAGIN HAS FAILED TO FULLY STOCK IT WITH ENOUGH GENERATOR FUEL, FOOD, AND BEDDING.

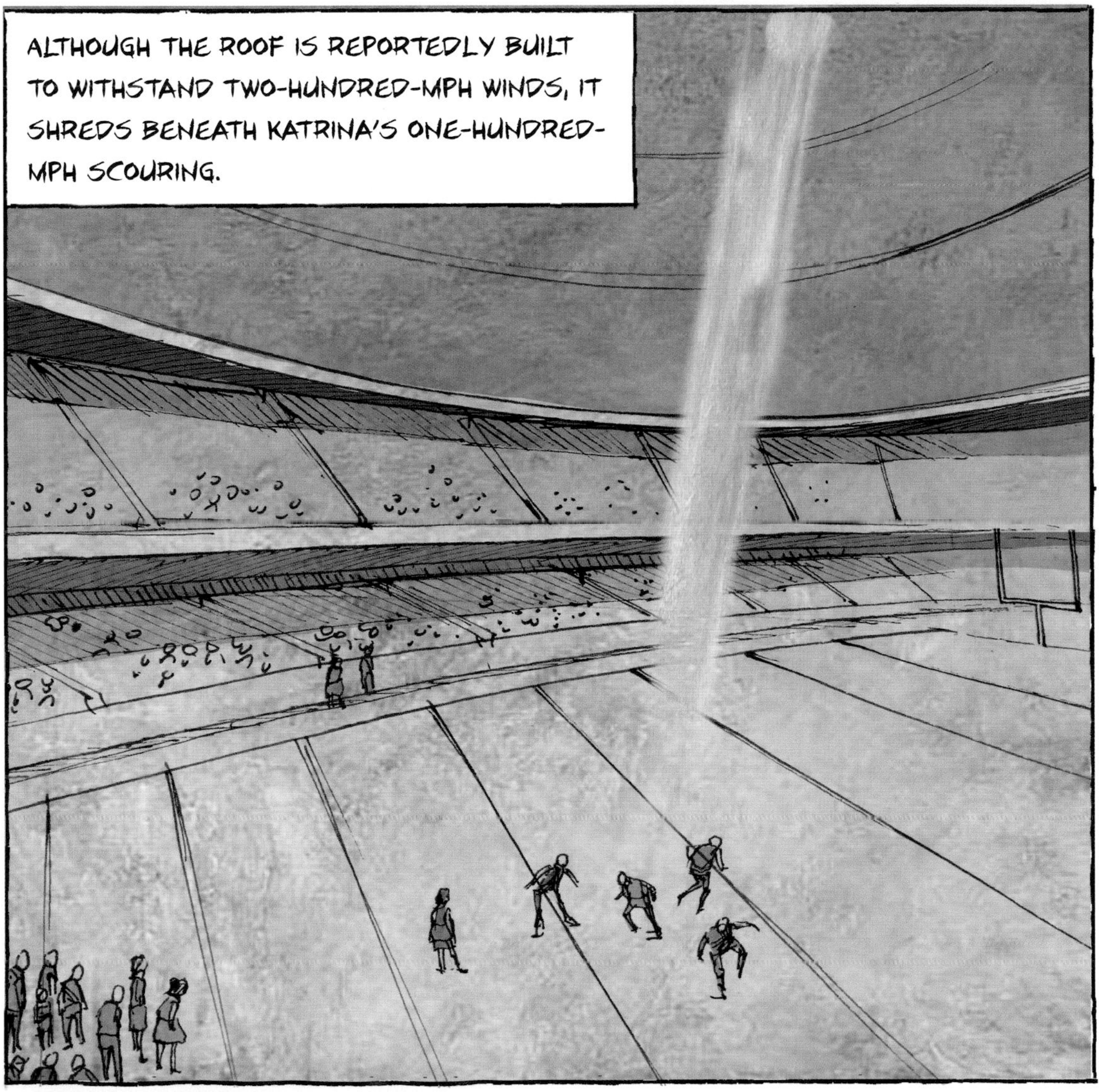
ALTHOUGH THE ROOF IS REPORTEDLY BUILT TO WITHSTAND TWO-HUNDRED-MPH WINDS, IT SHREDS BENEATH KATRINA'S ONE-HUNDRED-MPH SCOURING.

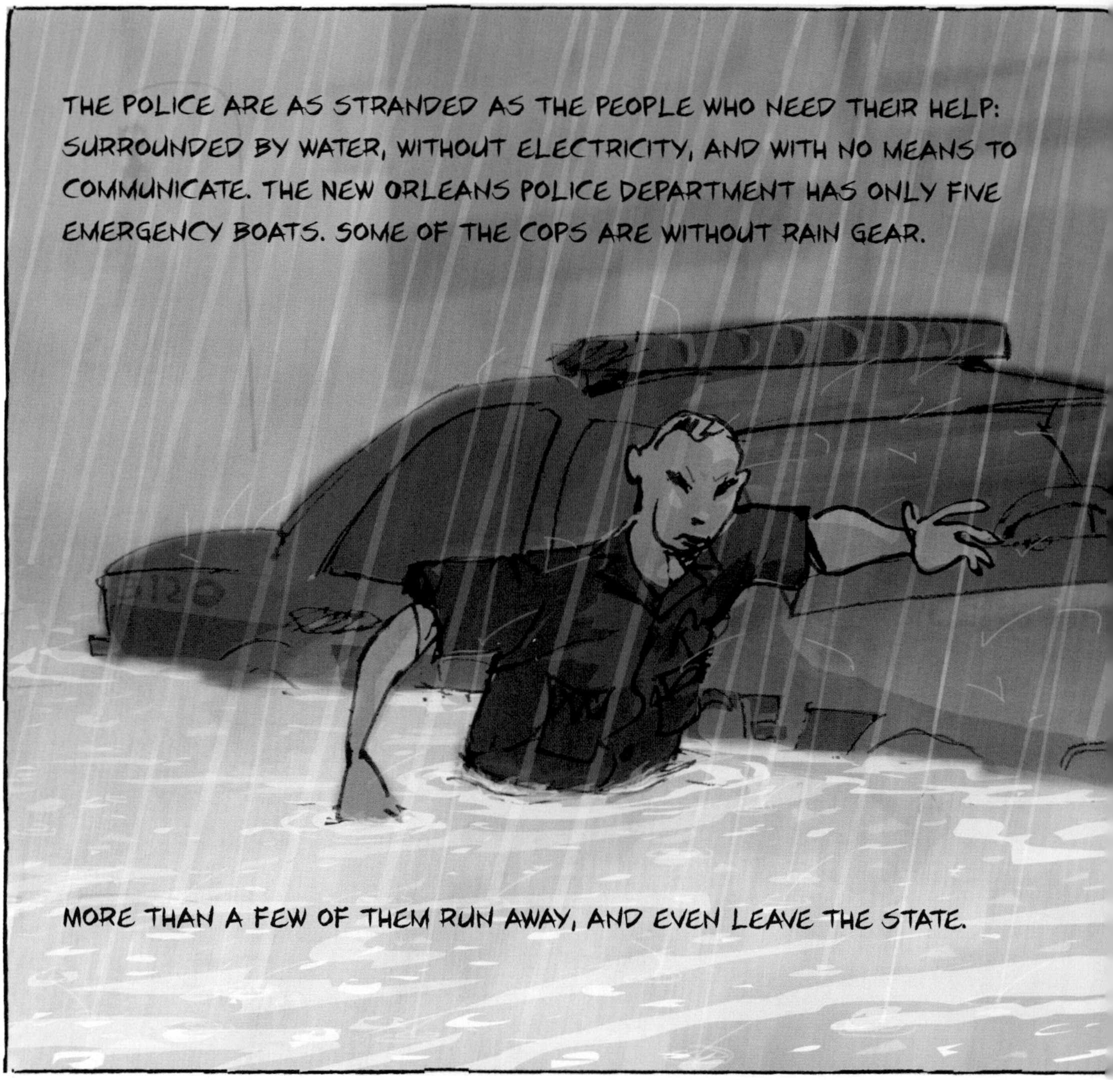
THE POLICE ARE AS STRANDED AS THE PEOPLE WHO NEED THEIR HELP: SURROUNDED BY WATER, WITHOUT ELECTRICITY, AND WITH NO MEANS TO COMMUNICATE. THE NEW ORLEANS POLICE DEPARTMENT HAS ONLY FIVE EMERGENCY BOATS. SOME OF THE COPS ARE WITHOUT RAIN GEAR.
MORE THAN A FEW OF THEM RUN AWAY, AND EVEN LEAVE THE STATE.

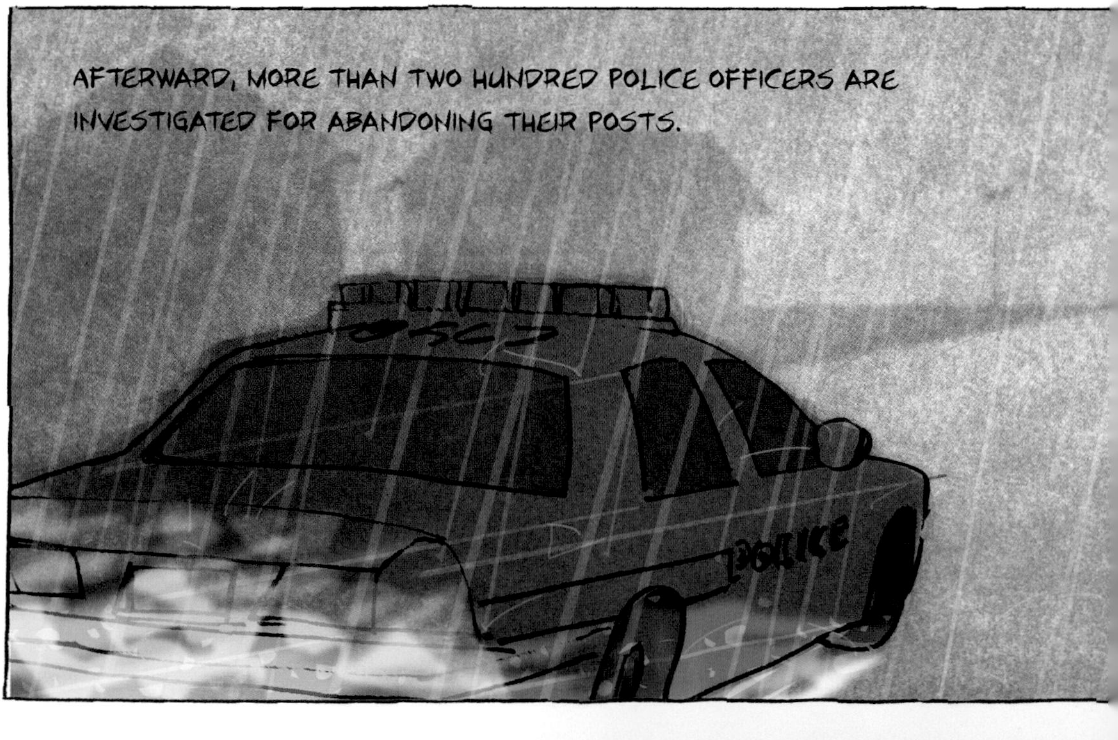
AFTERWARD, MORE THAN TWO HUNDRED POLICE OFFICERS ARE INVESTIGATED FOR ABANDONING THEIR POSTS.
POLICE

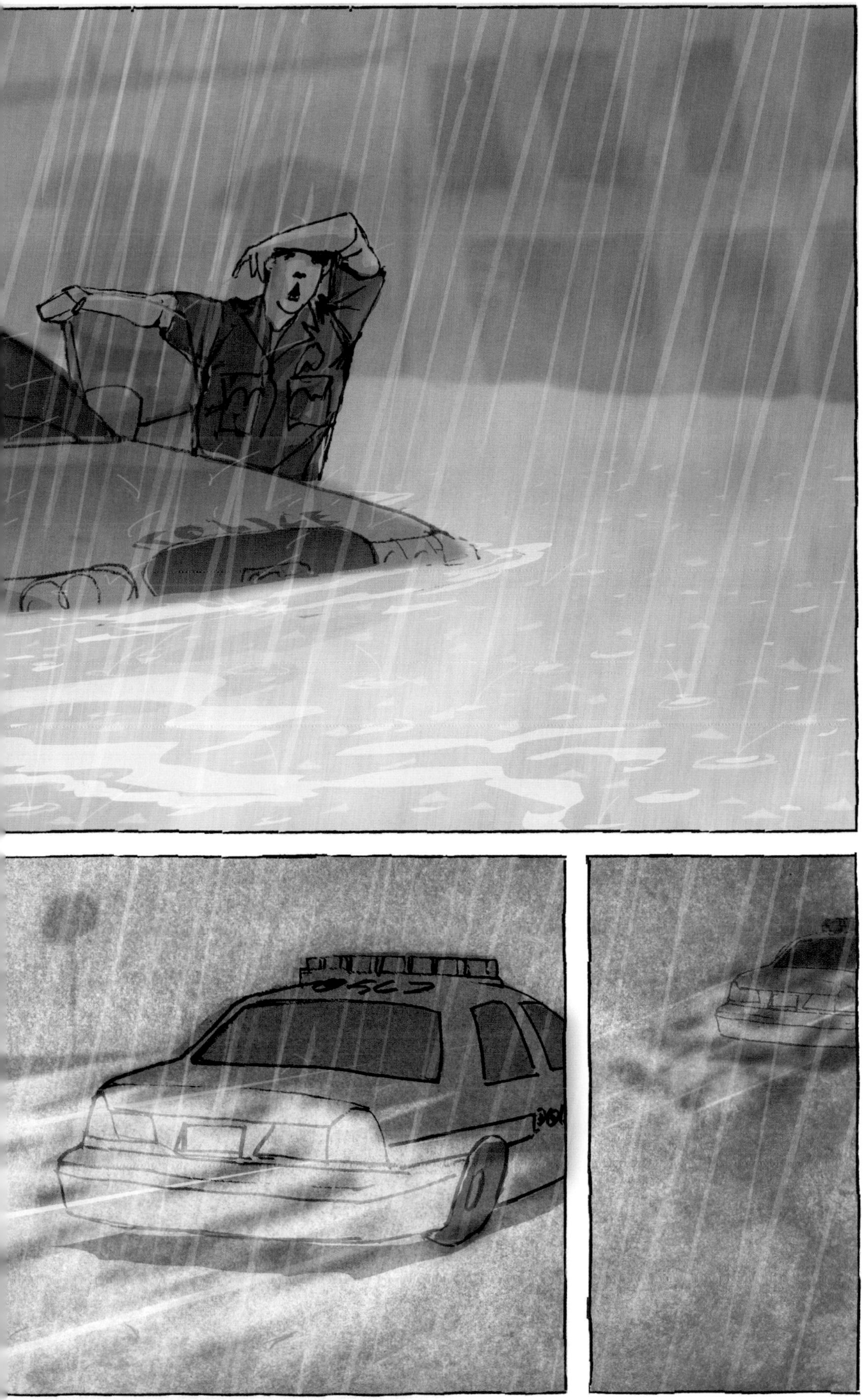

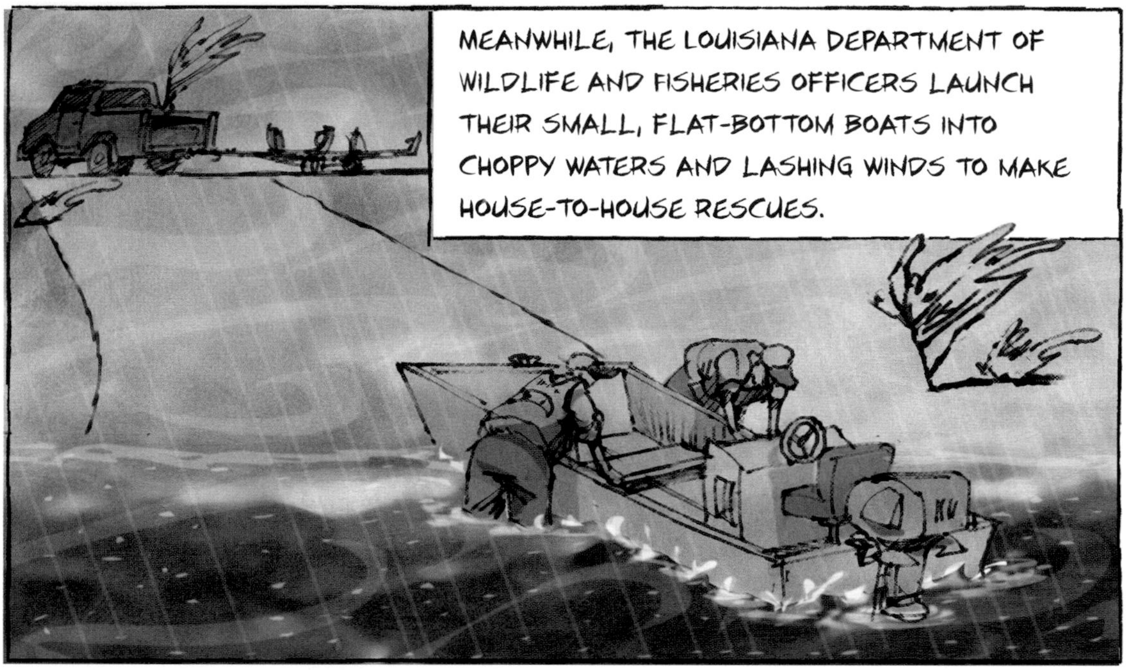
MEANWHILE, THE LOUISIANA DEPARTMENT OF WILDLIFE AND FISHERIES OFFICERS LAUNCH THEIR SMALL, FLAT-BOTTOM BOATS INTO CHOPPY WATERS AND LASHING WINDS TO MAKE HOUSE-TO-HOUSE RESCUES.

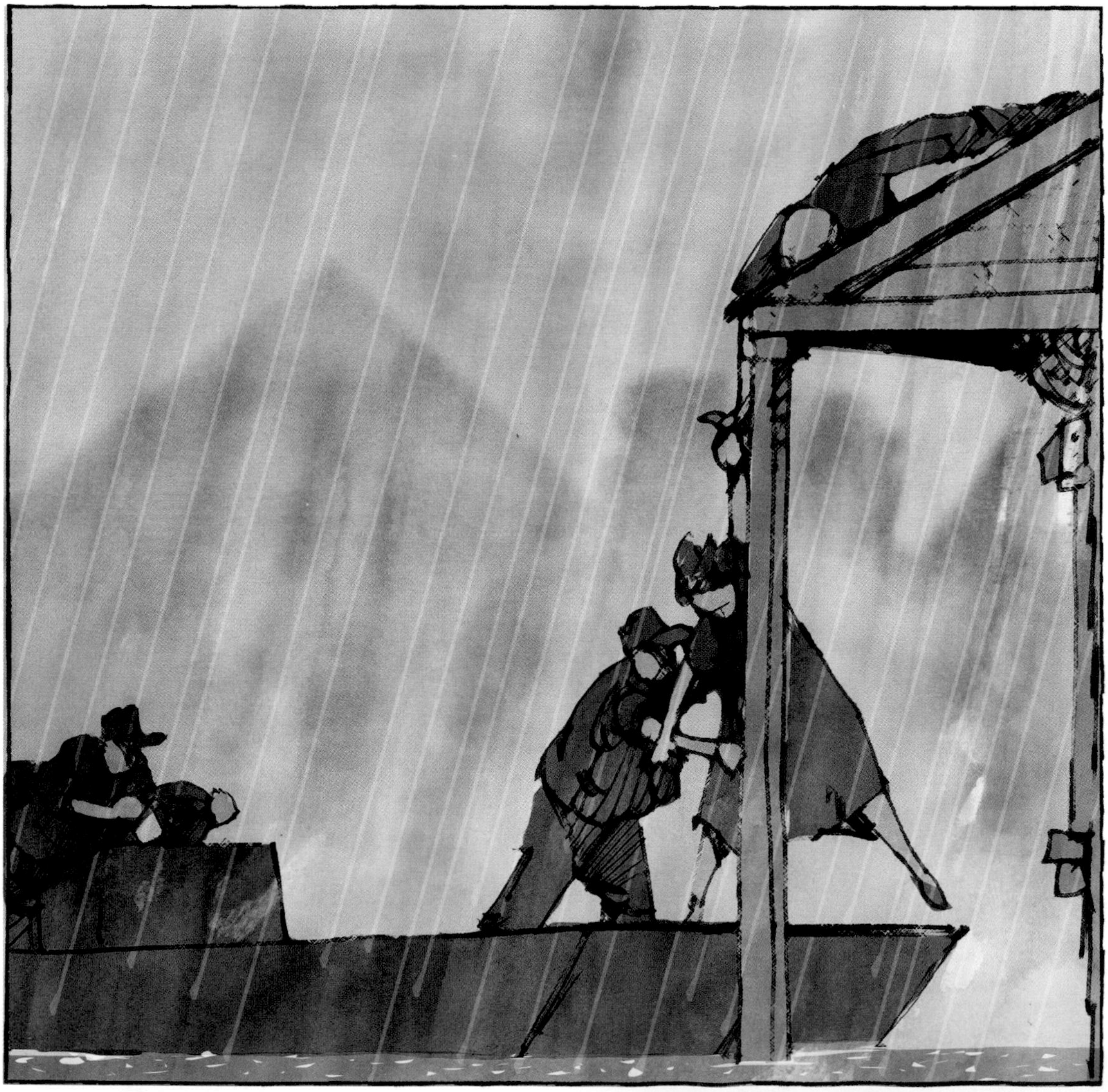

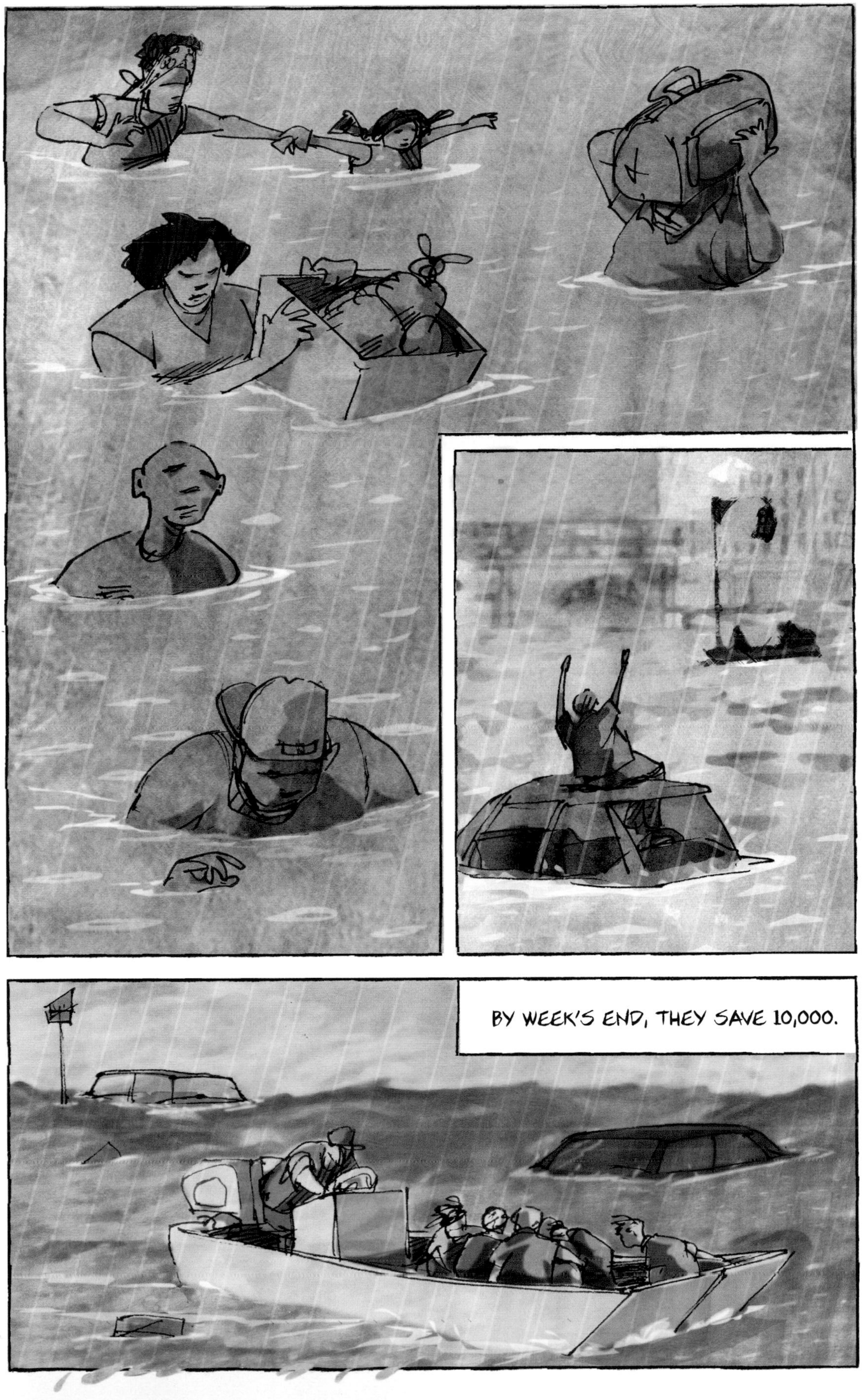
BY WEEK'S END, THEY SAVE 10,000.

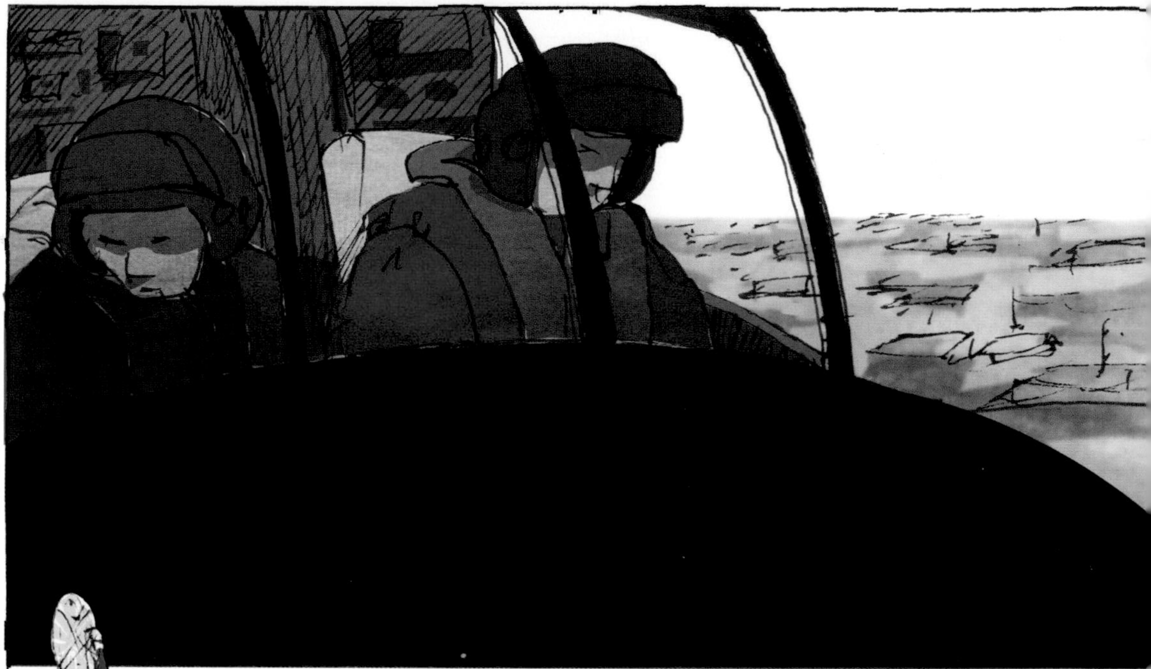

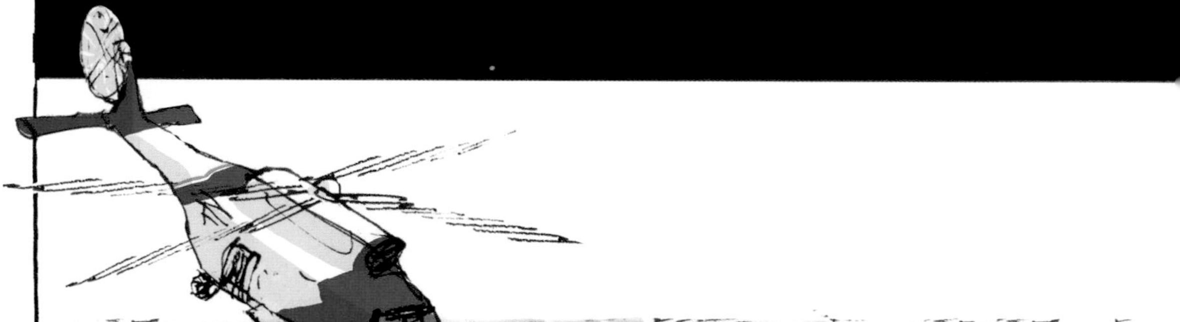

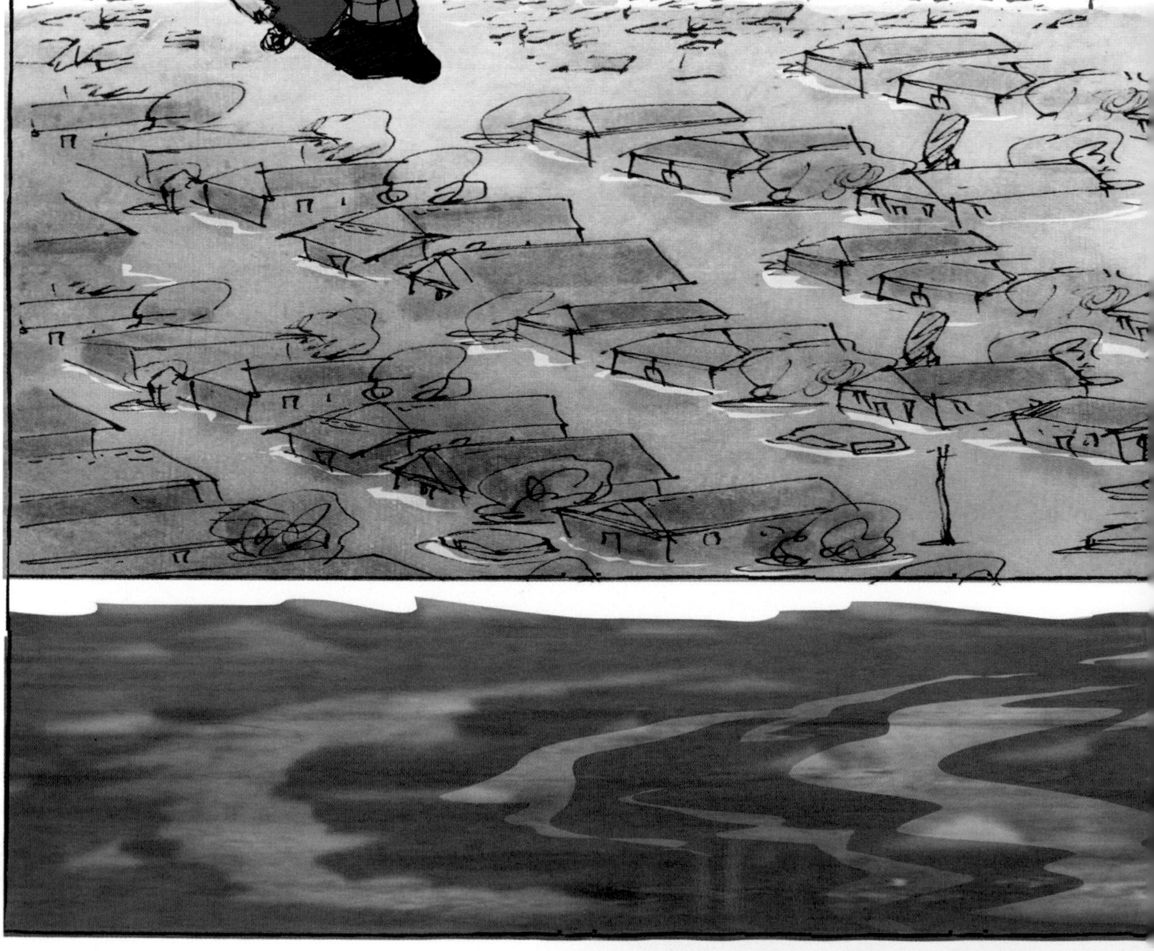

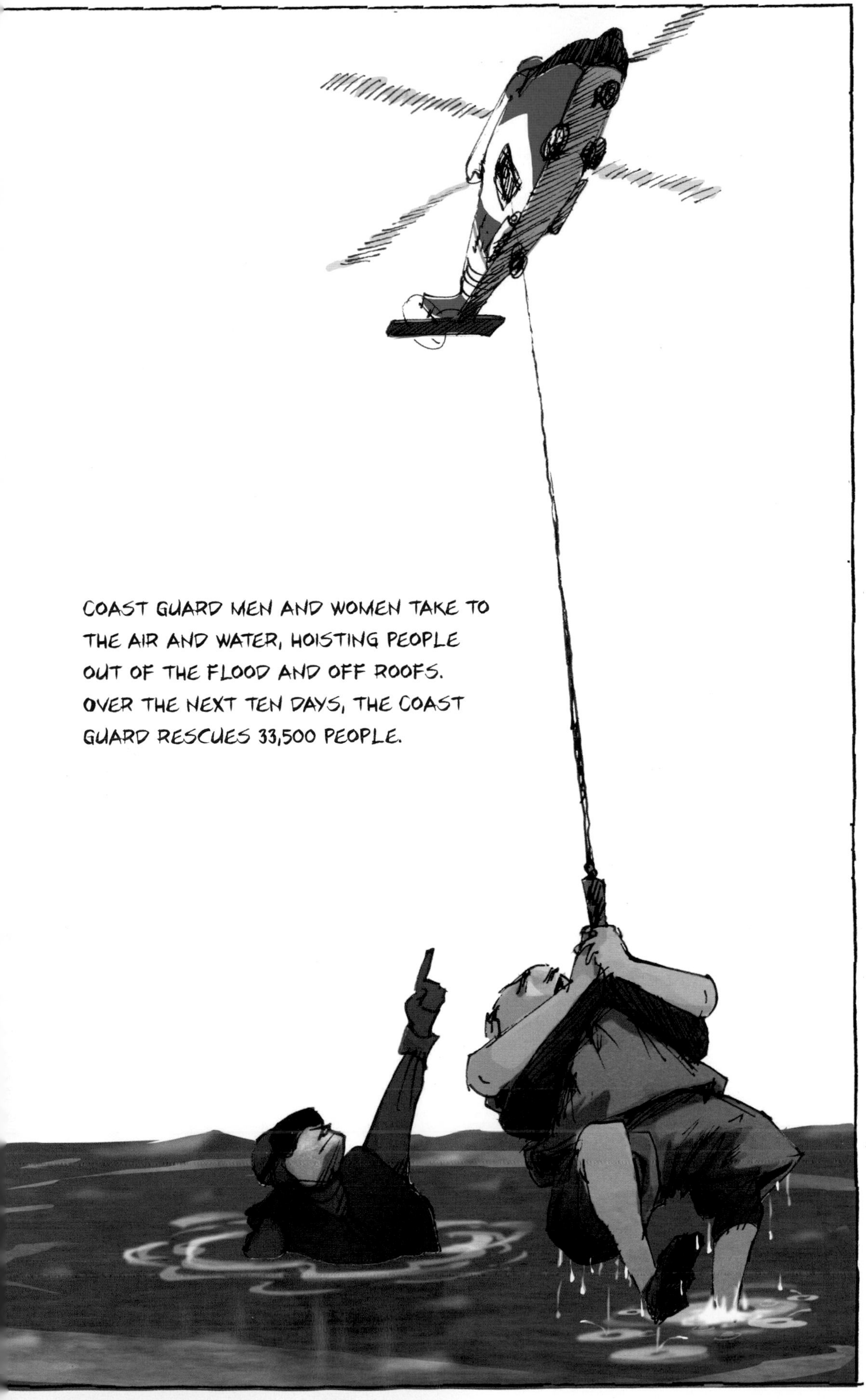
COAST GUARD MEN AND WOMEN TAKE TO THE AIR AND WATER, HOISTING PEOPLE OUT OF THE FLOOD AND OFF ROOFS. OVER THE NEXT TEN DAYS, THE COAST GUARD RESCUES 33,500 PEOPLE.

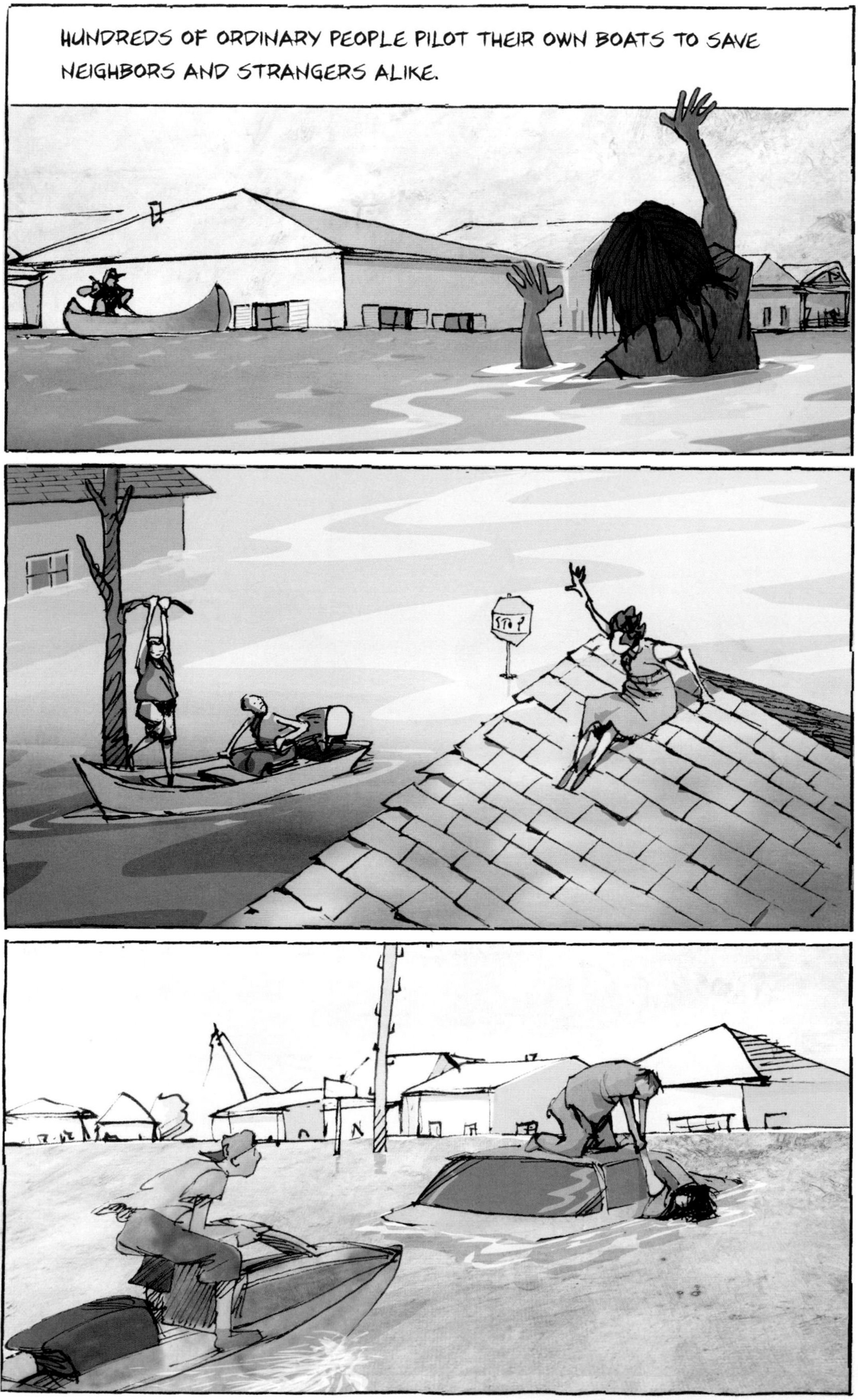
HUNDREDS OF ORDINARY PEOPLE PILOT THEIR OWN BOATS TO SAVE NEIGHBORS AND STRANGERS ALIKE.

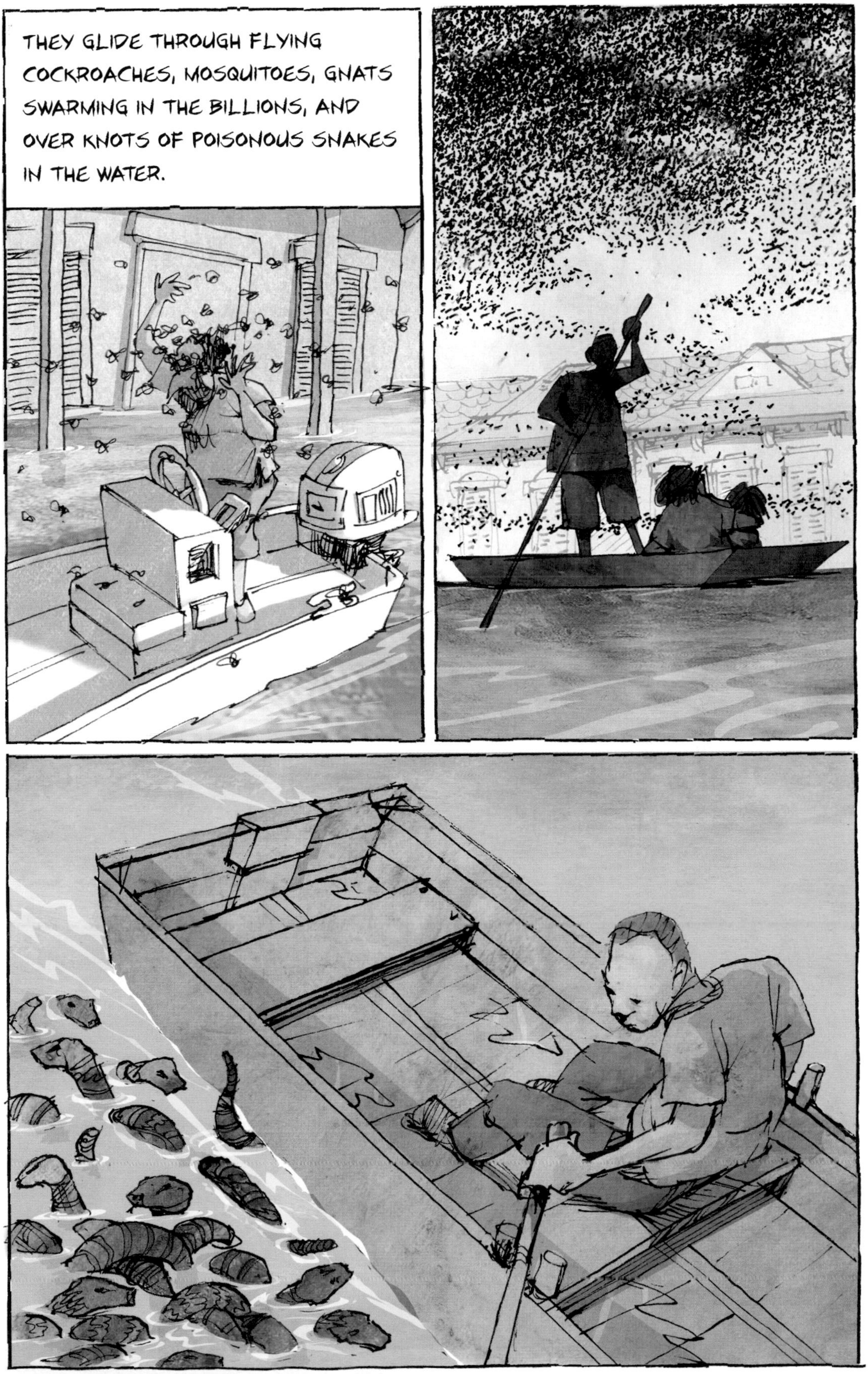
THEY GLIDE THROUGH FLYING COCKROACHES, MOSQUITOES, GNATS SWARMING IN THE BILLIONS, AND OVER KNOTS OF POISONOUS SNAKES IN THE WATER.

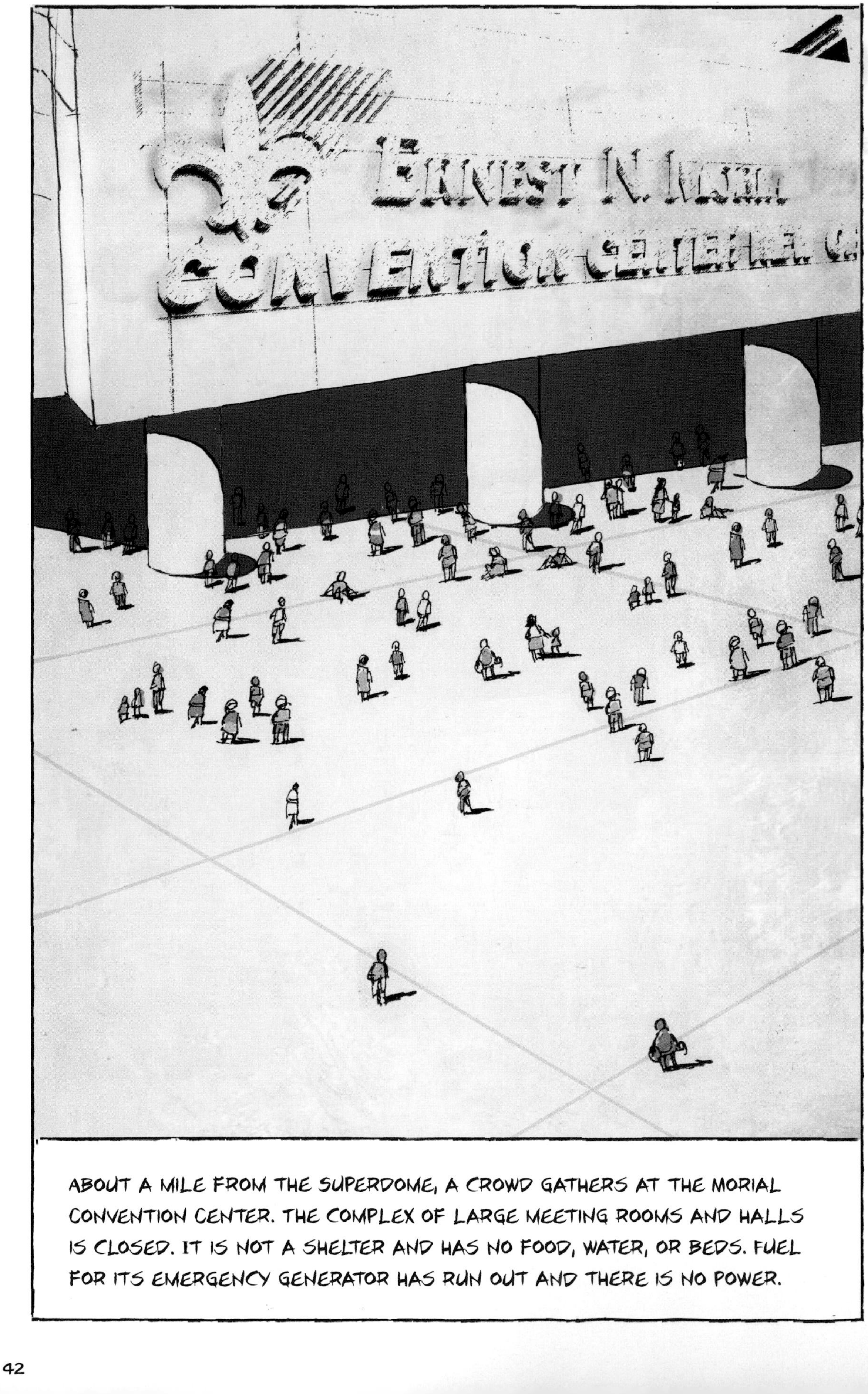
ERNEST N.
CONVENTION

ABOUT A MILE FROM THE SUPERDOME, A CROWD GATHERS AT THE MORIAL CONVENTION CENTER. THE COMPLEX OF LARGE MEETING ROOMS AND HALLS IS CLOSED. IT IS NOT A SHELTER AND HAS NO FOOD, WATER, OR BEDS. FUEL FOR ITS EMERGENCY GENERATOR HAS RUN OUT AND THERE IS NO POWER.

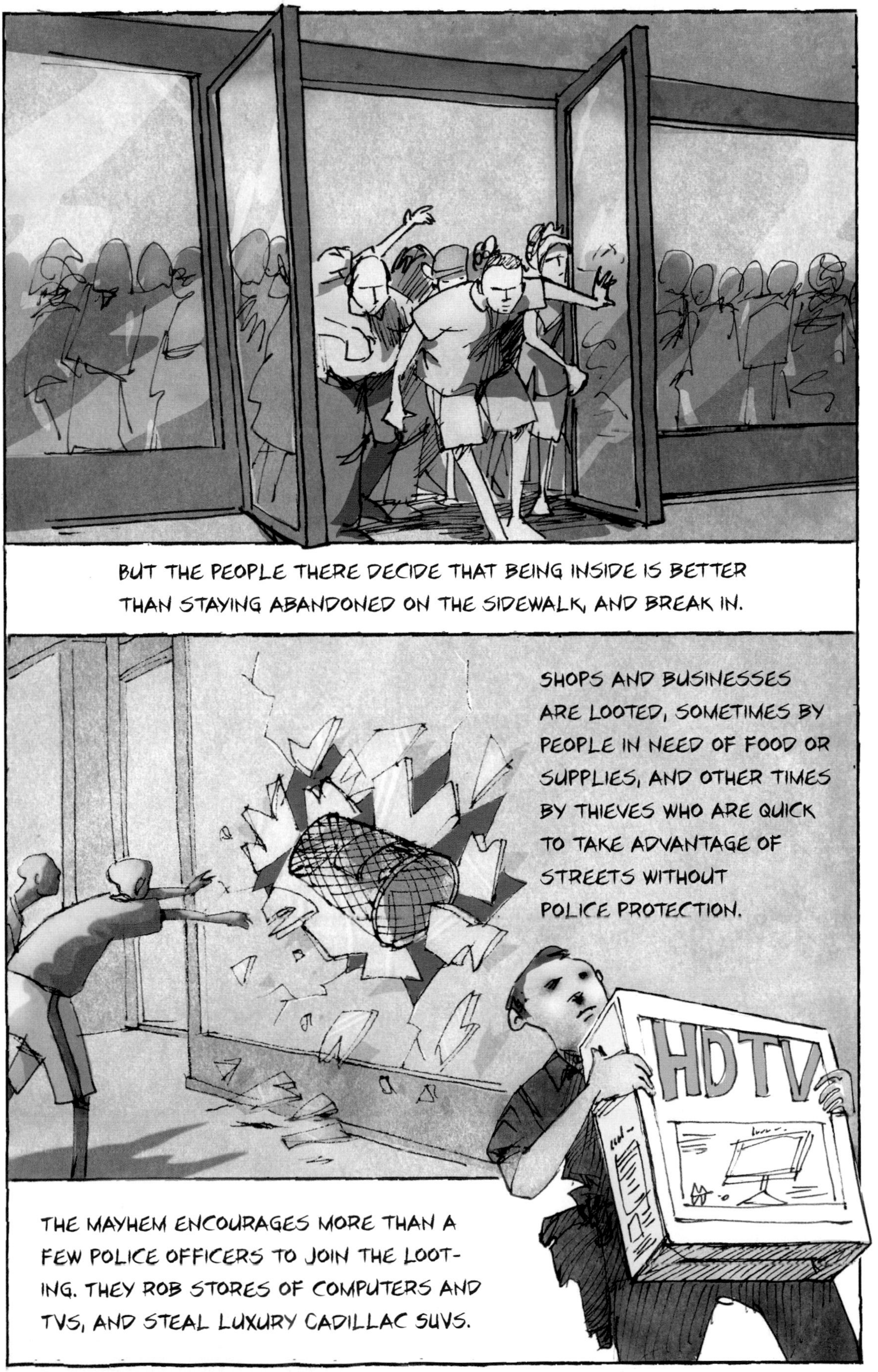
BUT THE PEOPLE THERE DECIDE THAT BEING INSIDE IS BETTER THAN STAYING ABANDONED ON THE SIDEWALK, AND BREAK IN.
SHOPS AND BUSINESSES ARE LOOTED, SOMETIMES BY PEOPLE IN NEED OF FOOD OR SUPPLIES, AND OTHER TIMES BY THIEVES WHO ARE QUICK TO TAKE ADVANTAGE OF STREETS WITHOUT POLICE PROTECTION.
HDTV
THE MAYHEM ENCOURAGES MORE THAN A FEW POLICE OFFICERS TO JOIN THE LOOT-ING. THEY ROB STORES OF COMPUTERS AND TVS, AND STEAL LUXURY CADILLAC SUVS.

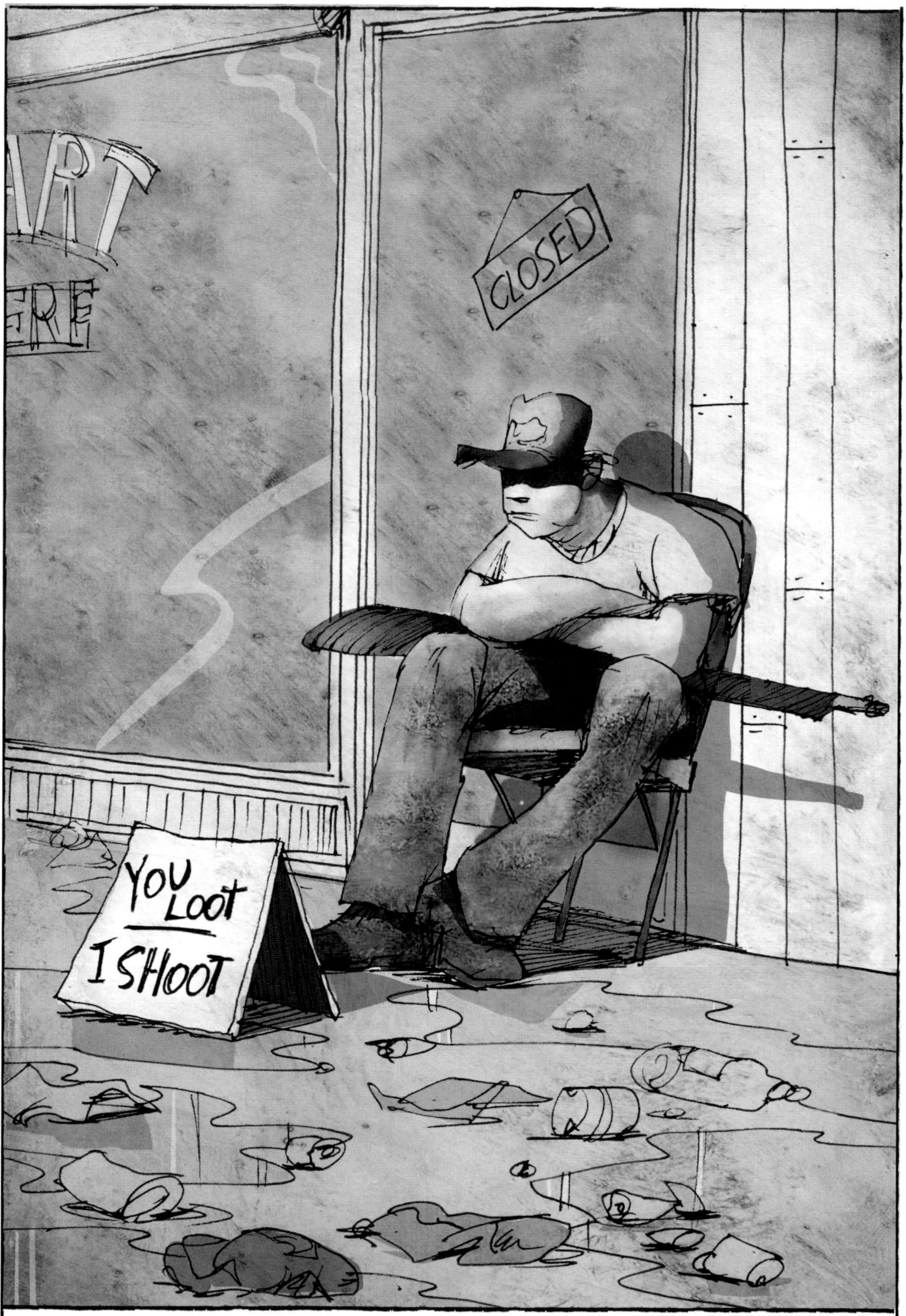
ART
ERE
CLOSED
YOU LOOT
I SHOOT

SOME GUN-TOTING BUSINESS OWNERS ARRIVE TO PROTECT THEIR SHOPS AND OFFICES.

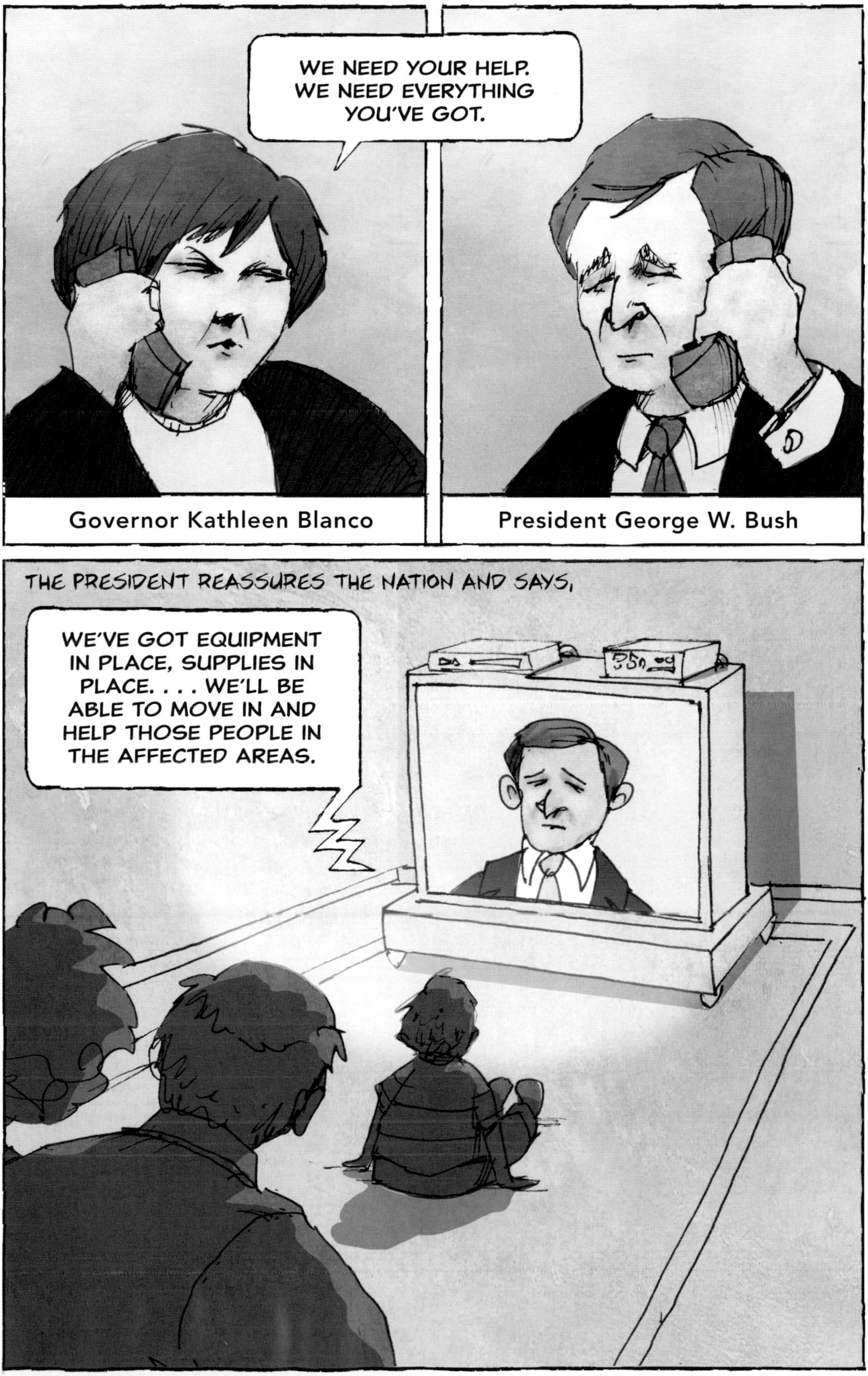
WE NEED YOUR HELP. WE NEED EVERYTHING YOU'VE GOT.
Governor Kathleen Blanco
President George W. Bush
THE PRESIDENT REASSURES THE NATION AND SAYS,
WE'VE GOT EQUIPMENT IN PLACE, SUPPLIES IN PLACE. . . . WE'LL BE ABLE TO MOVE IN AND HELP THOSE PEOPLE IN THE AFFECTED AREAS.

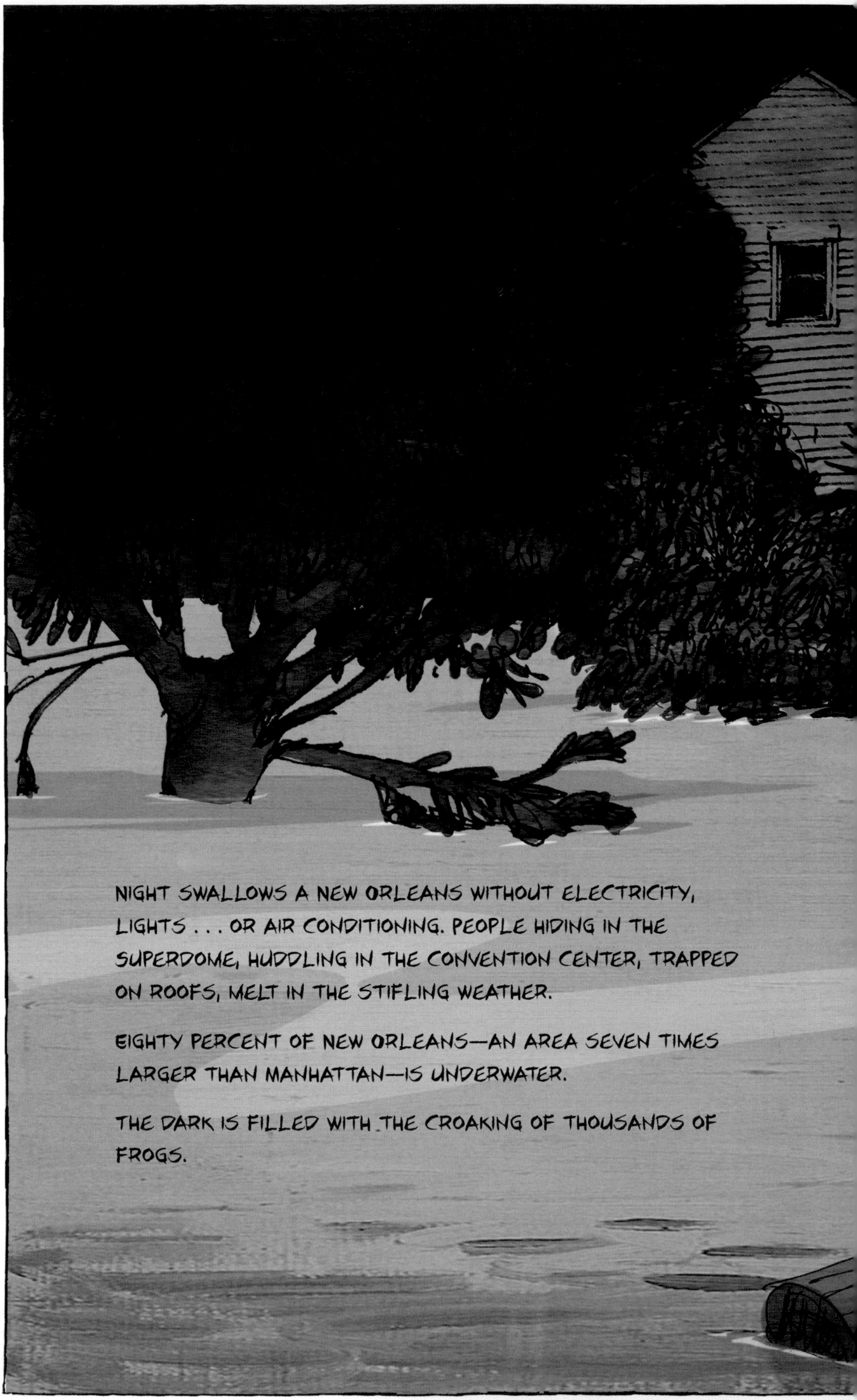
NIGHT SWALLOWS A NEW ORLEANS WITHOUT ELECTRICITY, LIGHTS . . . OR AIR CONDITIONING. PEOPLE HIDING IN THE SUPERDOME, HUDDLING IN THE CONVENTION CENTER, TRAPPED ON ROOFS, MELT IN THE STIFLING WEATHER.
EIGHTY PERCENT OF NEW ORLEANS—AN AREA SEVEN TIMES LARGER THAN MANHATTAN—IS UNDERWATER.
THE DARK IS FILLED WITH THE CROAKING OF THOUSANDS OF FROGS.

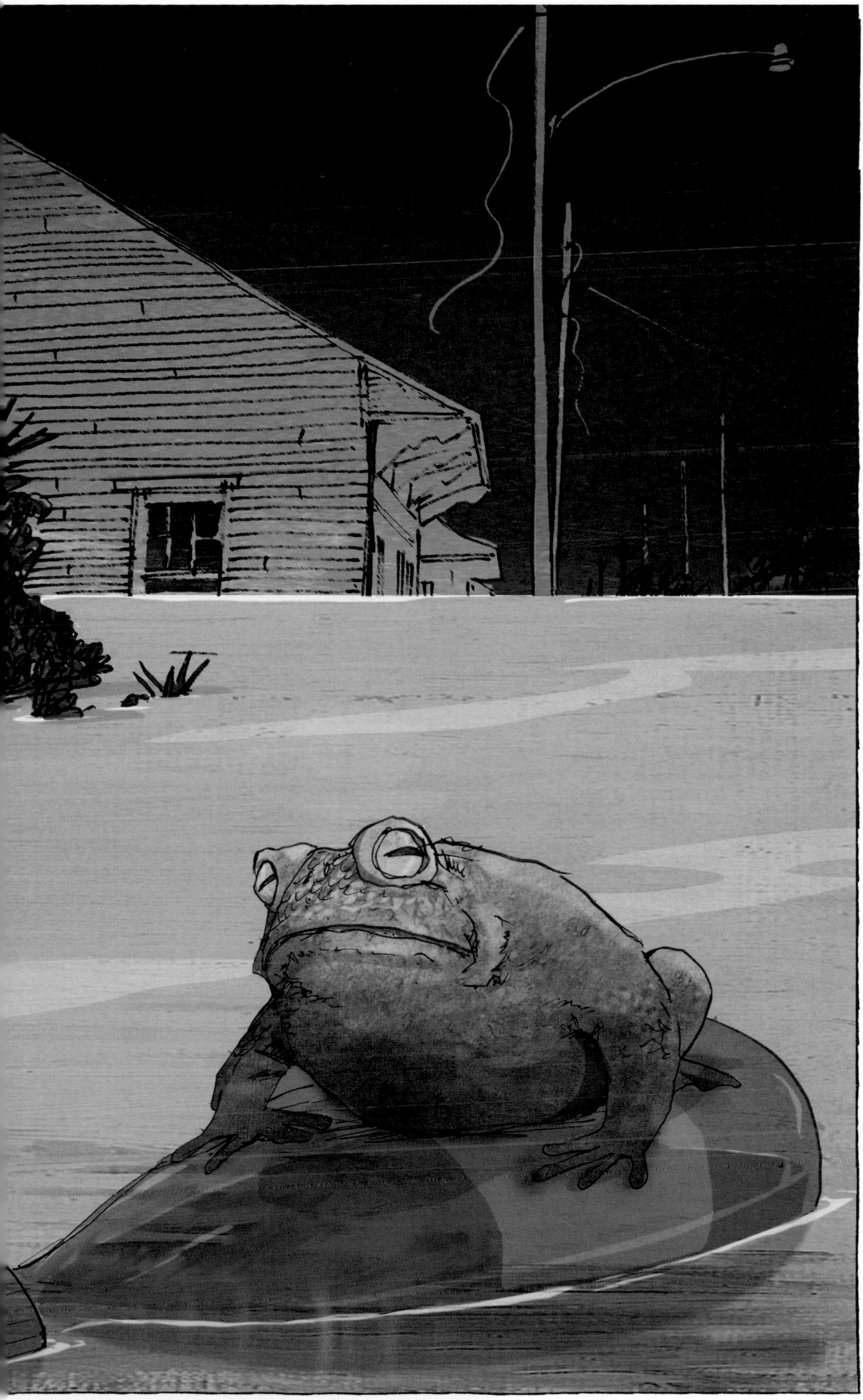

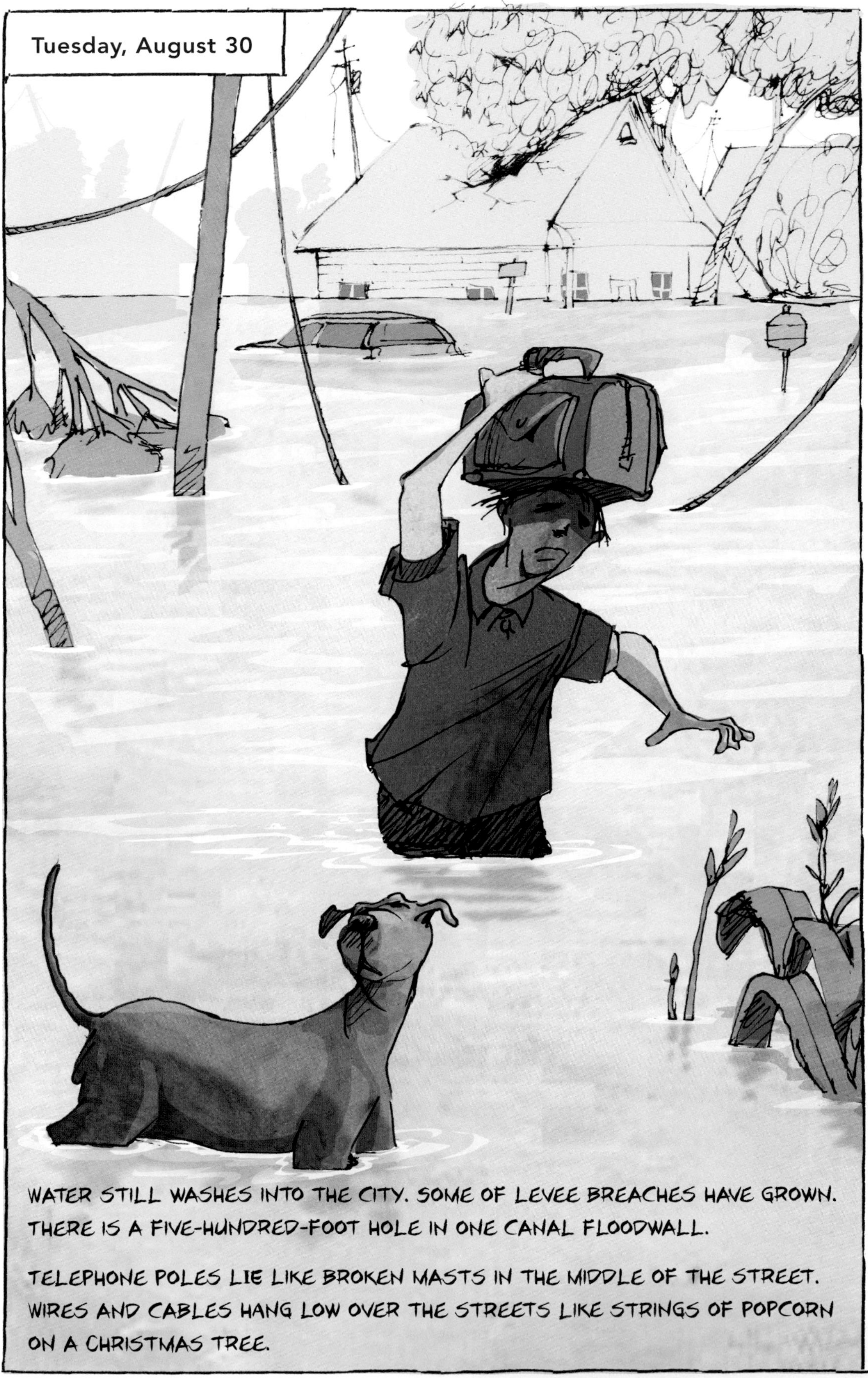
Tuesday, August 30
WATER STILL WASHES INTO THE CITY. SOME OF LEVEE BREACHES HAVE GROWN. THERE IS A FIVE-HUNDRED-FOOT HOLE IN ONE CANAL FLOODWALL.
TELEPHONE POLES LIE LIKE BROKEN MASTS IN THE MIDDLE OF THE STREET. WIRES AND CABLES HANG LOW OVER THE STREETS LIKE STRINGS OF POPCORN ON A CHRISTMAS TREE.

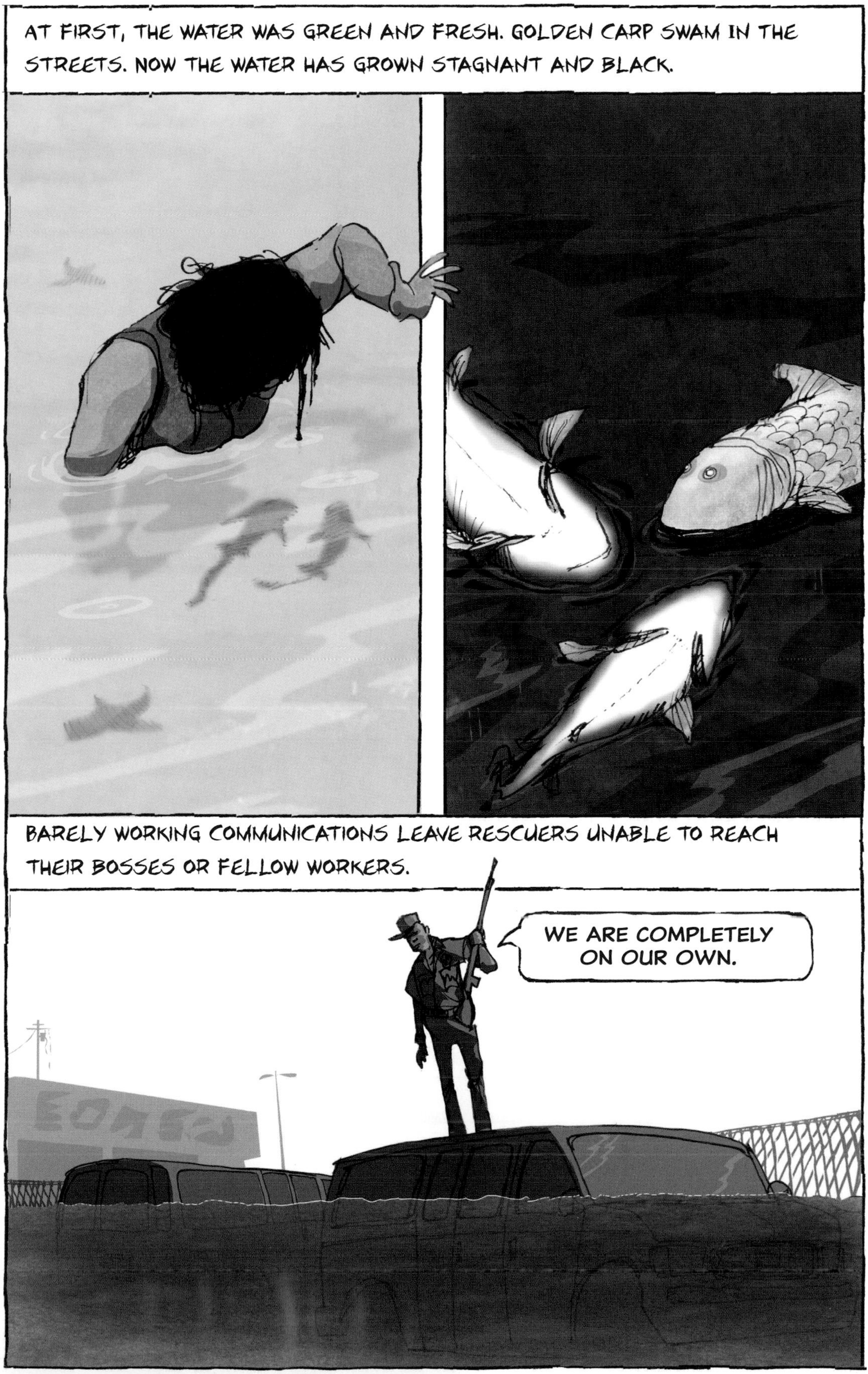
AT FIRST, THE WATER WAS GREEN AND FRESH. GOLDEN CARP SWAM IN THE STREETS. NOW THE WATER HAS GROWN STAGNANT AND BLACK.
BARELY WORKING COMMUNICATIONS LEAVE RESCUERS UNABLE TO REACH THEIR BOSSES OR FELLOW WORKERS.
WE ARE COMPLETELY ON OUR OWN.

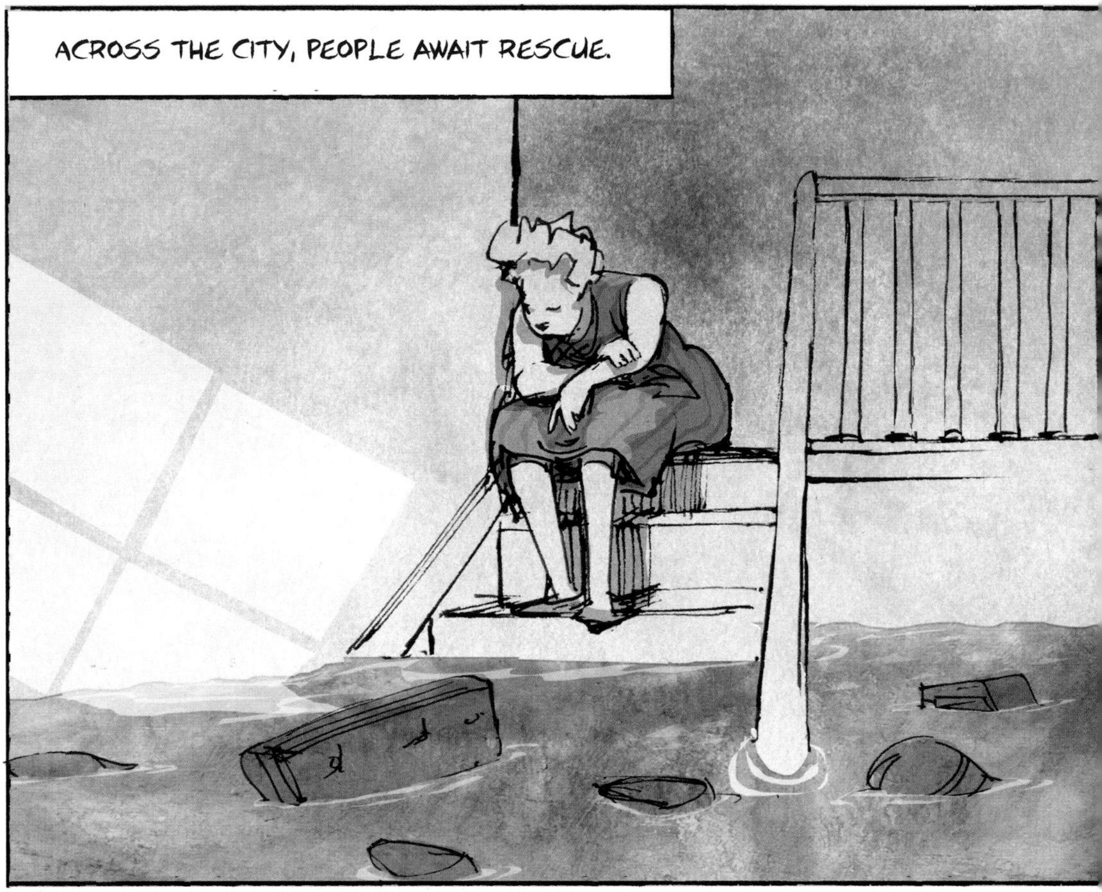
ACROSS THE CITY, PEOPLE AWAIT RESCUE.

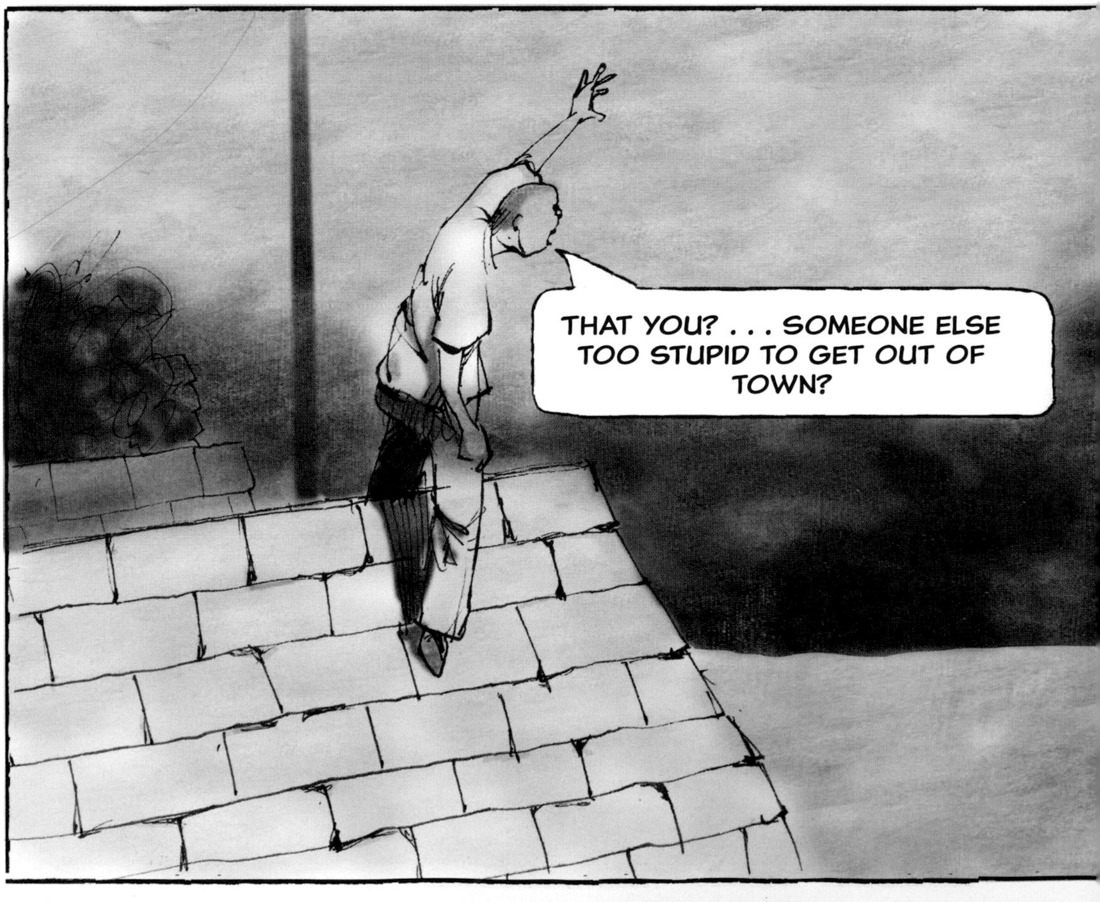
THAT YOU? . . . SOMEONE ELSE TOO STUPID TO GET OUT OF TOWN?

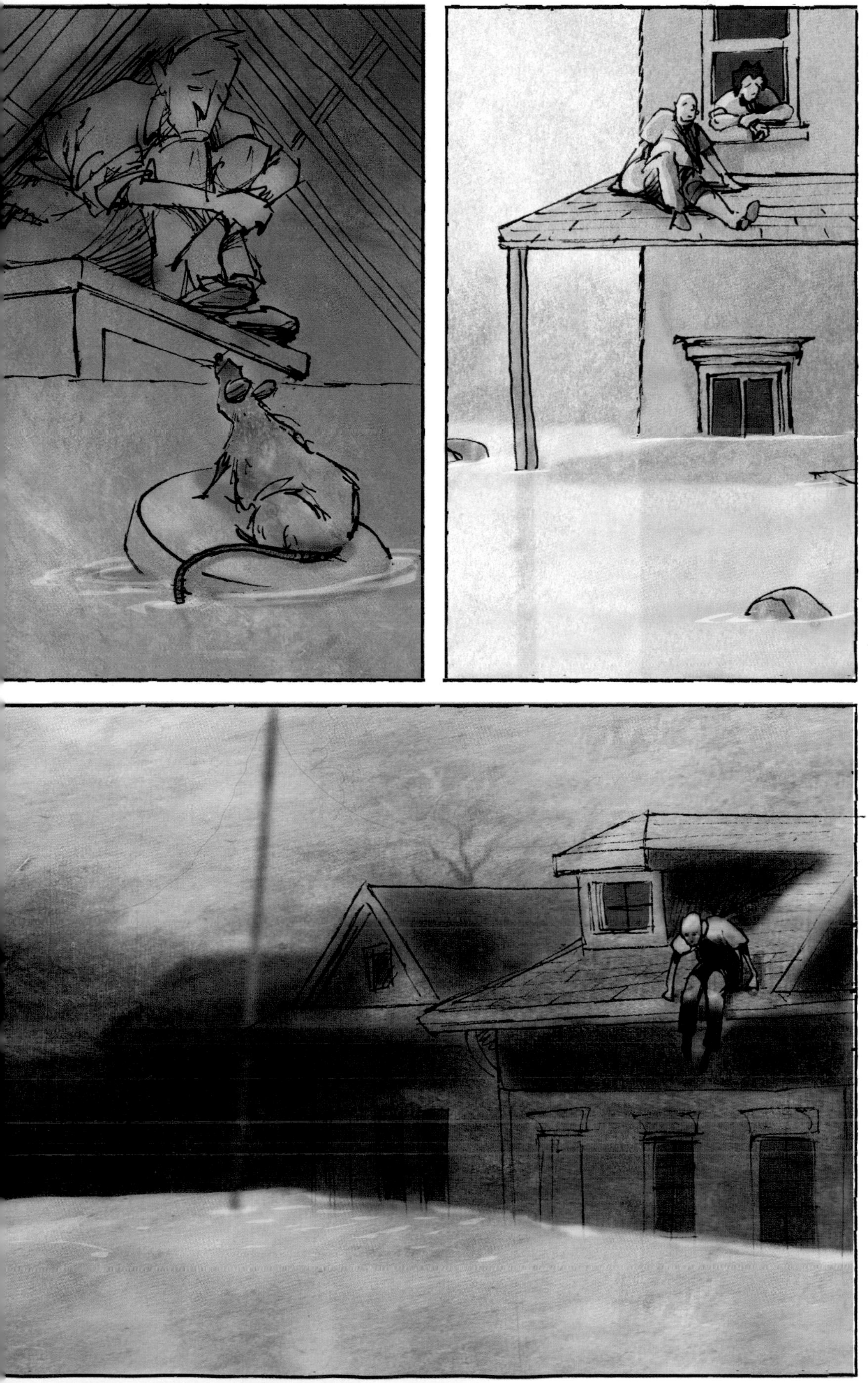

MICHAEL BROWN, CHIEF OF THE FEDERAL EMERGENCY MANAGEMENT AGENCY—FEMA—ALERTS HIS BOSS, MICHAEL CHERTOFF, THE SECRETARY OF HOMELAND SECURITY, AND PRESIDENT BUSH OF THE PROBLEMS, EXPLAINING, "THIS WAS THE BIG ONE."

IN FACT, KATRINA WAS WEAKER THAN THE FEARED BIG ONE. STILL, IT HAS WRECKED NEW ORLEANS.

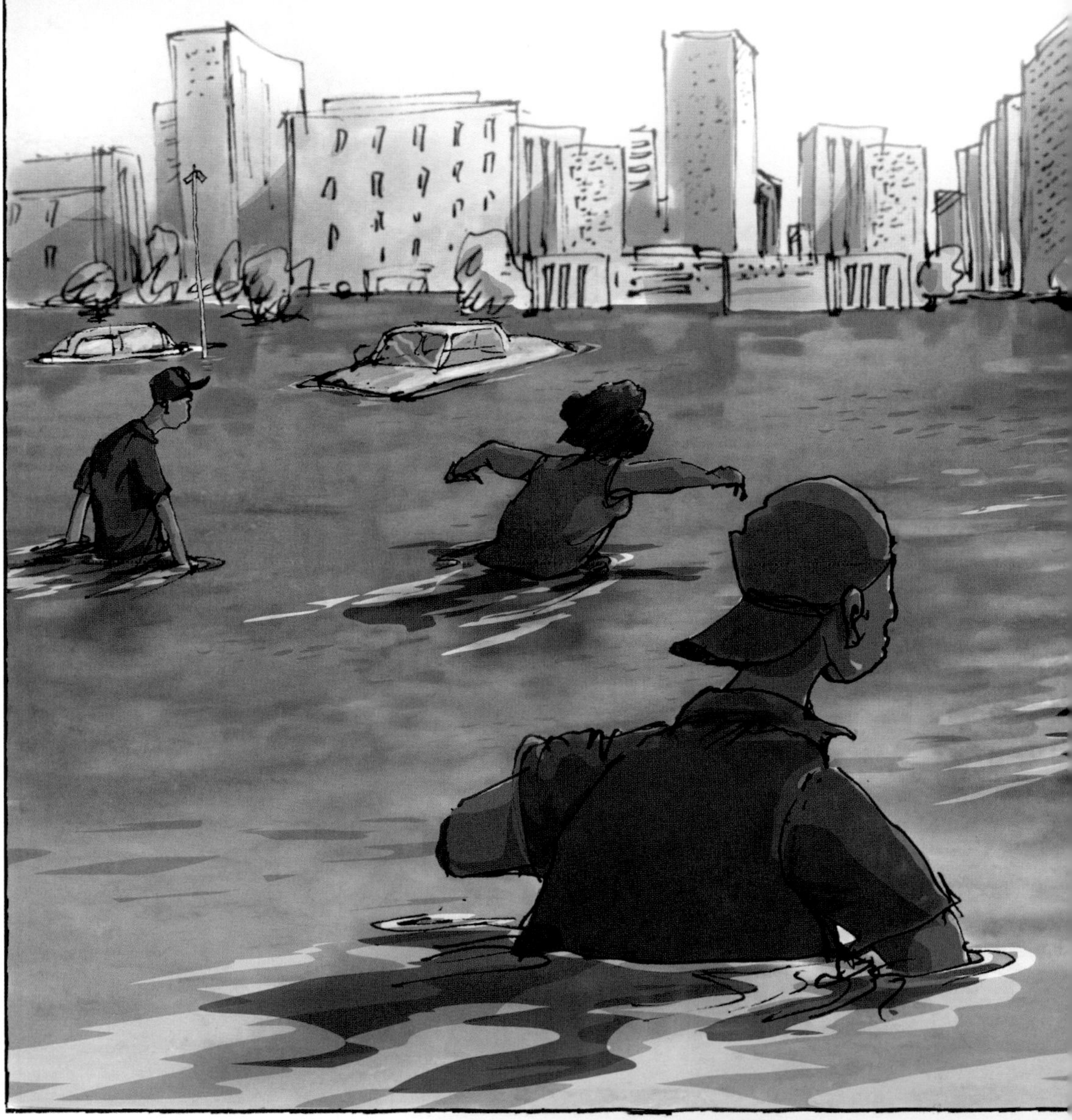

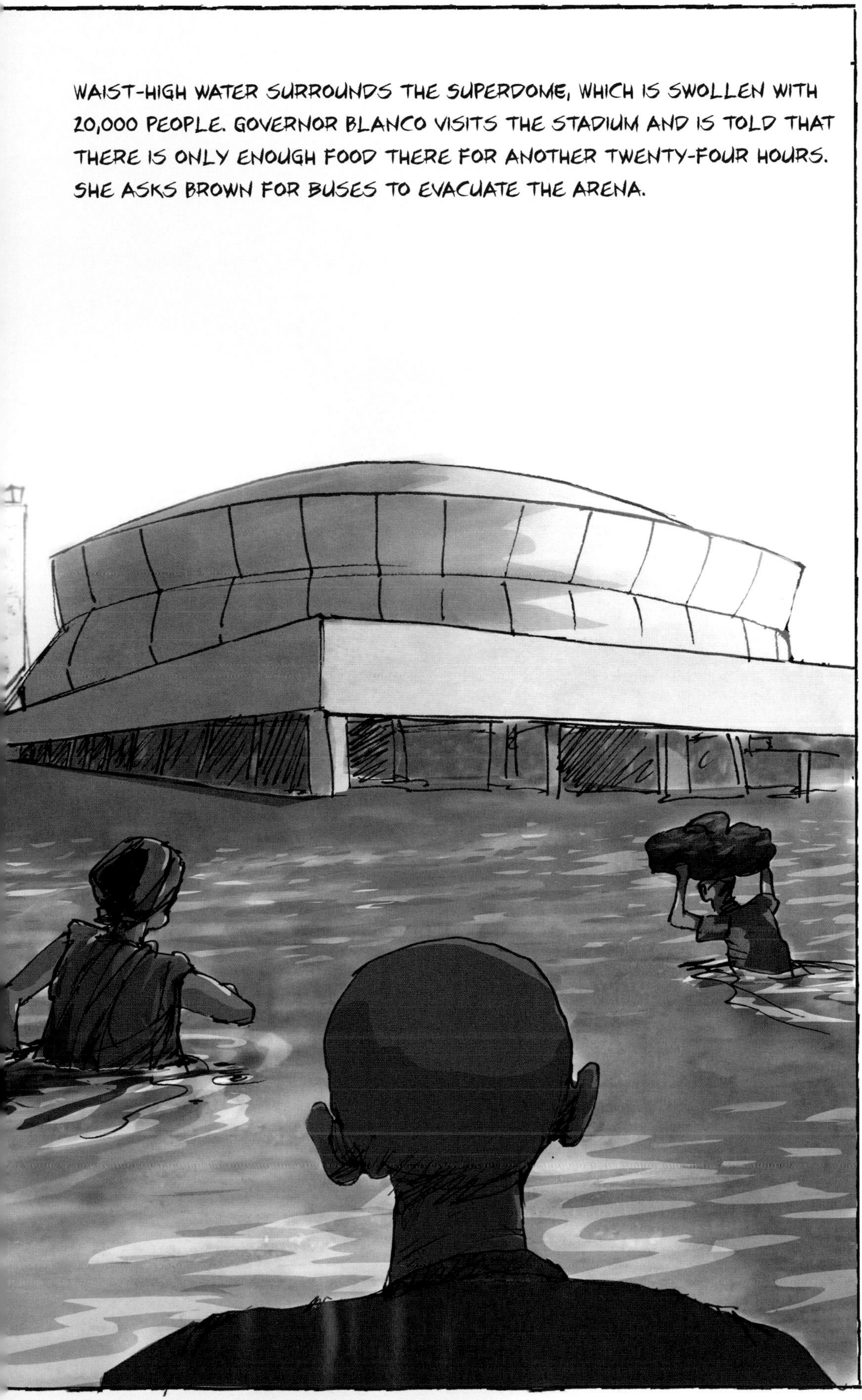
WAIST-HIGH WATER SURROUNDS THE SUPERDOME, WHICH IS SWOLLEN WITH 20,000 PEOPLE. GOVERNOR BLANCO VISITS THE STADIUM AND IS TOLD THAT THERE IS ONLY ENOUGH FOOD THERE FOR ANOTHER TWENTY-FOUR HOURS. SHE ASKS BROWN FOR BUSES TO EVACUATE THE ARENA.

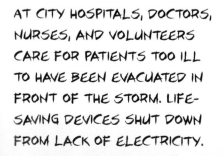

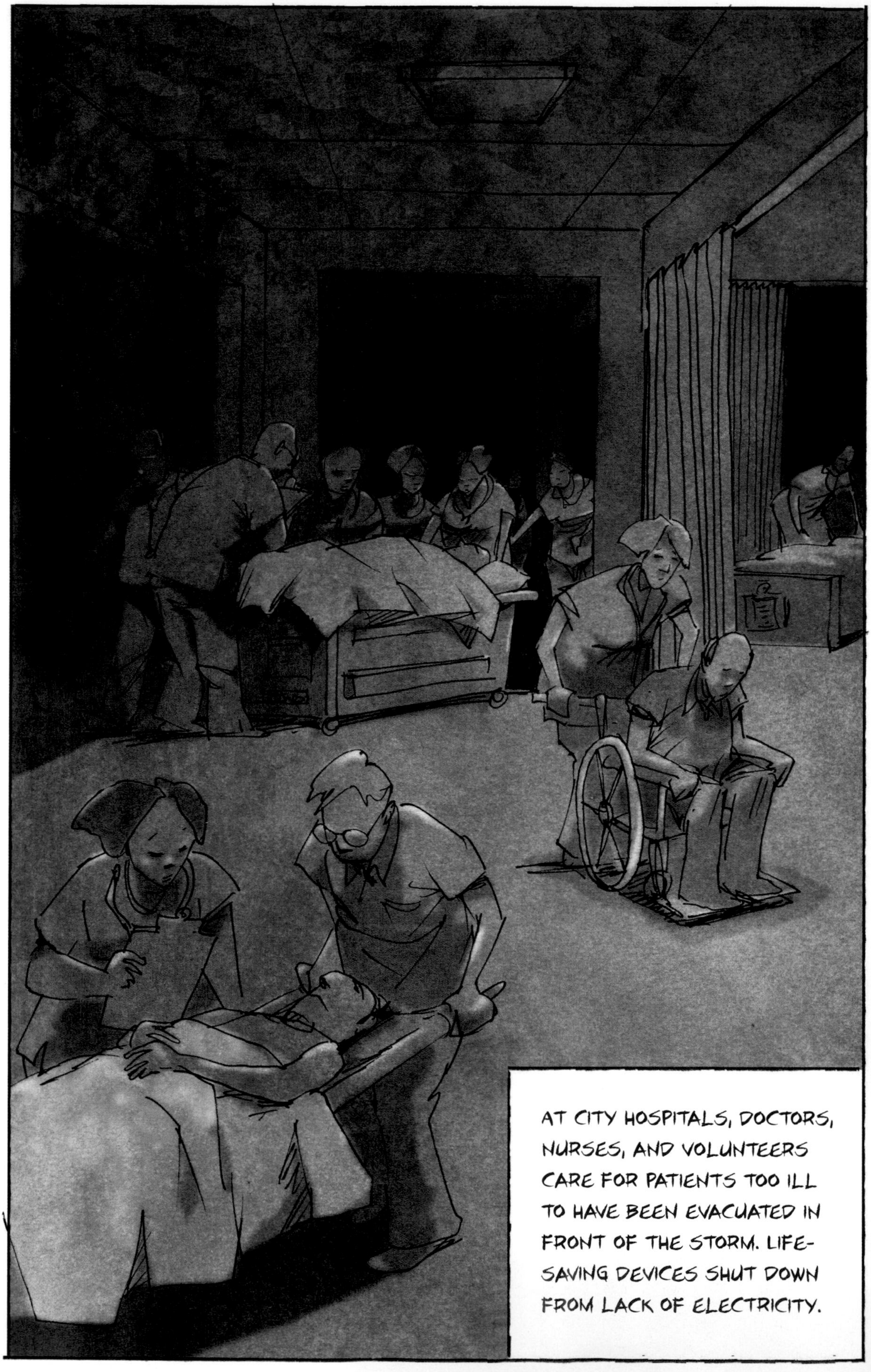

AT CITY HOSPITALS, DOCTORS, NURSES, AND VOLUNTEERS CARE FOR PATIENTS TOO ILL TO HAVE BEEN EVACUATED IN FRONT OF THE STORM. LIFE-SAVING DEVICES SHUT DOWN FROM LACK OF ELECTRICITY.

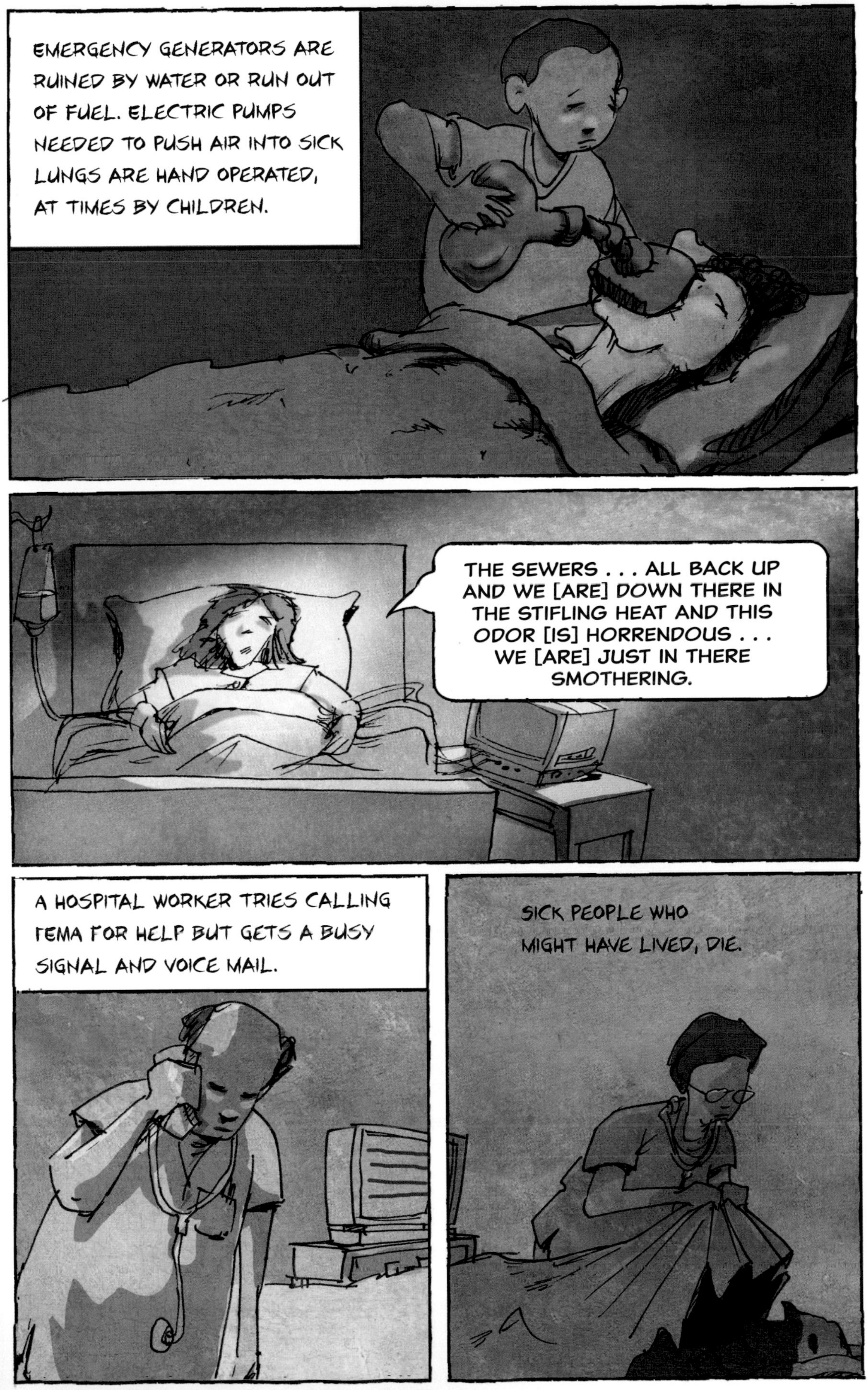
EMERGENCY GENERATORS ARE RUINED BY WATER OR RUN OUT OF FUEL. ELECTRIC PUMPS NEEDED TO PUSH AIR INTO SICK LUNGS ARE HAND OPERATED, AT TIMES BY CHILDREN.
THE SEWERS . . . ALL BACK UP AND WE [ARE] DOWN THERE IN THE STIFLING HEAT AND THIS ODOR [IS] HORRENDOUS . . . WE [ARE] JUST IN THERE SMOTHERING.
A HOSPITAL WORKER TRIES CALLING FEMA FOR HELP BUT GETS A BUSY SIGNAL AND VOICE MAIL.
SICK PEOPLE WHO MIGHT HAVE LIVED, DIE.

PEOPLE RESCUED FROM THE WATER, FROM BUILDINGS AND HOMES, ARE DROPPED OFF ON REMOTE BITS OF HIGH GROUND. PARTLY FLOODED HIGHWAY RAMPS ACT AS MAKESHIFT PIERS.

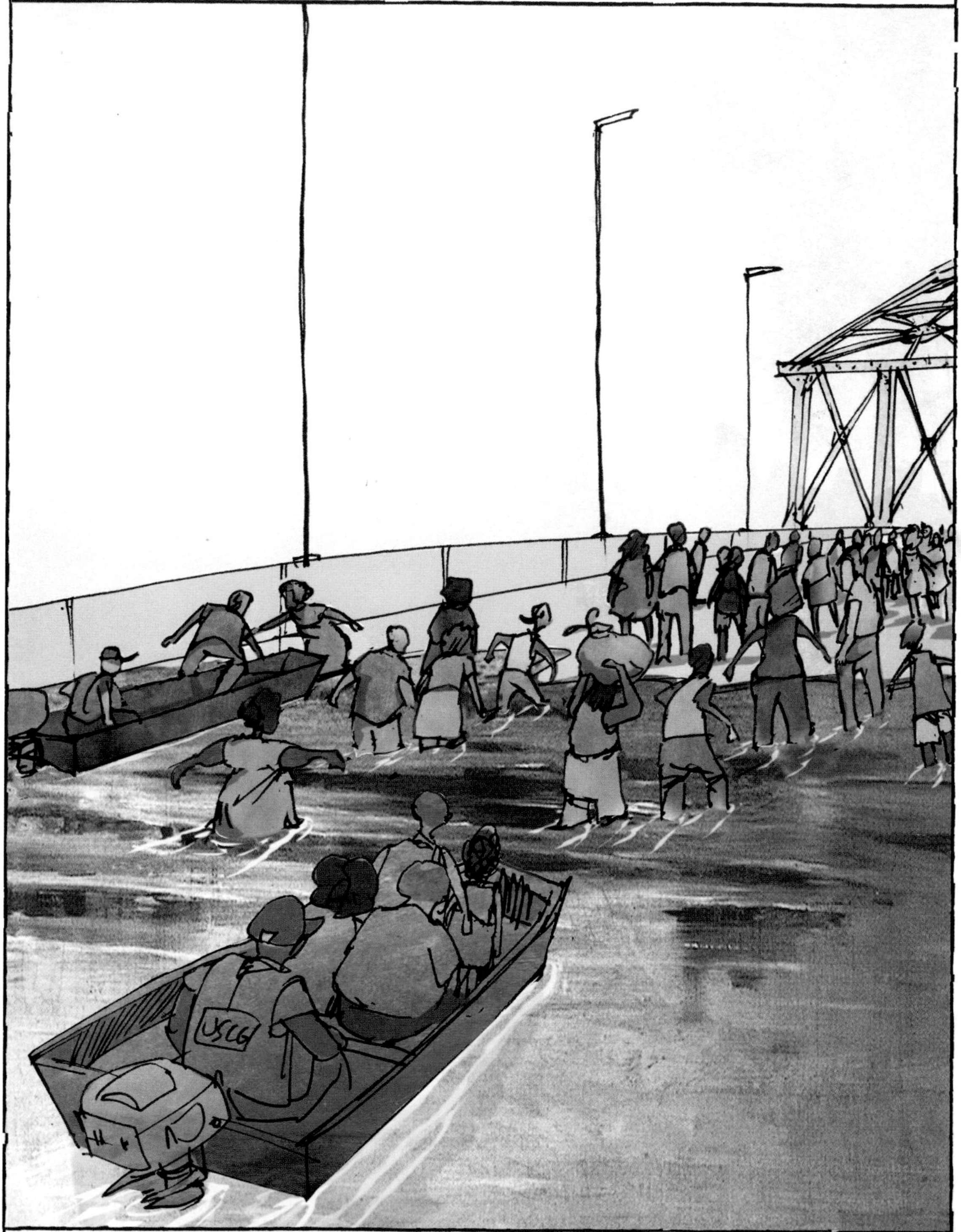
USCG

ALL MANNER OF SAVED PEOPLE ARRIVE: YOUNG, OLD, HEALTHY, SICK, ALERT, AND STUNNED. THEY DON'T KNOW WHERE TO GO, AND THERE IS NO ONE TO HELP THEM.

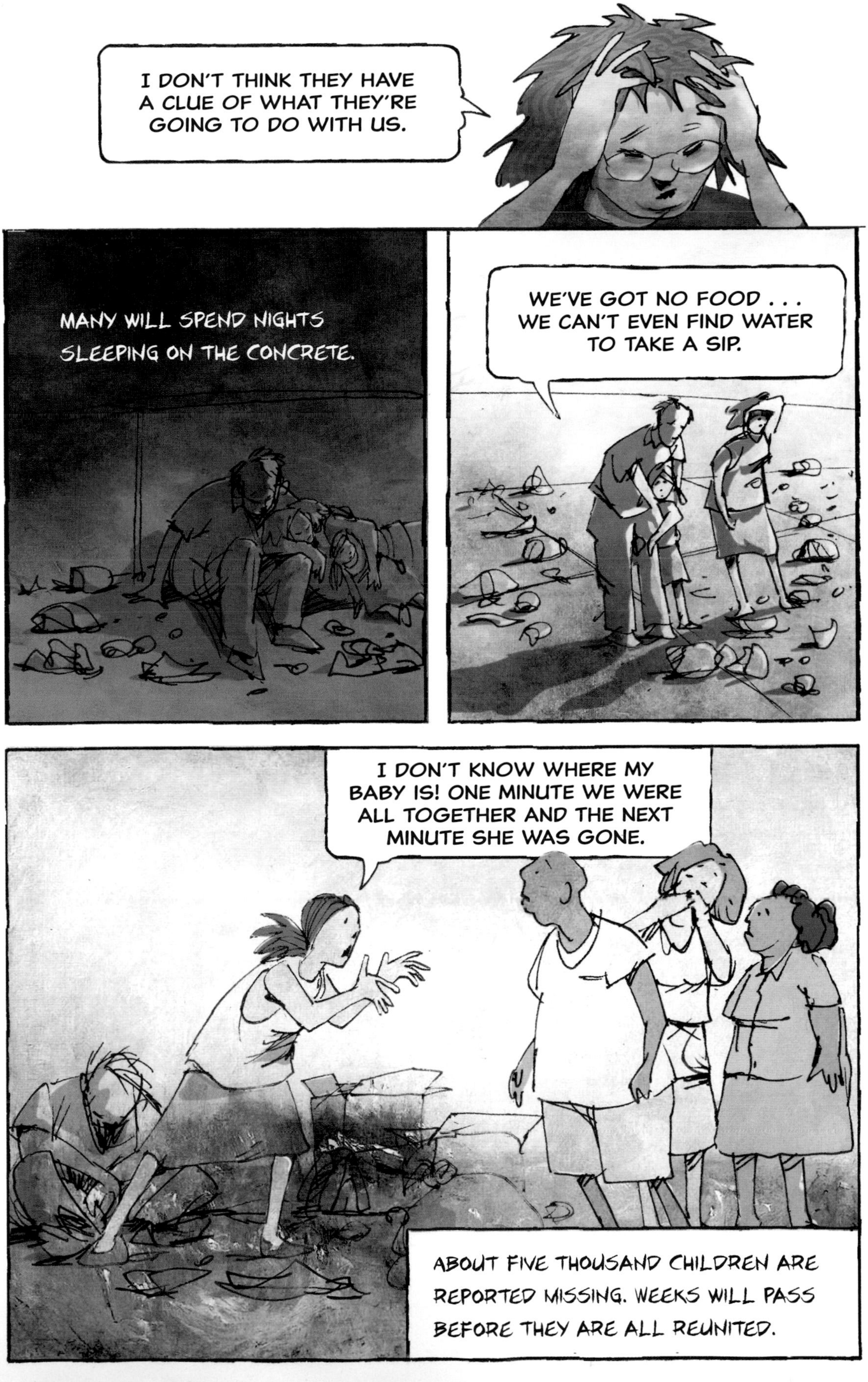
I DON'T THINK THEY HAVE A CLUE OF WHAT THEY'RE GOING TO DO WITH US.
MANY WILL SPEND NIGHTS SLEEPING ON THE CONCRETE.
WE'VE GOT NO FOOD . . . WE CAN'T EVEN FIND WATER TO TAKE A SIP.
I DON'T KNOW WHERE MY BABY IS! ONE MINUTE WE WERE ALL TOGETHER AND THE NEXT MINUTE SHE WAS GONE.
ABOUT FIVE THOUSAND CHILDREN ARE REPORTED MISSING. WEEKS WILL PASS BEFORE THEY ARE ALL REUNITED.

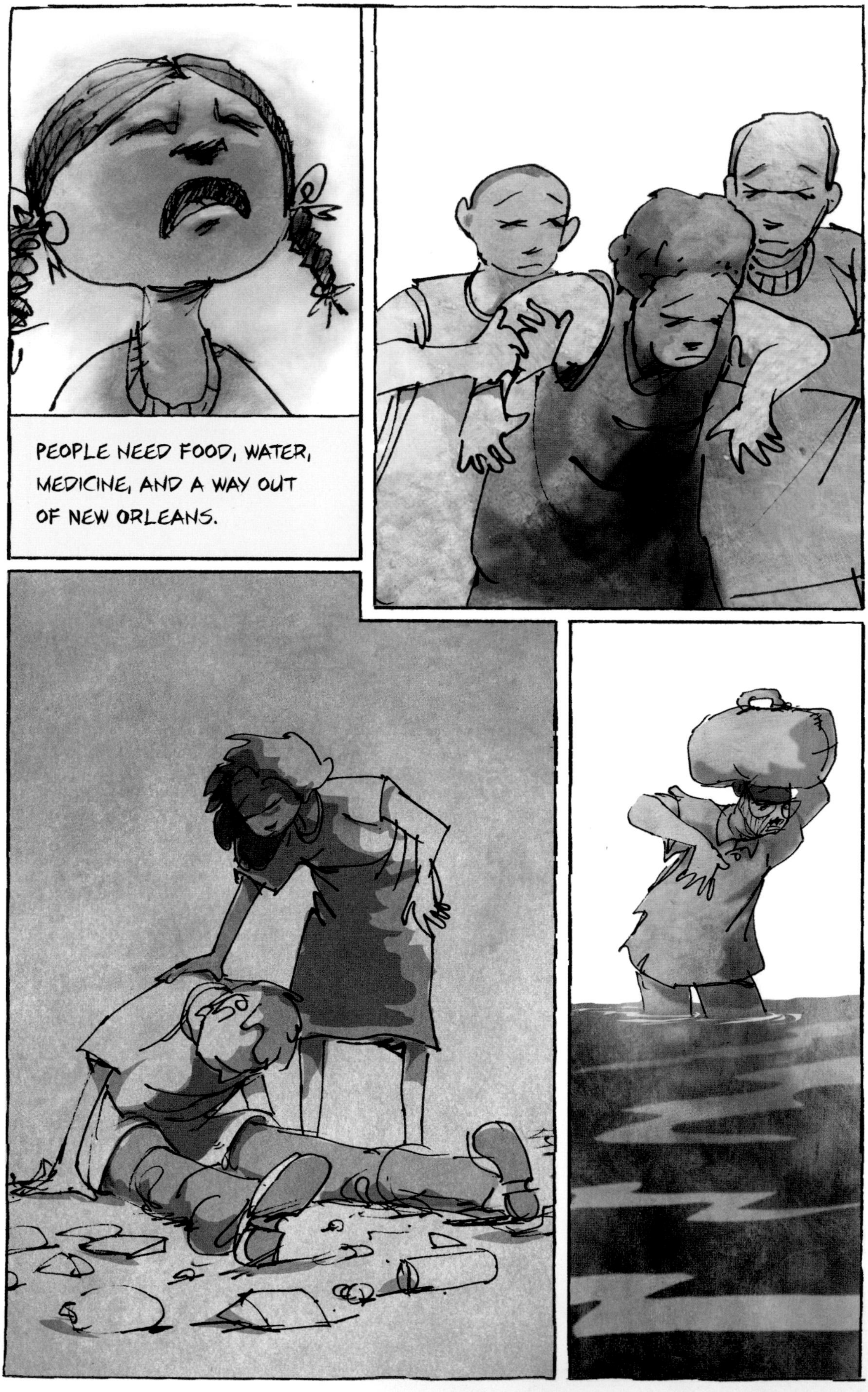
PEOPLE NEED FOOD, WATER, MEDICINE, AND A WAY OUT OF NEW ORLEANS.

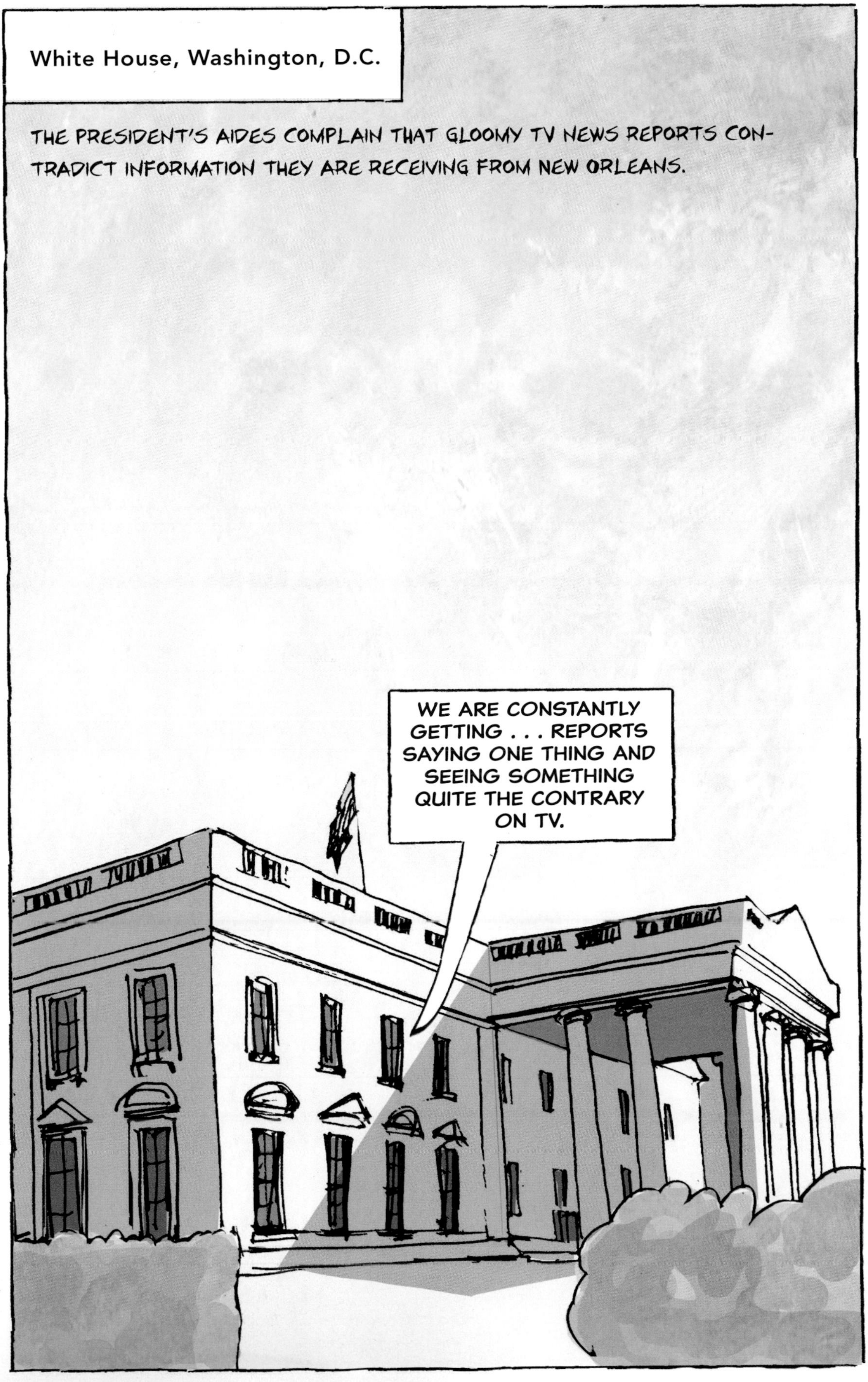
White House, Washington, D.C.
THE PRESIDENT'S AIDES COMPLAIN THAT GLOOMY TV NEWS REPORTS CONTRADICT INFORMATION THEY ARE RECEIVING FROM NEW ORLEANS.
WE ARE CONSTANTLY GETTING . . . REPORTS SAYING ONE THING AND SEEING SOMETHING QUITE THE CONTRARY ON TV.

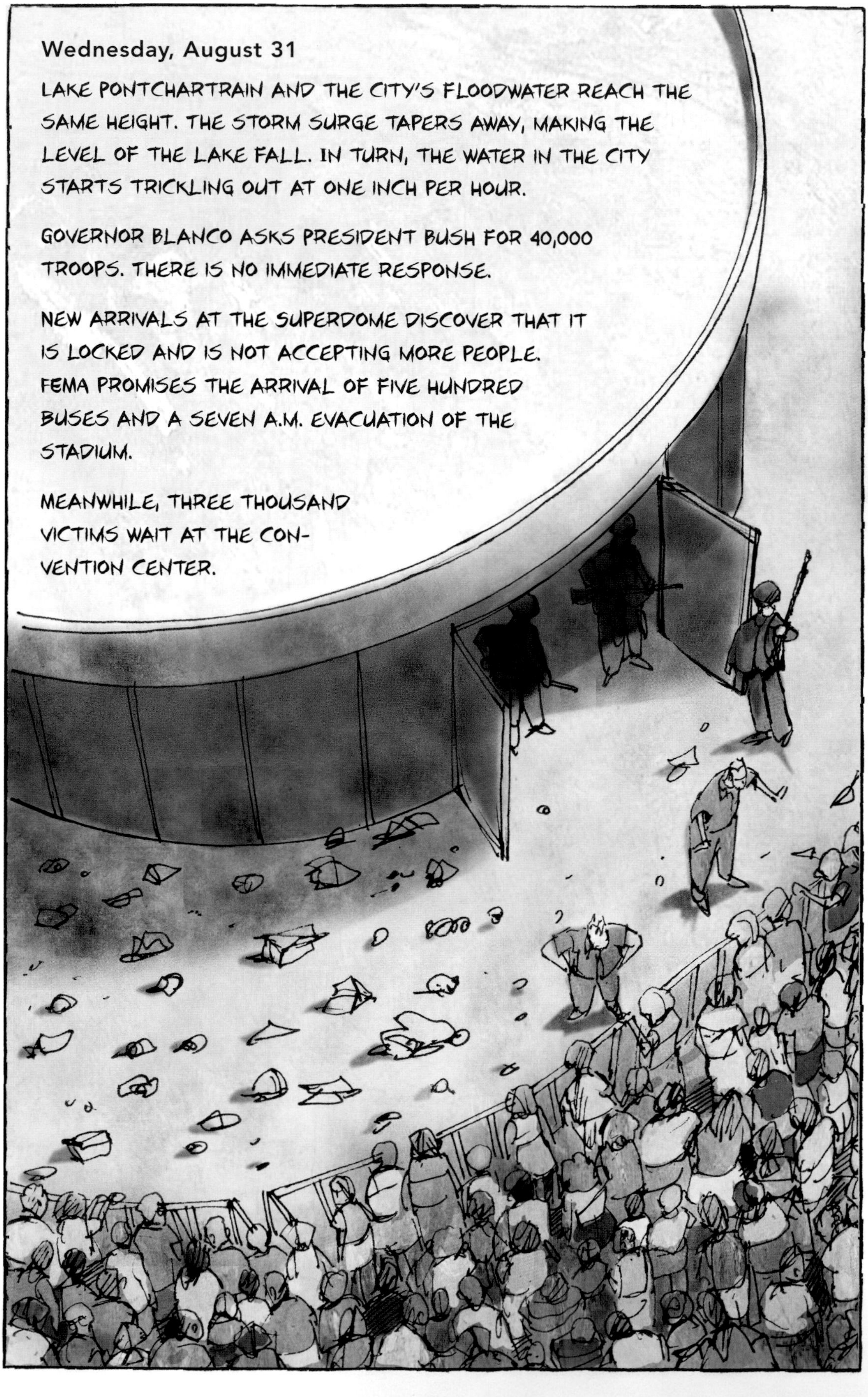
Wednesday, August 31
LAKE PONTCHARTRAIN AND THE CITY'S FLOODWATER REACH THE SAME HEIGHT. THE STORM SURGE TAPERS AWAY, MAKING THE LEVEL OF THE LAKE FALL. IN TURN, THE WATER IN THE CITY STARTS TRICKLING OUT AT ONE INCH PER HOUR.
GOVERNOR BLANCO ASKS PRESIDENT BUSH FOR 40,000 TROOPS. THERE IS NO IMMEDIATE RESPONSE.
NEW ARRIVALS AT THE SUPERDOME DISCOVER THAT IT IS LOCKED AND IS NOT ACCEPTING MORE PEOPLE. FEMA PROMISES THE ARRIVAL OF FIVE HUNDRED BUSES AND A SEVEN A.M. EVACUATION OF THE STADIUM.
MEANWHILE, THREE THOUSAND VICTIMS WAIT AT THE CON-VENTION CENTER.

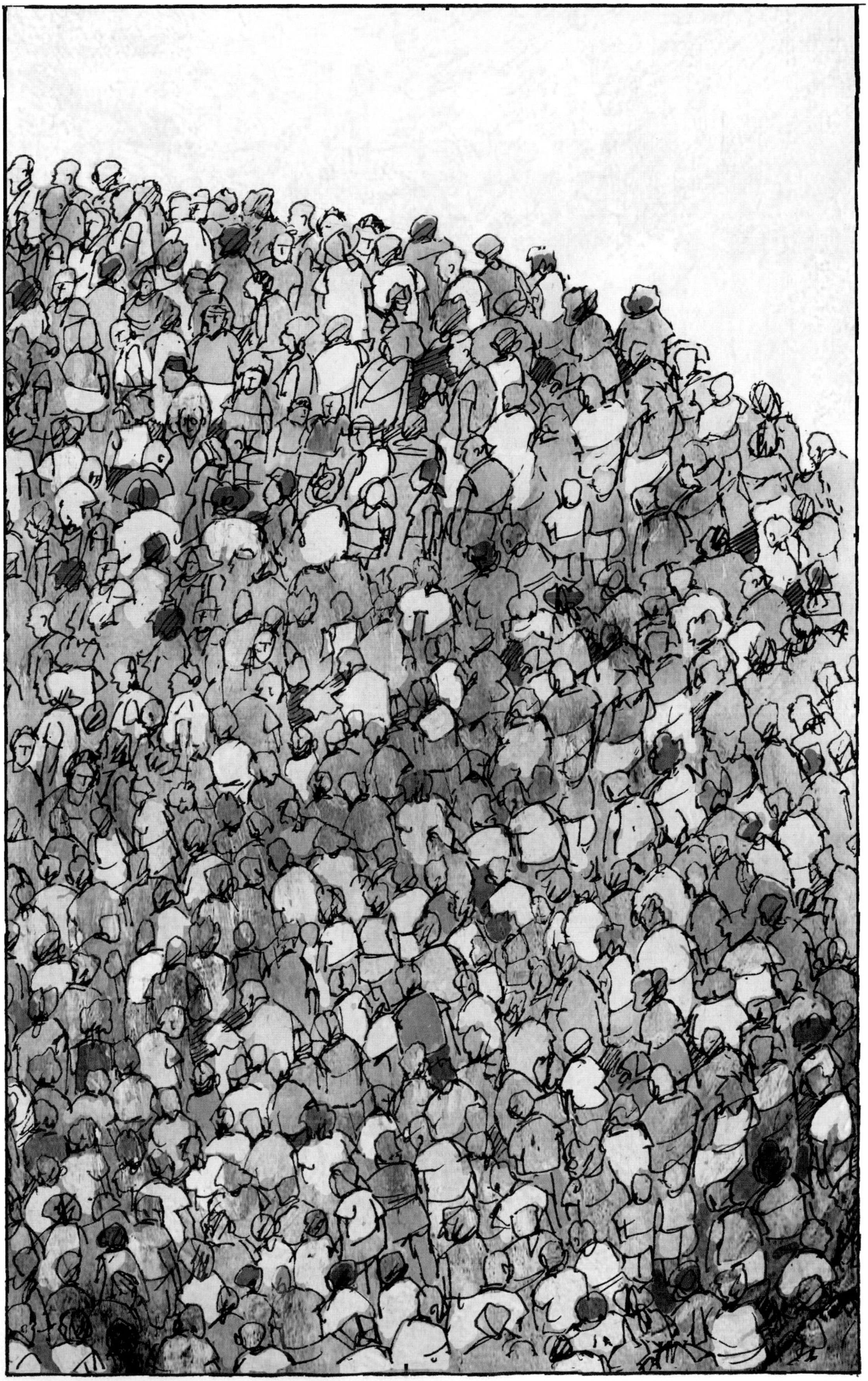

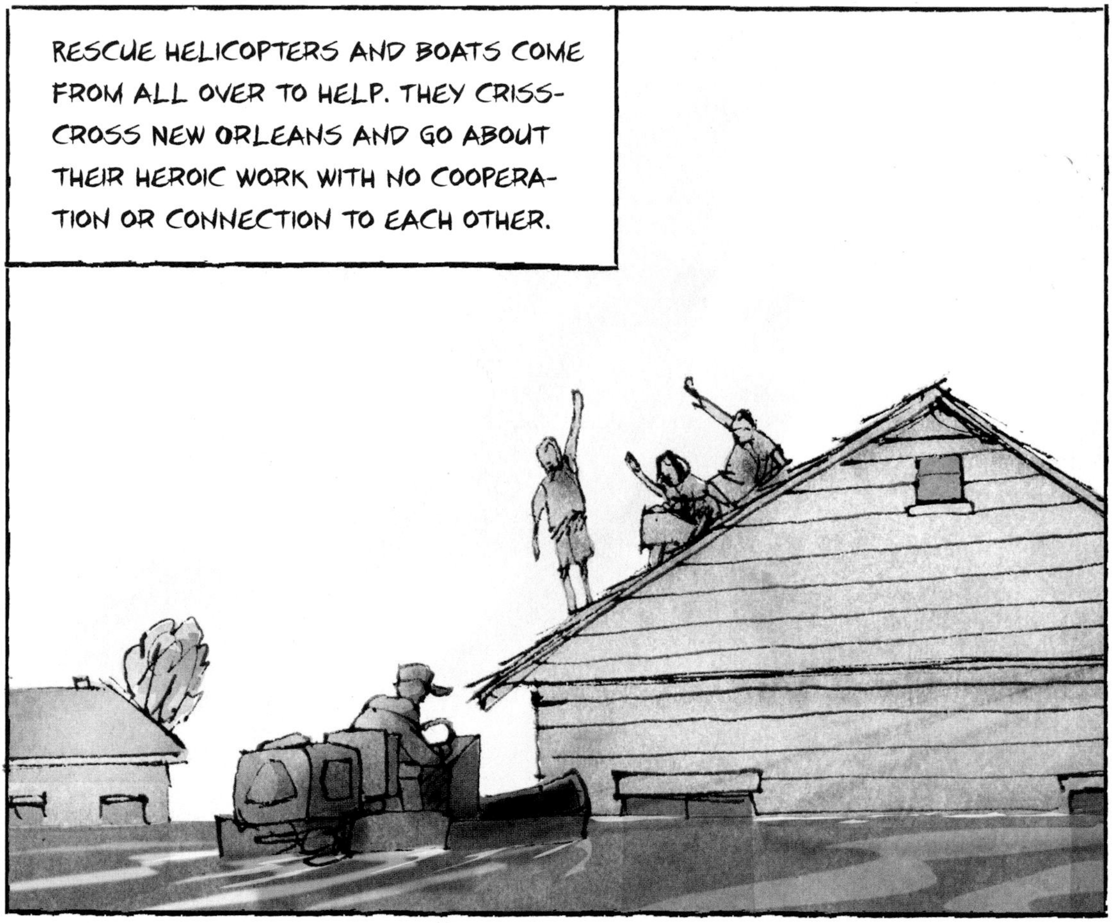
RESCUE HELICOPTERS AND BOATS COME FROM ALL OVER TO HELP. THEY CRISS-CROSS NEW ORLEANS AND GO ABOUT THEIR HEROIC WORK WITH NO COOPERATION OR CONNECTION TO EACH OTHER.

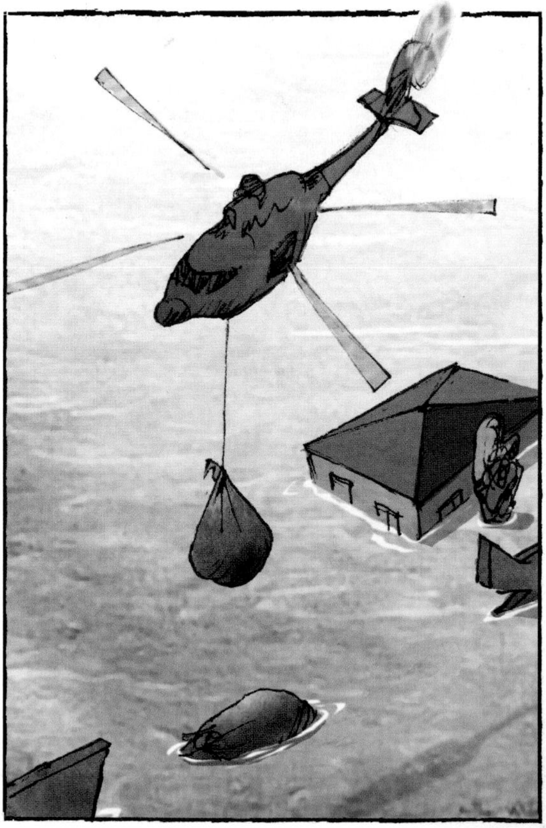

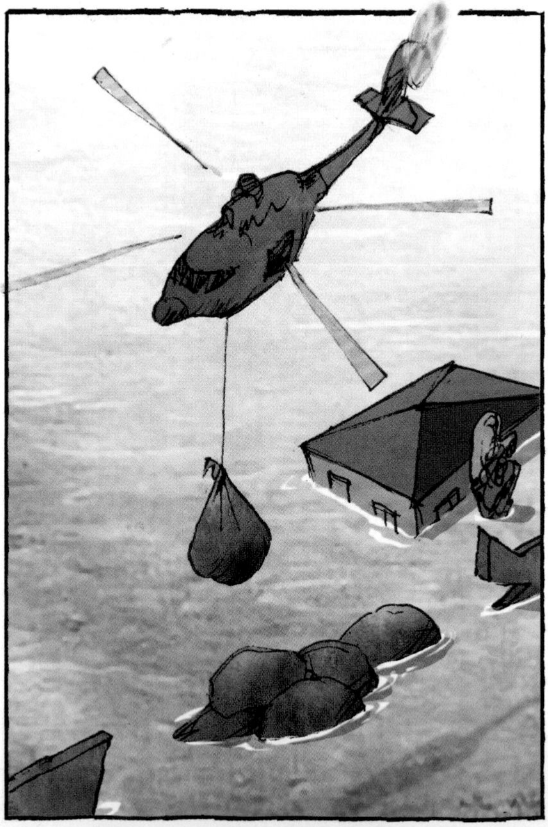

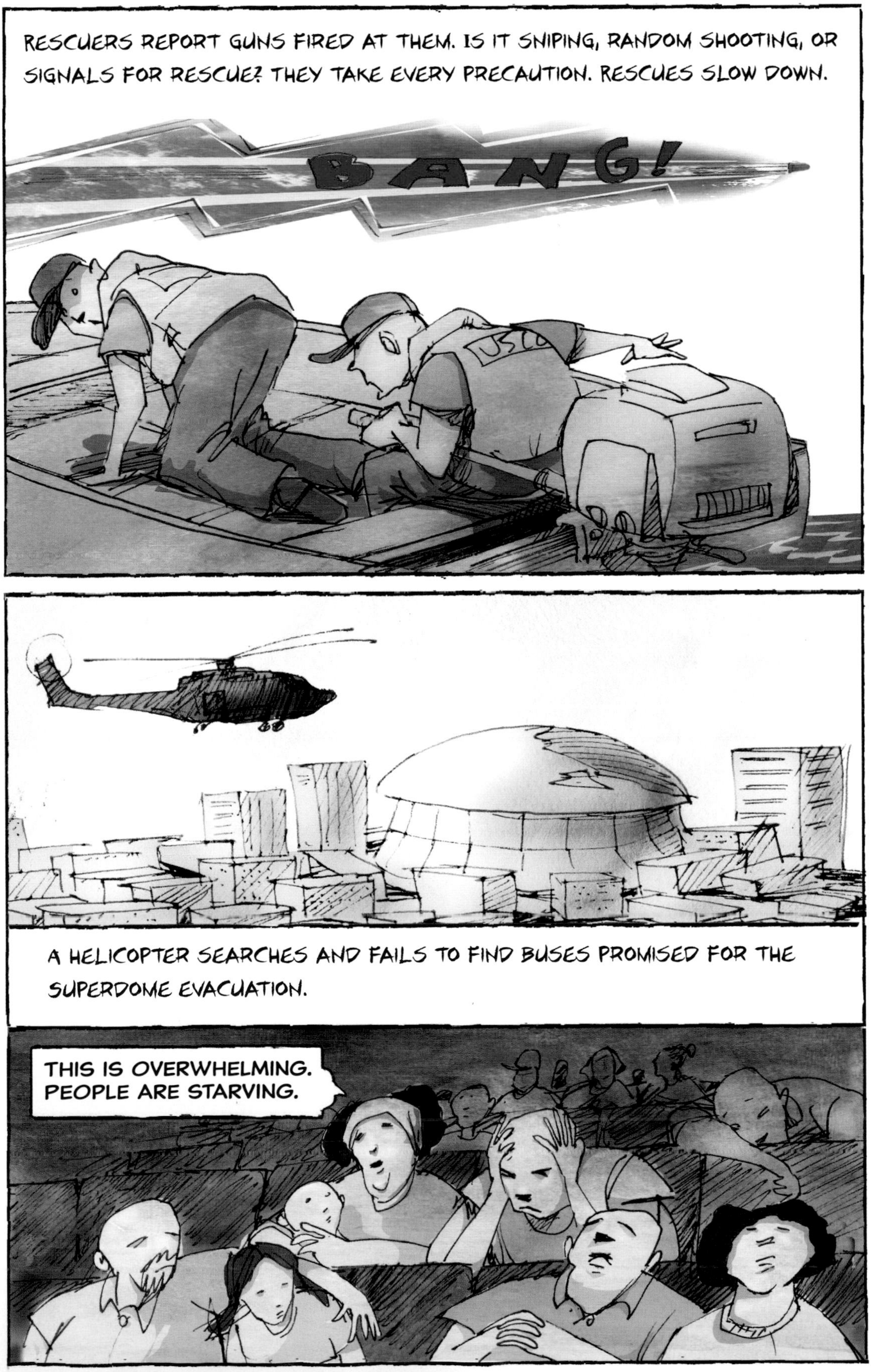
RESCUERS REPORT GUNS FIRED AT THEM. IS IT SNIPING, RANDOM SHOOTING, OR SIGNALS FOR RESCUE? THEY TAKE EVERY PRECAUTION. RESCUES SLOW DOWN.
BANG!
A HELICOPTER SEARCHES AND FAILS TO FIND BUSES PROMISED FOR THE SUPERDOME EVACUATION.
THIS IS OVERWHELMING. PEOPLE ARE STARVING.

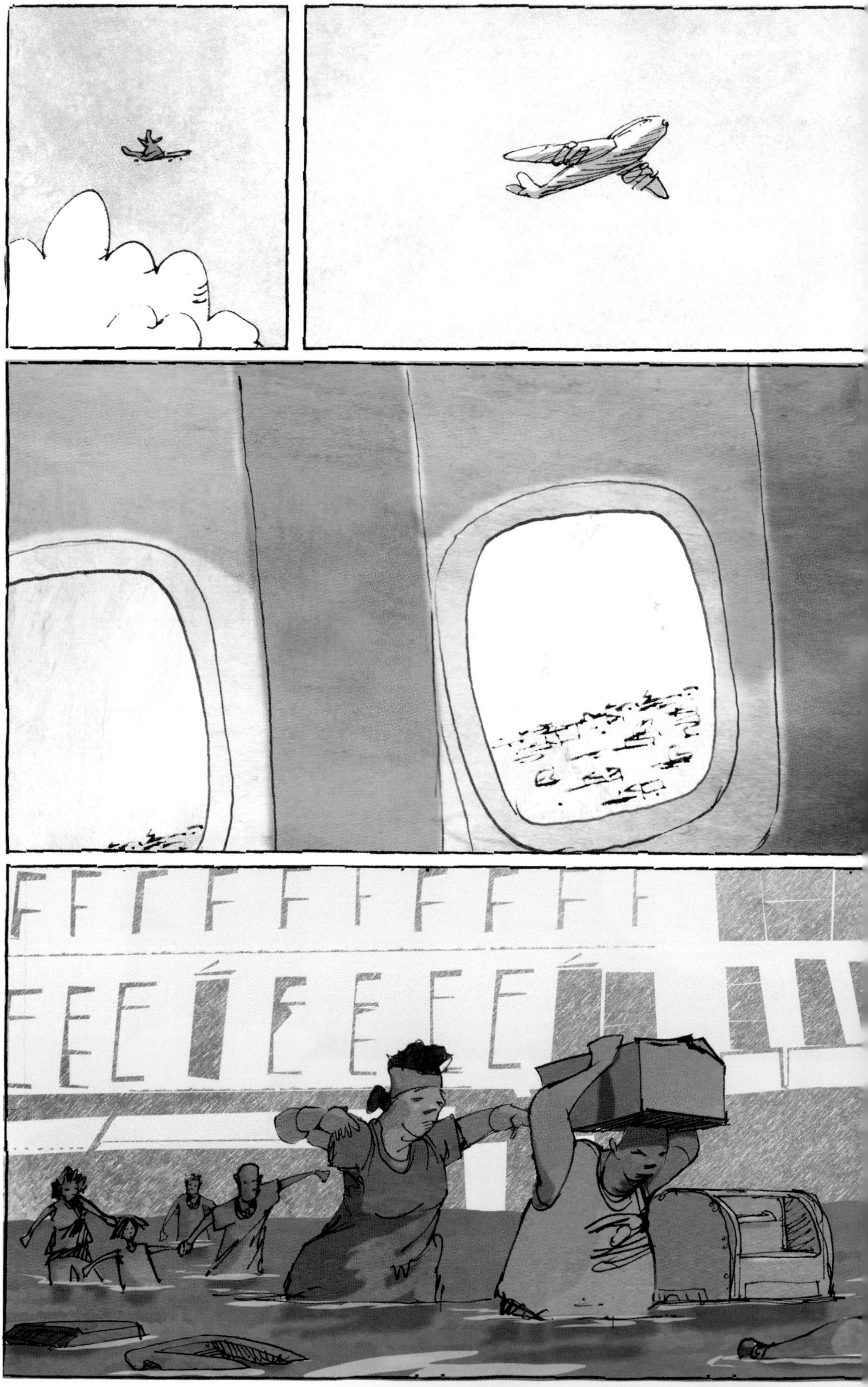

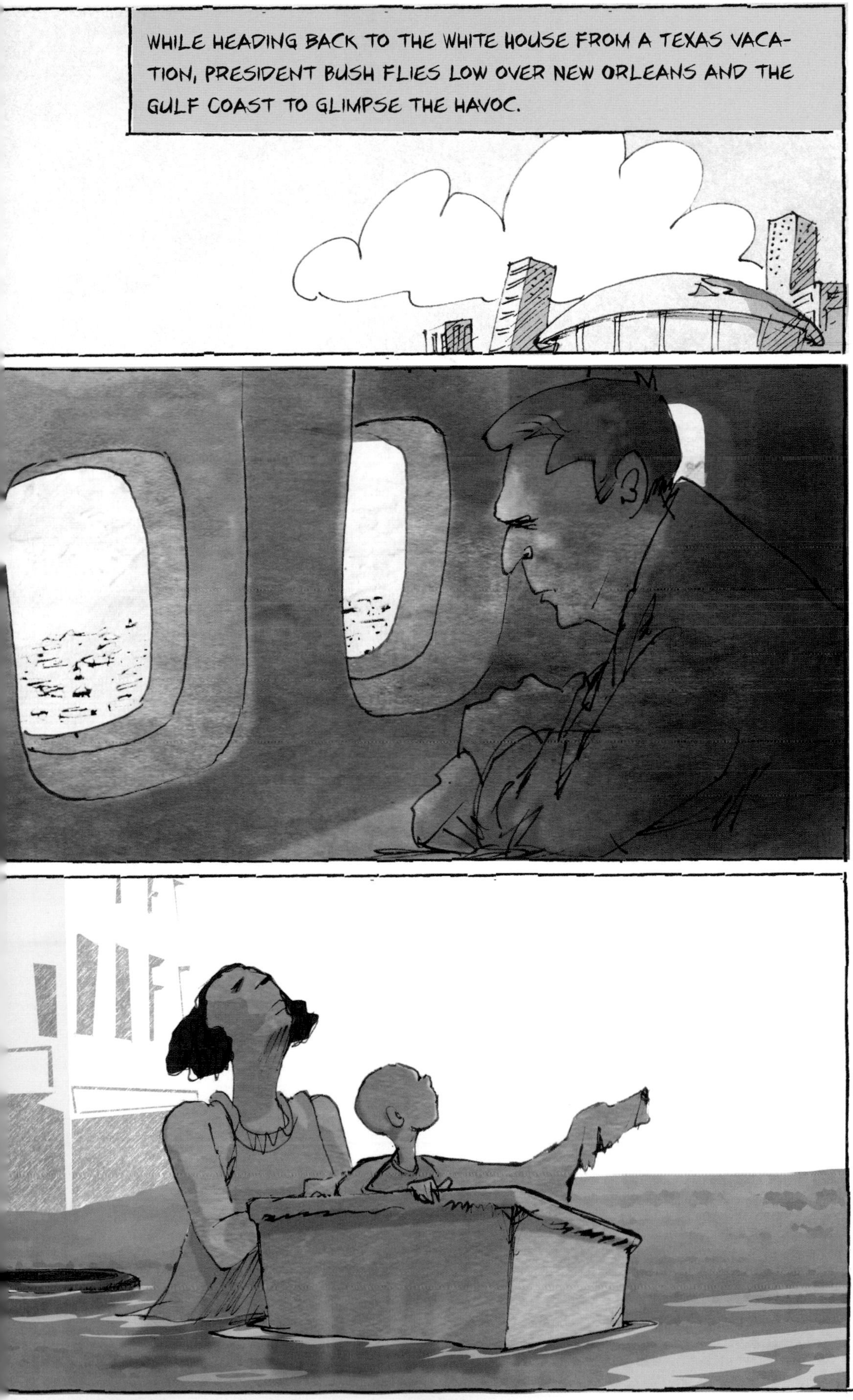
WHILE HEADING BACK TO THE WHITE HOUSE FROM A TEXAS VACATION, PRESIDENT BUSH FLIES LOW OVER NEW ORLEANS AND THE GULF COAST TO GLIMPSE THE HAVOC.

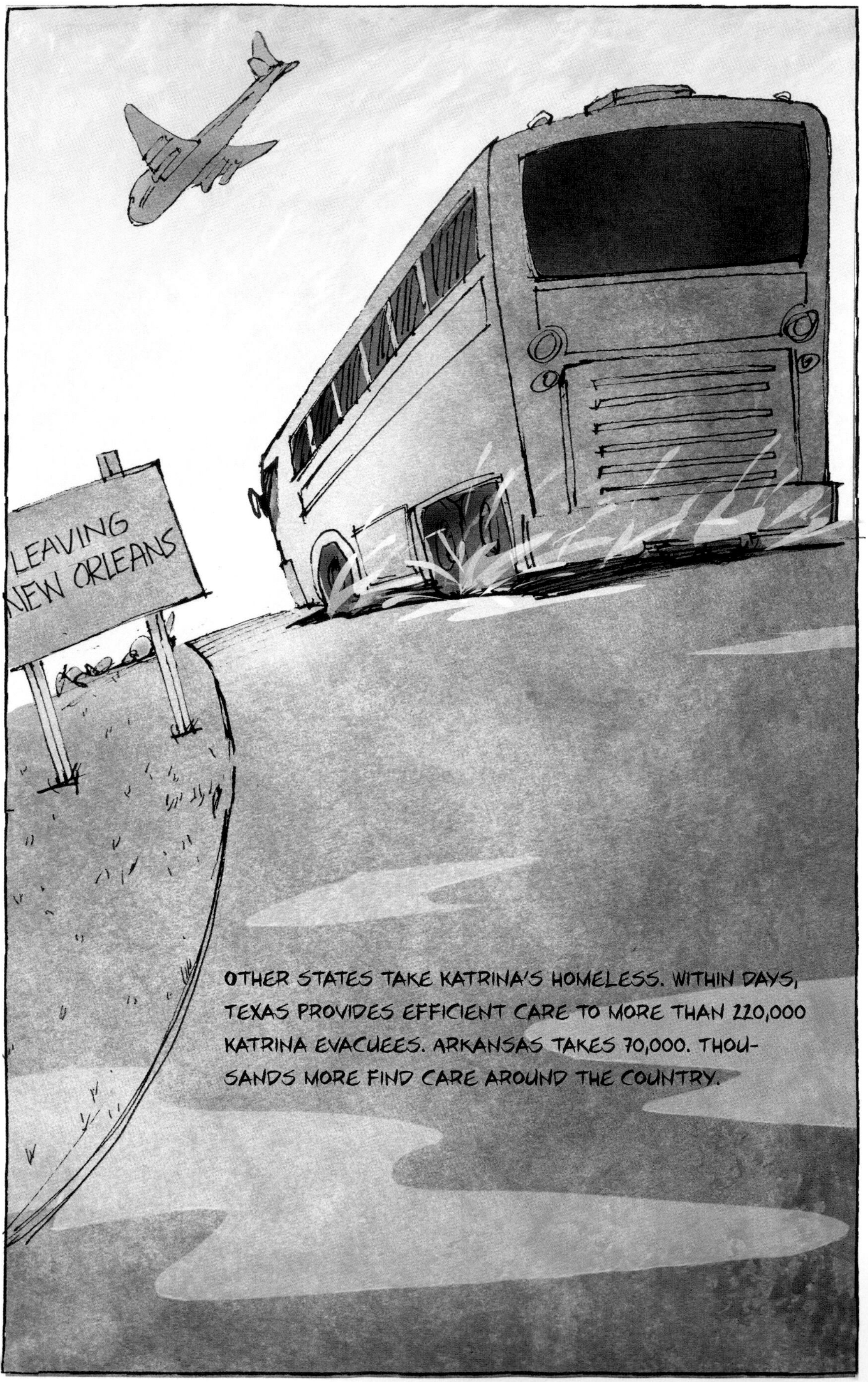
LEAVING NEW ORLEANS
OTHER STATES TAKE KATRINA'S HOMELESS. WITHIN DAYS, TEXAS PROVIDES EFFICIENT CARE TO MORE THAN 220,000 KATRINA EVACUEES. ARKANSAS TAKES 70,000. THOUSANDS MORE FIND CARE AROUND THE COUNTRY.

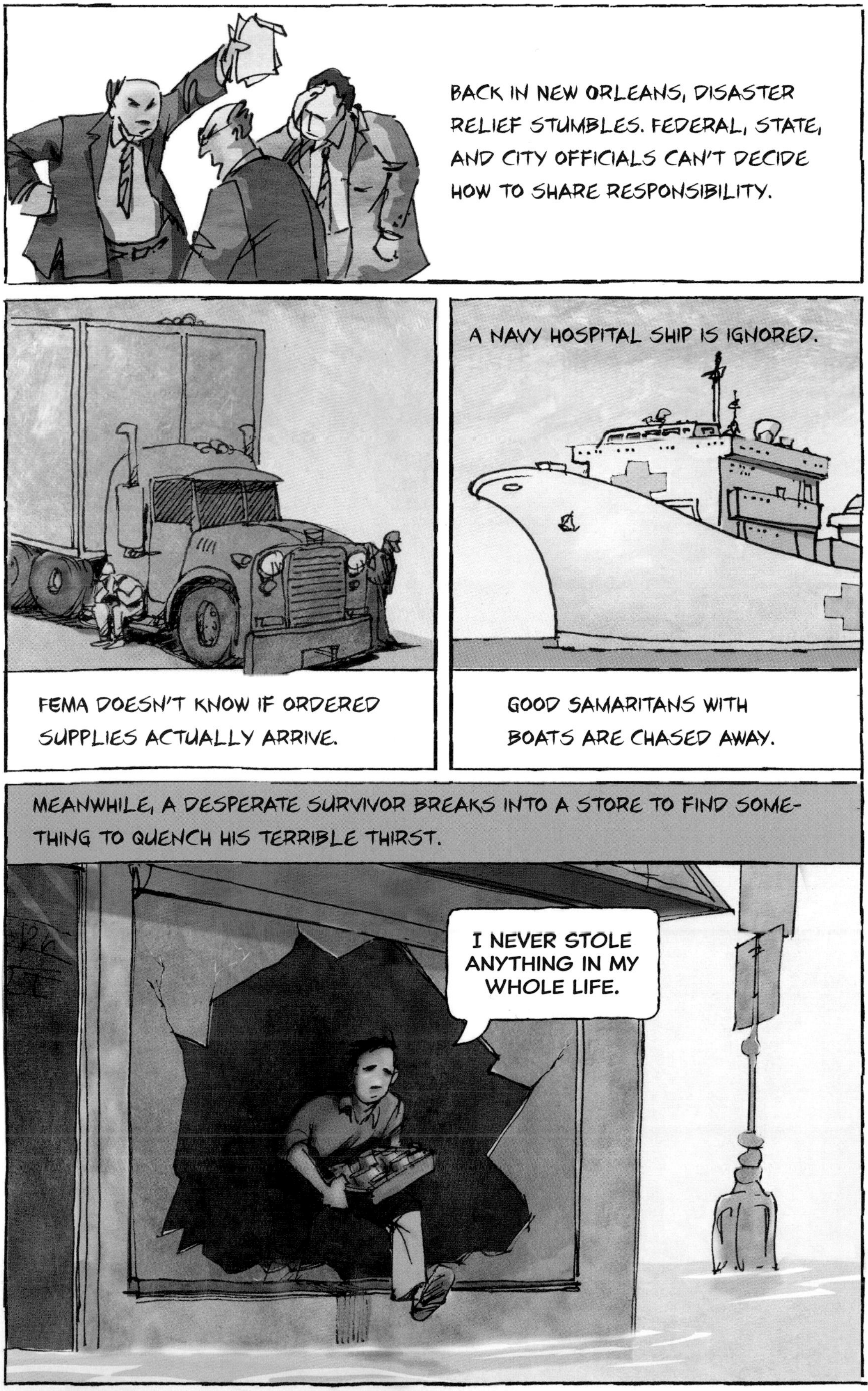
BACK IN NEW ORLEANS, DISASTER RELIEF STUMBLES. FEDERAL, STATE, AND CITY OFFICIALS CAN'T DECIDE HOW TO SHARE RESPONSIBILITY.
FEMA DOESN'T KNOW IF ORDERED SUPPLIES ACTUALLY ARRIVE.
A NAVY HOSPITAL SHIP IS IGNORED.
GOOD SAMARITANS WITH BOATS ARE CHASED AWAY.
MEANWHILE, A DESPERATE SURVIVOR BREAKS INTO A STORE TO FIND SOMETHING TO QUENCH HIS TERRIBLE THIRST.
I NEVER STOLE ANYTHING IN MY WHOLE LIFE.

Thursday, September 1

RUMORS SWEEP THE CITY: HUNDREDS DEAD IN THE SUPERDOME, GANG ASSAULTS ON CHILDREN, SHARKS AND ALLIGATORS SWIMMING DOWN THE AVENUES, LEVEES DYNAMITED TO DRIVE OUT POOR RESIDENTS. MAYOR NAGIN CLAIMS THERE ARE 10,000 DEAD IN NEW ORLEANS, AND THAT HUNDREDS OF ARMED GANG MEMBERS ARE TERRORIZING SURVIVORS.

NONE OF THE RUMORS IS TRUE, BUT PEOPLE WON'T LEARN DIFFERENTLY FOR WEEKS.

MORE THAN 15,000 PEOPLE CROWD THE CONVENTION CENTER.

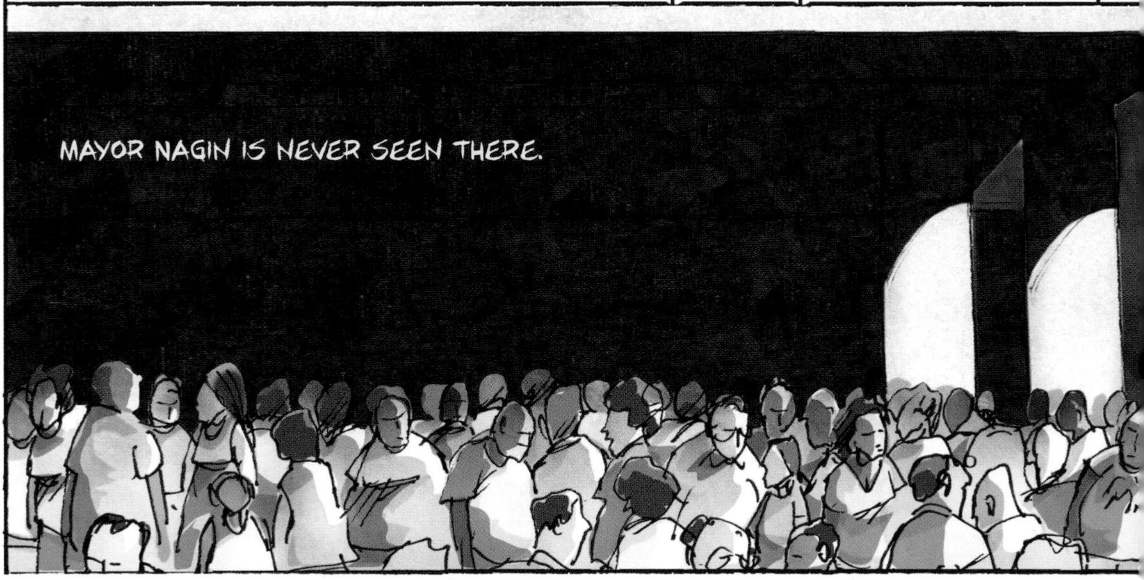
MAYOR NAGIN IS NEVER SEEN THERE.

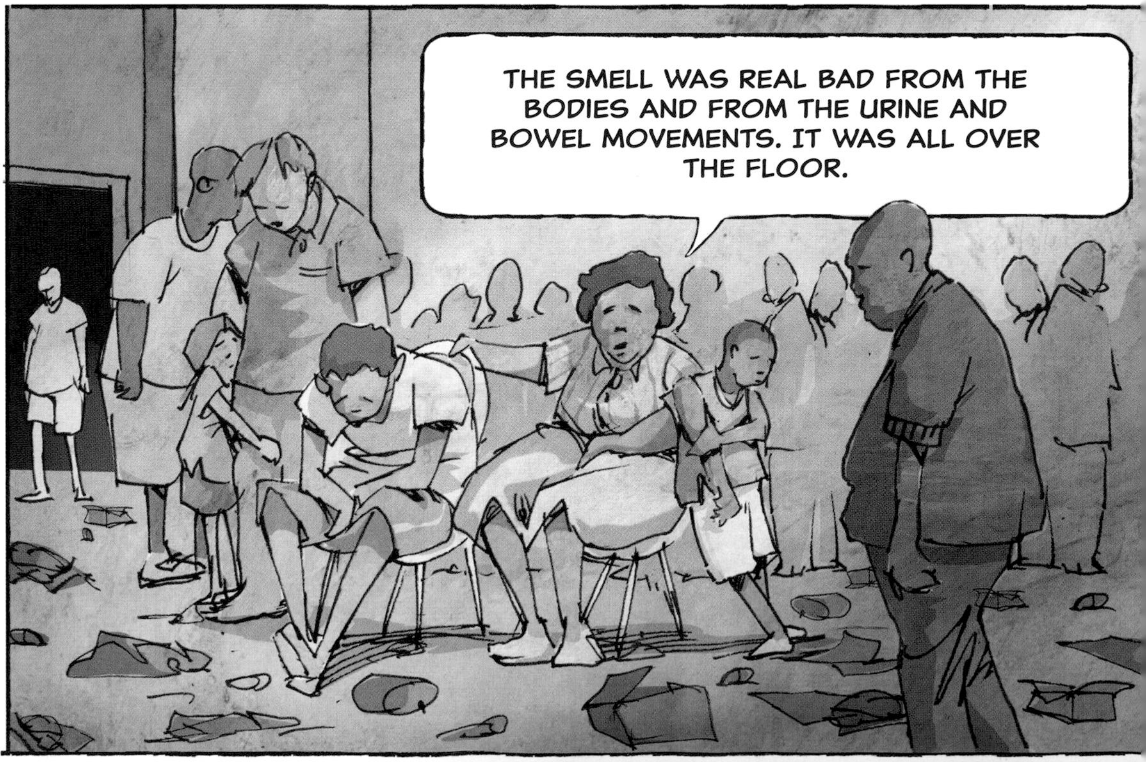
THE SMELL WAS REAL BAD FROM THE BODIES AND FROM THE URINE AND BOWEL MOVEMENTS. IT WAS ALL OVER THE FLOOR.

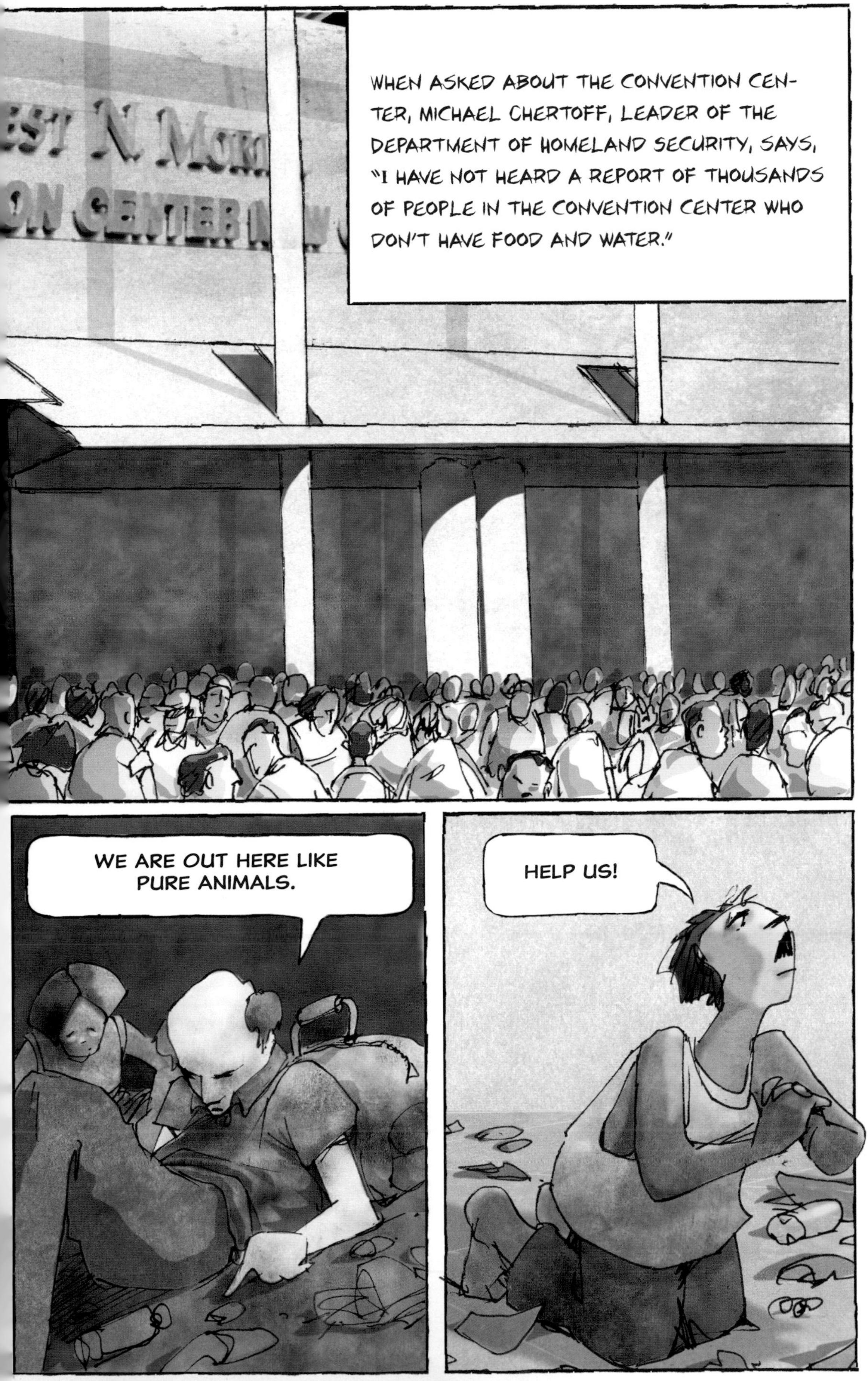
WHEN ASKED ABOUT THE CONVENTION CENTER, MICHAEL CHERTOFF, LEADER OF THE DEPARTMENT OF HOMELAND SECURITY, SAYS, "I HAVE NOT HEARD A REPORT OF THOUSANDS OF PEOPLE IN THE CONVENTION CENTER WHO DON'T HAVE FOOD AND WATER."
WE ARE OUT HERE LIKE PURE ANIMALS.
HELP US!

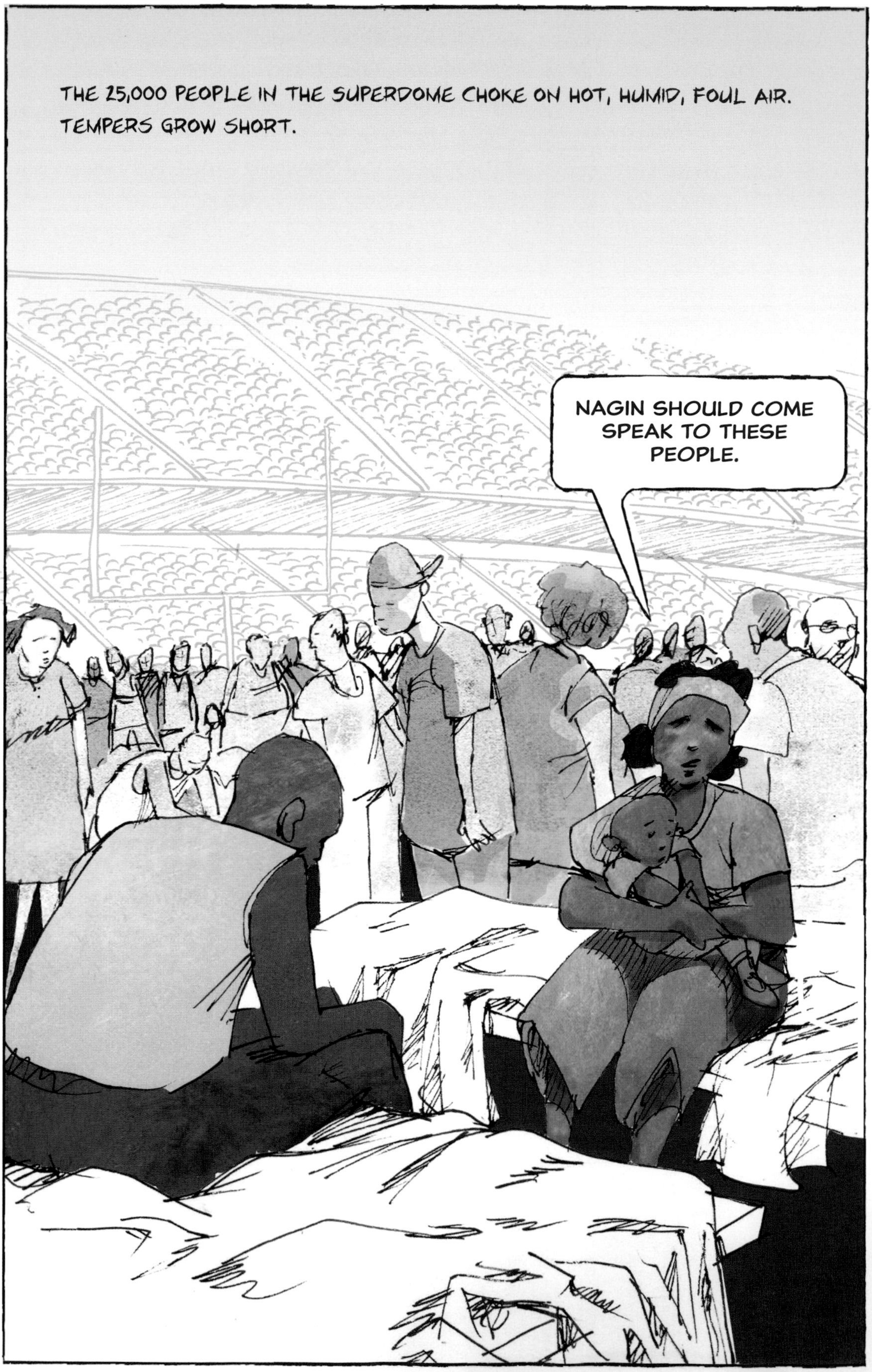
THE 25,000 PEOPLE IN THE SUPERDOME CHOKE ON HOT, HUMID, FOUL AIR. TEMPERS GROW SHORT.
NAGIN SHOULD COME SPEAK TO THESE PEOPLE.

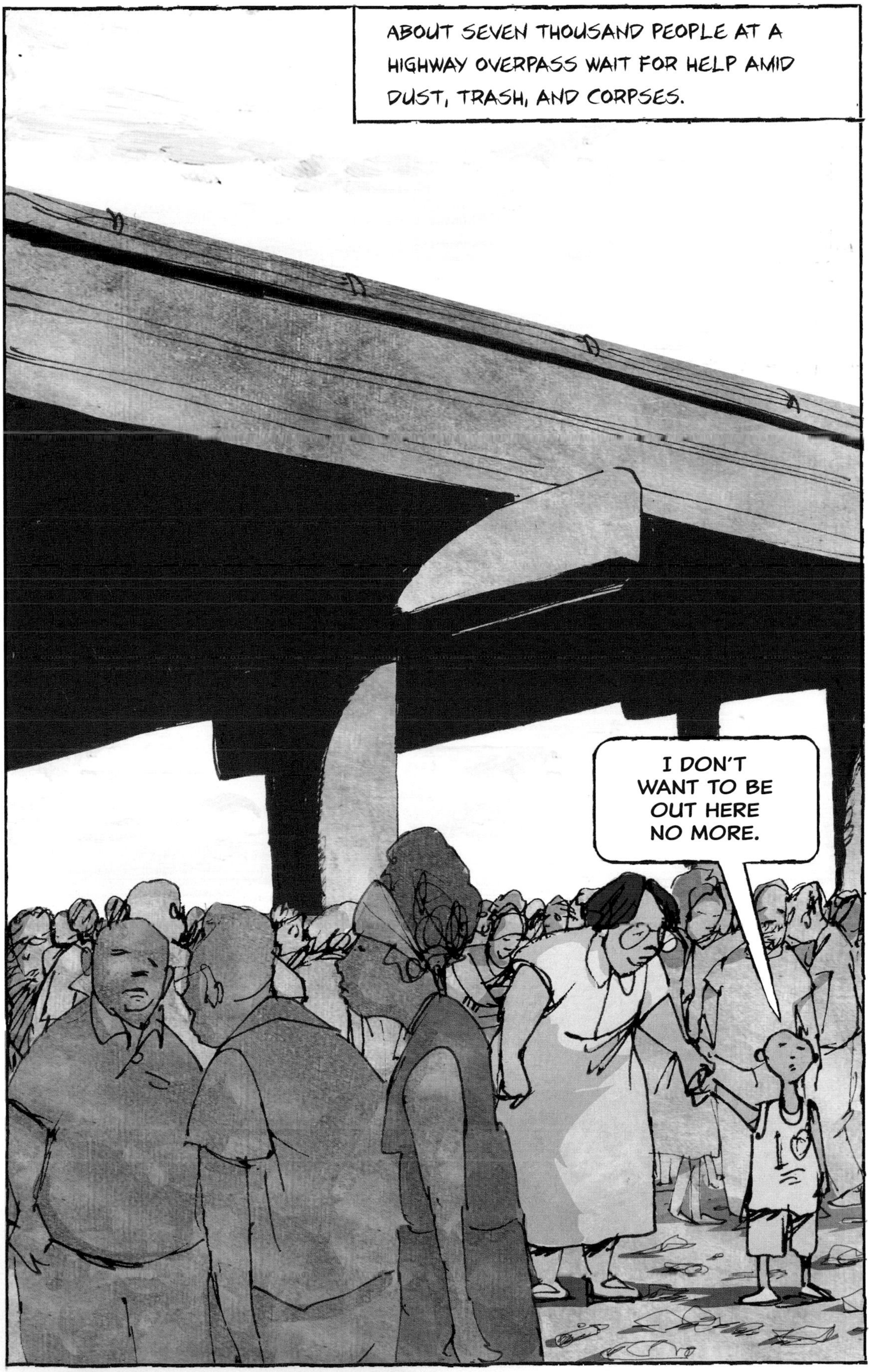
ABOUT SEVEN THOUSAND PEOPLE AT A HIGHWAY OVERPASS WAIT FOR HELP AMID DUST, TRASH, AND CORPSES.
I DON'T WANT TO BE OUT HERE NO MORE.

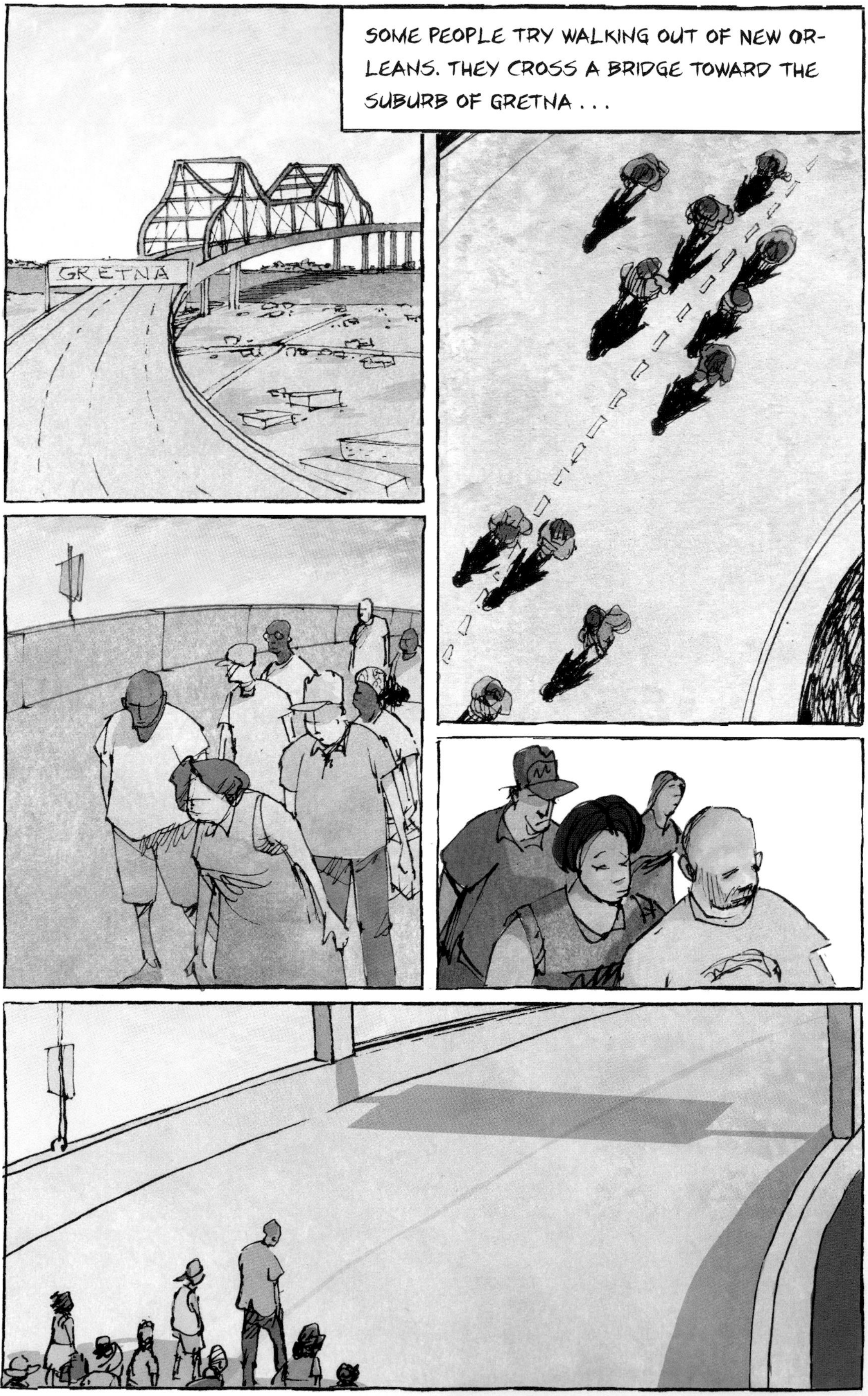
SOME PEOPLE TRY WALKING OUT OF NEW OR-LEANS. THEY CROSS A BRIDGE TOWARD THE SUBURB OF GRETNA . . .
GRETNA

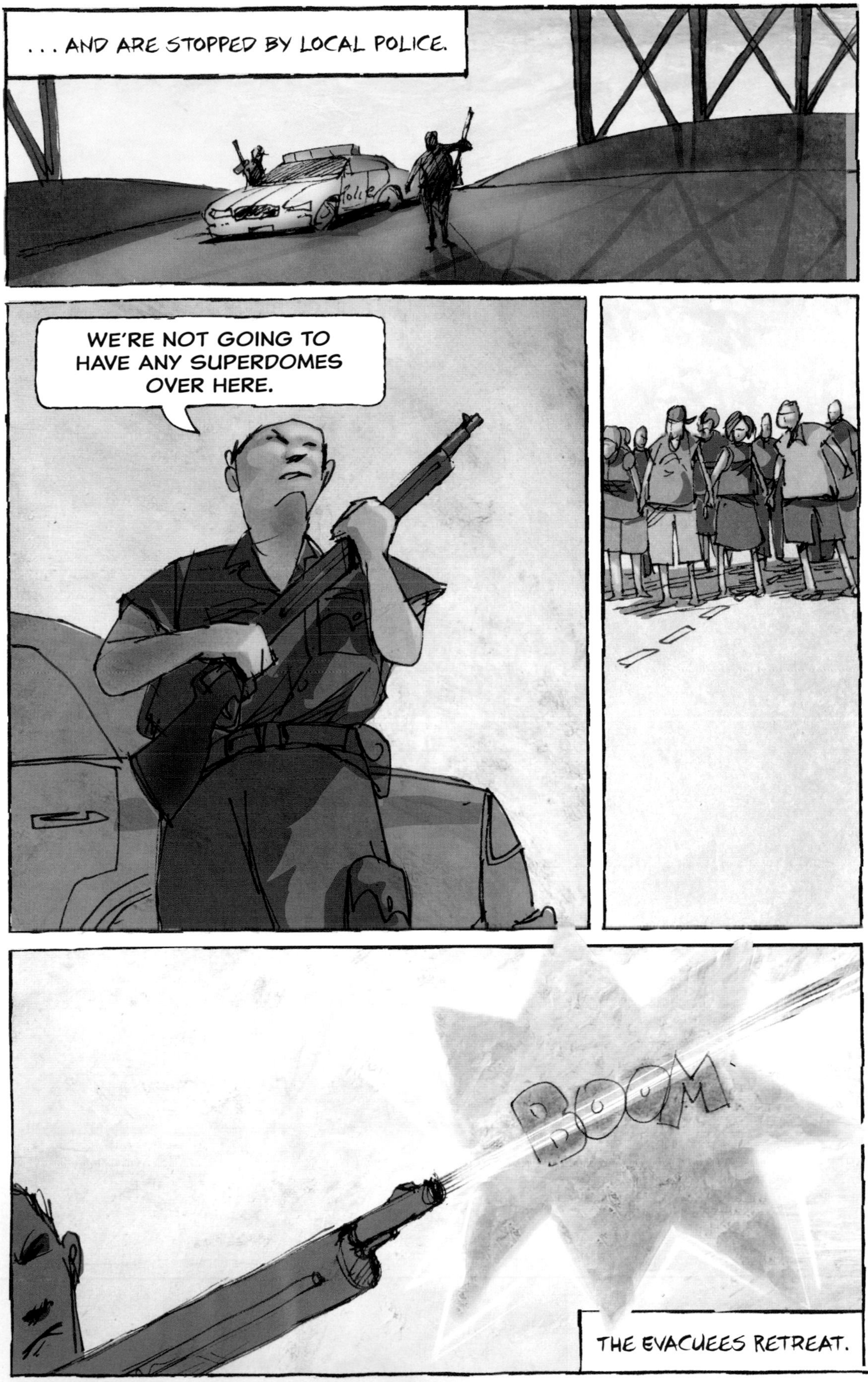
. . . AND ARE STOPPED BY LOCAL POLICE.
POLICE
WE'RE NOT GOING TO HAVE ANY SUPERDOMES OVER HERE.
BOOM
THE EVACUEES RETREAT.

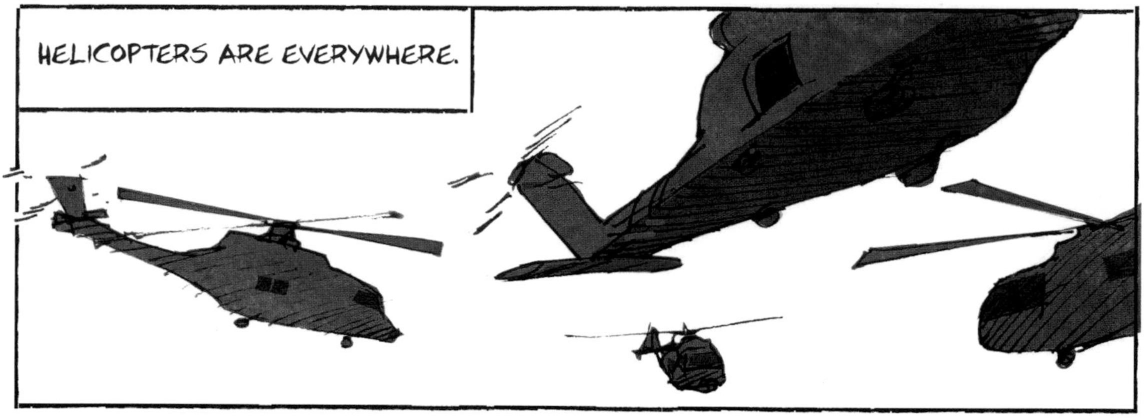
HELICOPTERS ARE EVERYWHERE.

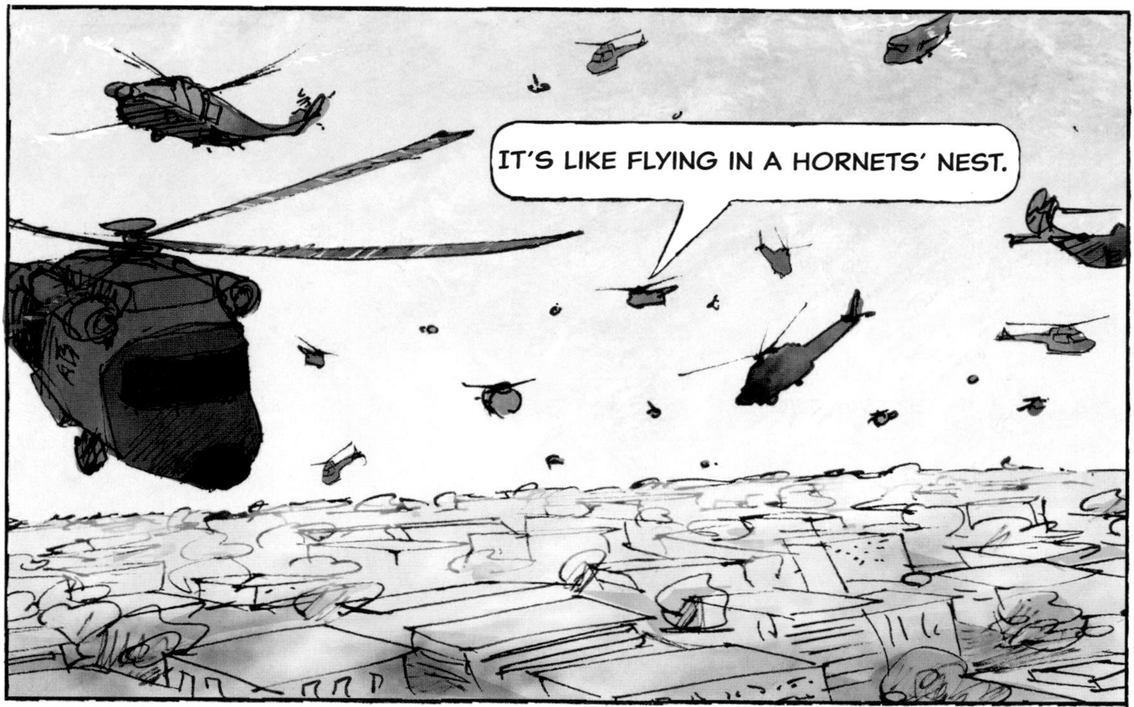
IT'S LIKE FLYING IN A HORNETS' NEST.

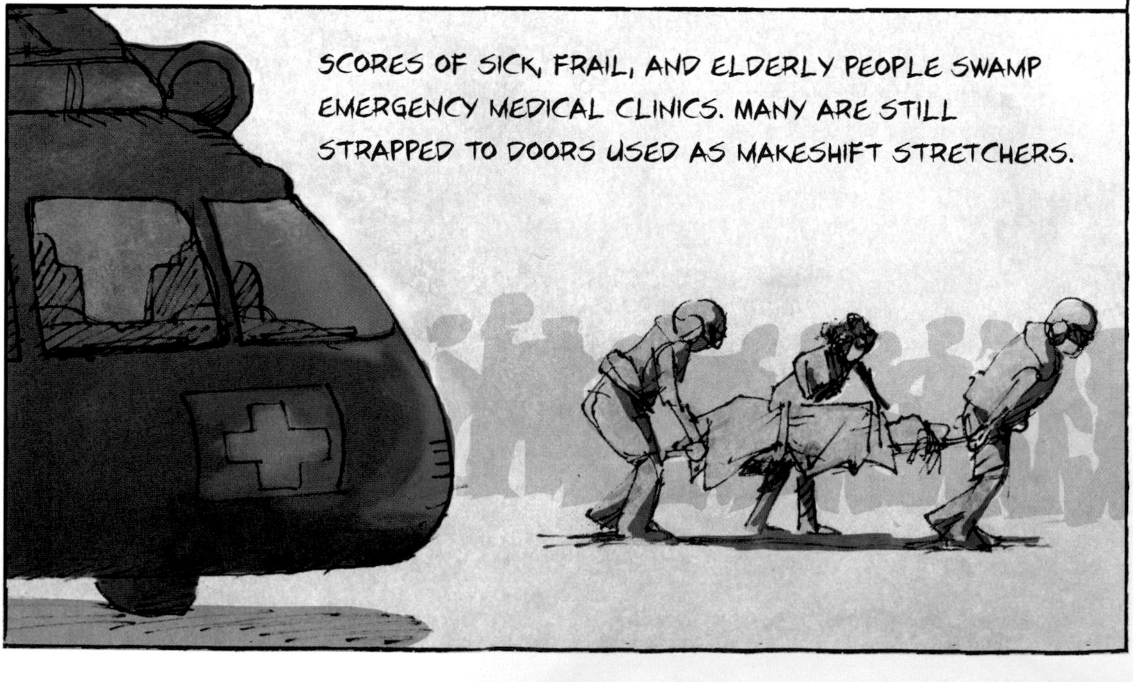
SCORES OF SICK, FRAIL, AND ELDERLY PEOPLE SWAMP EMERGENCY MEDICAL CLINICS. MANY ARE STILL STRAPPED TO DOORS USED AS MAKESHIFT STRETCHERS.

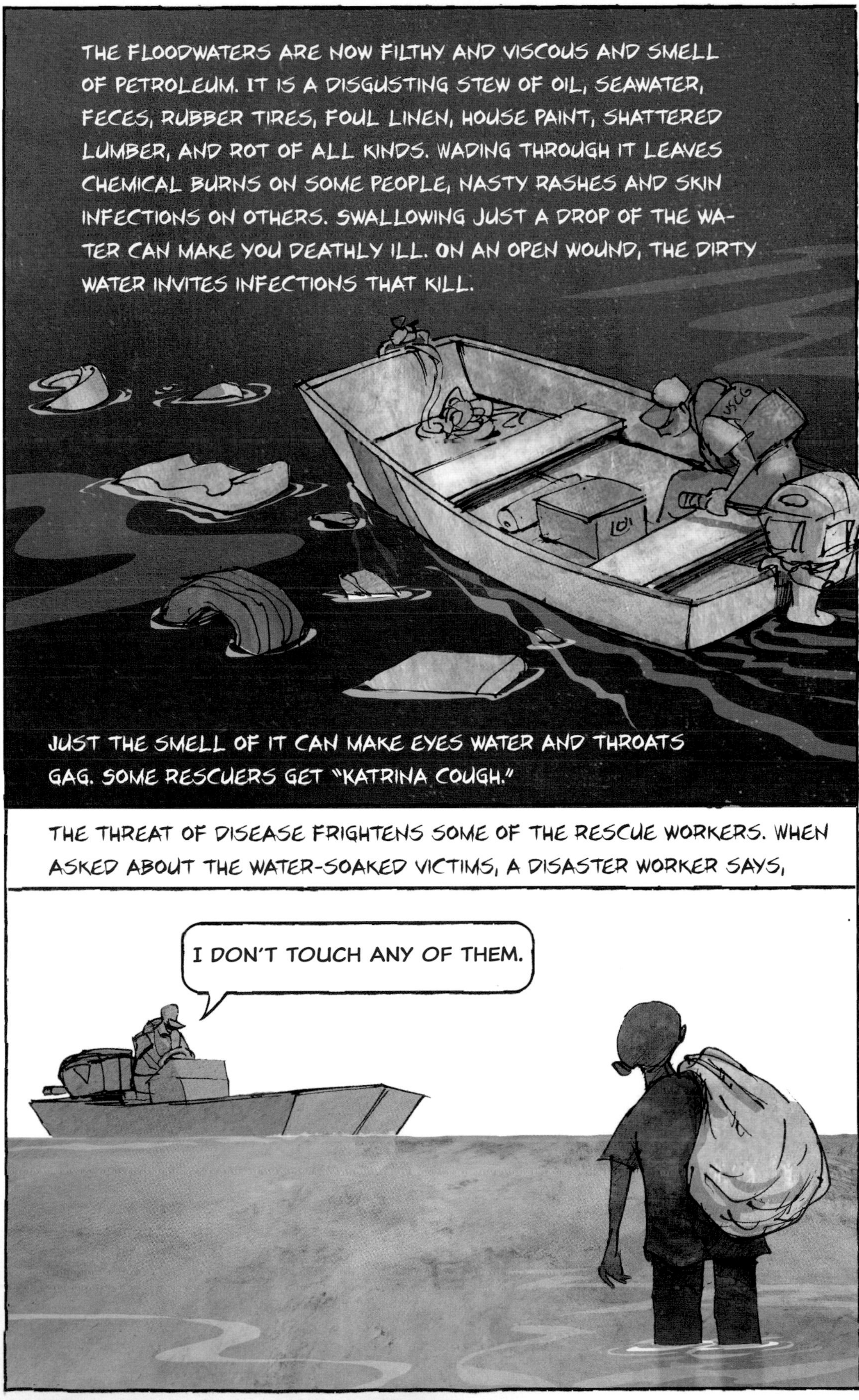
THE FLOODWATERS ARE NOW FILTHY AND VISCOUS AND SMELL OF PETROLEUM. IT IS A DISGUSTING STEW OF OIL, SEAWATER, FECES, RUBBER TIRES, FOUL LINEN, HOUSE PAINT, SHATTERED LUMBER, AND ROT OF ALL KINDS. WADING THROUGH IT LEAVES CHEMICAL BURNS ON SOME PEOPLE, NASTY RASHES AND SKIN INFECTIONS ON OTHERS. SWALLOWING JUST A DROP OF THE WATER CAN MAKE YOU DEATHLY ILL. ON AN OPEN WOUND, THE DIRTY WATER INVITES INFECTIONS THAT KILL.
USCG
JUST THE SMELL OF IT CAN MAKE EYES WATER AND THROATS GAG. SOME RESCUERS GET "KATRINA COUGH."
THE THREAT OF DISEASE FRIGHTENS SOME OF THE RESCUE WORKERS. WHEN ASKED ABOUT THE WATER-SOAKED VICTIMS, A DISASTER WORKER SAYS,
I DON'T TOUCH ANY OF THEM.

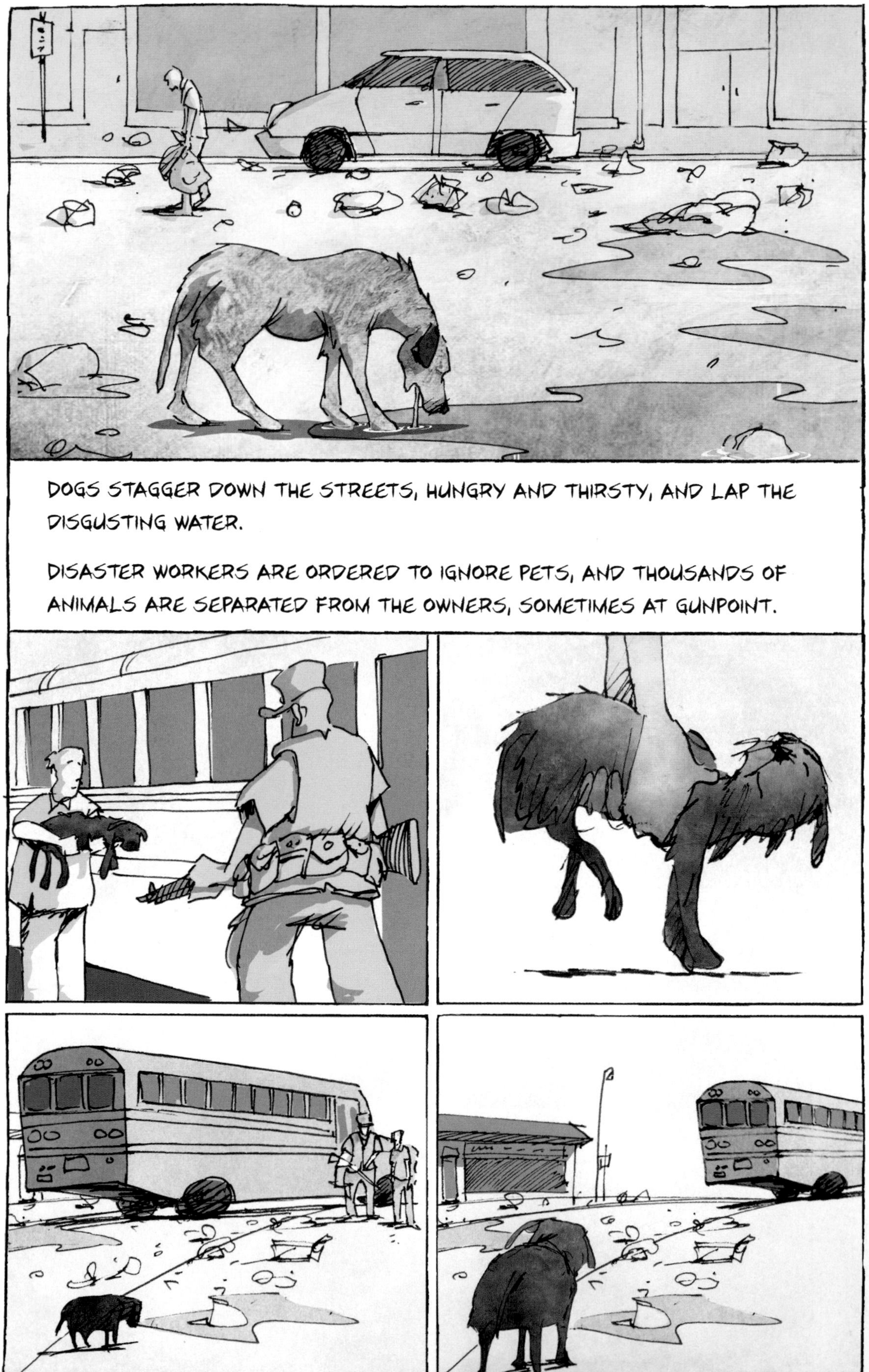
DOGS STAGGER DOWN THE STREETS, HUNGRY AND THIRSTY, AND LAP THE DISGUSTING WATER.
DISASTER WORKERS ARE ORDERED TO IGNORE PETS, AND THOUSANDS OF ANIMALS ARE SEPARATED FROM THE OWNERS, SOMETIMES AT GUNPOINT.

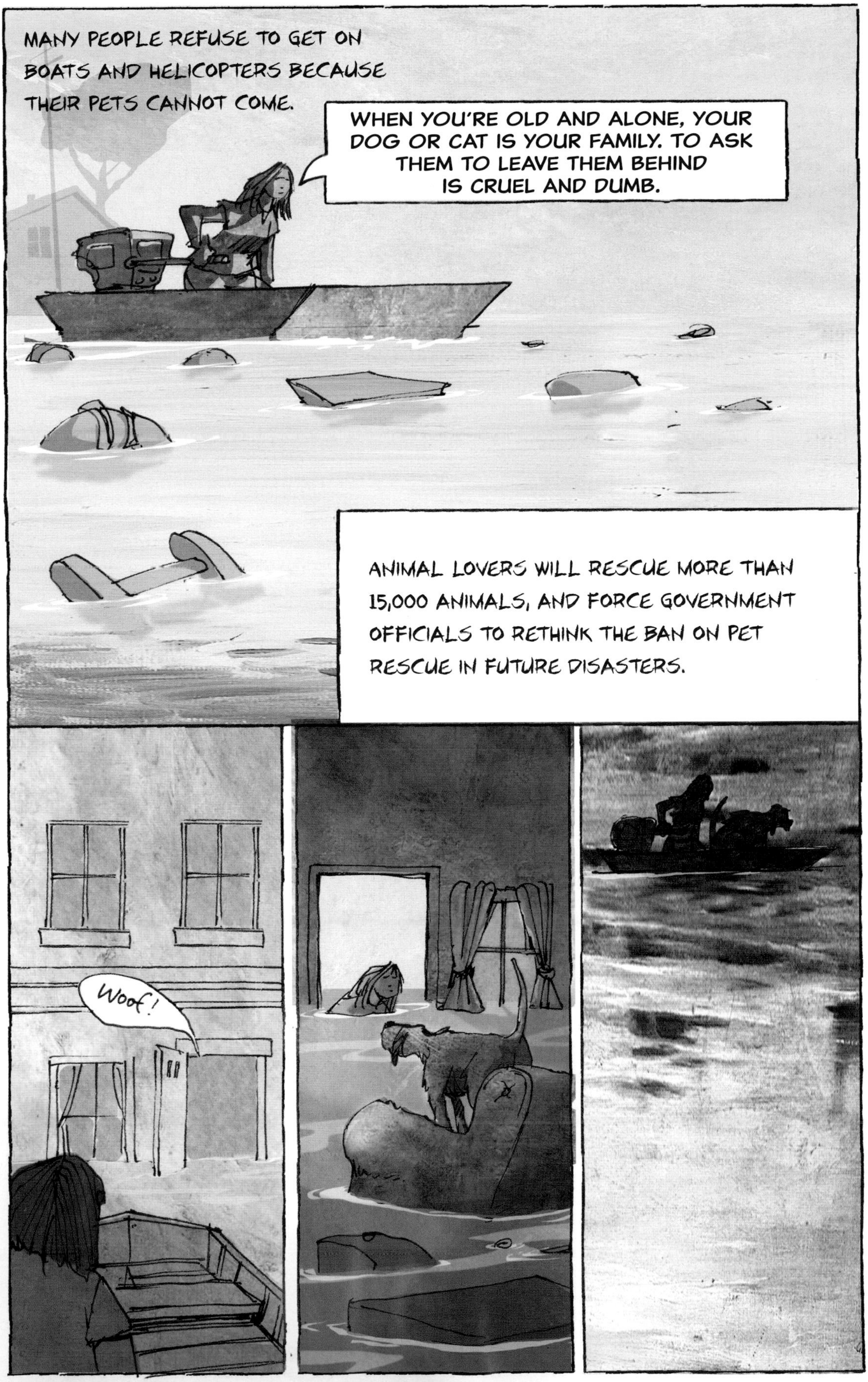
MANY PEOPLE REFUSE TO GET ON BOATS AND HELICOPTERS BECAUSE THEIR PETS CANNOT COME.
WHEN YOU'RE OLD AND ALONE, YOUR DOG OR CAT IS YOUR FAMILY. TO ASK THEM TO LEAVE THEM BEHIND IS CRUEL AND DUMB.
ANIMAL LOVERS WILL RESCUE MORE THAN 15,000 ANIMALS, AND FORCE GOVERNMENT OFFICIALS TO RETHINK THE BAN ON PET RESCUE IN FUTURE DISASTERS.
Woof!

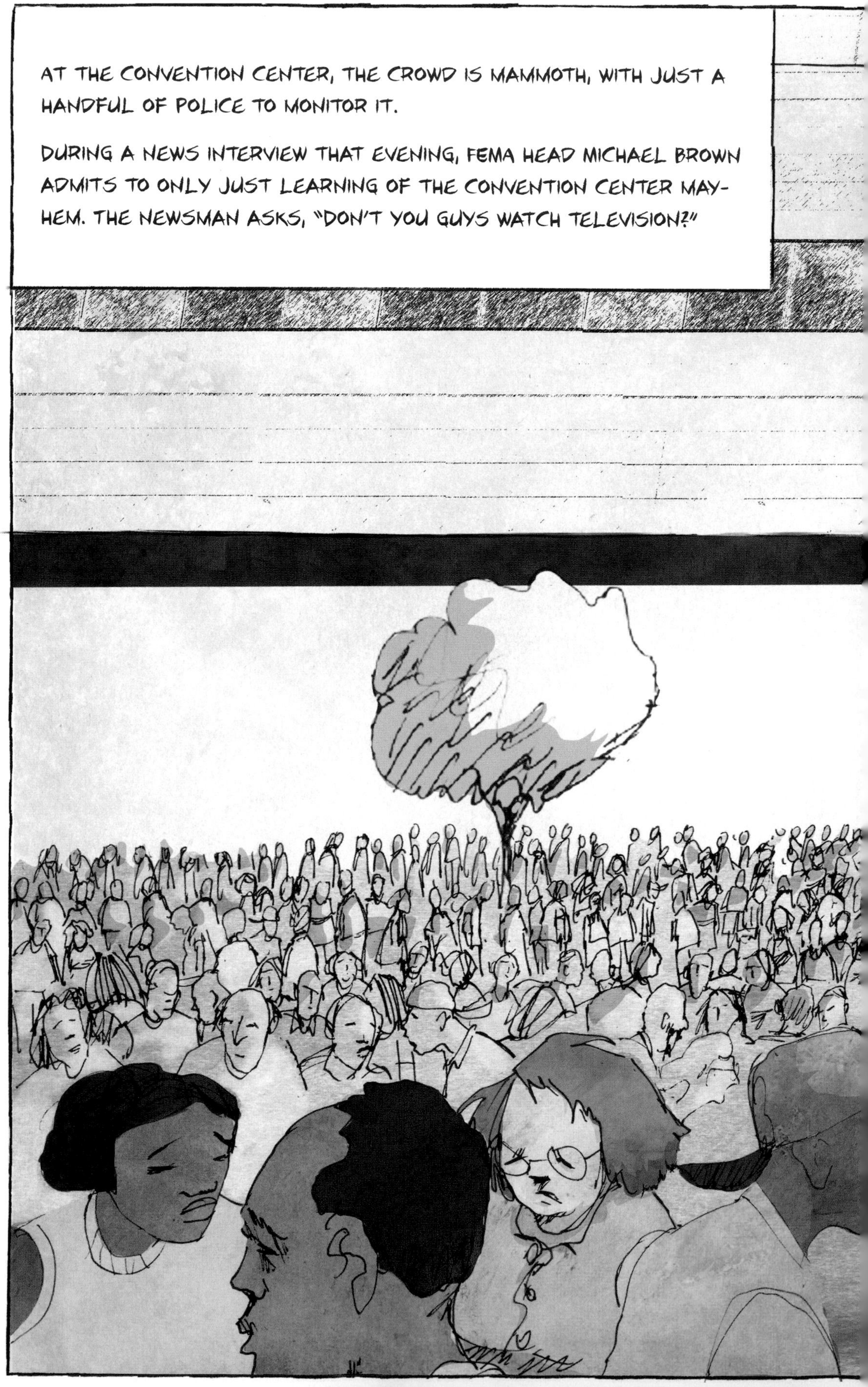
AT THE CONVENTION CENTER, THE CROWD IS MAMMOTH, WITH JUST A HANDFUL OF POLICE TO MONITOR IT.
DURING A NEWS INTERVIEW THAT EVENING, FEMA HEAD MICHAEL BROWN ADMITS TO ONLY JUST LEARNING OF THE CONVENTION CENTER MAYHEM. THE NEWSMAN ASKS, "DON'T YOU GUYS WATCH TELEVISION?"

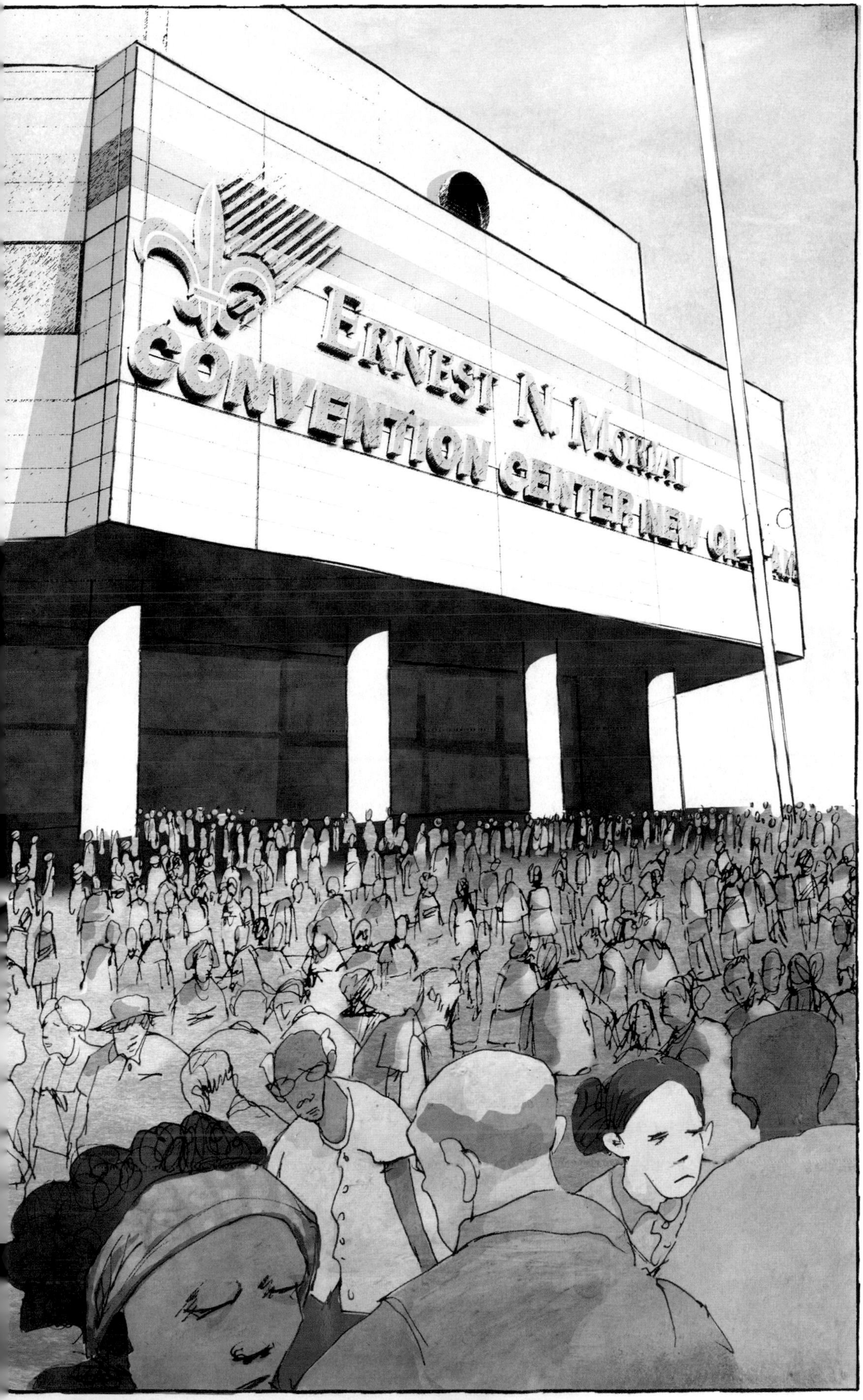
ERNEST N. MORIAL
CONVENTION CENTER

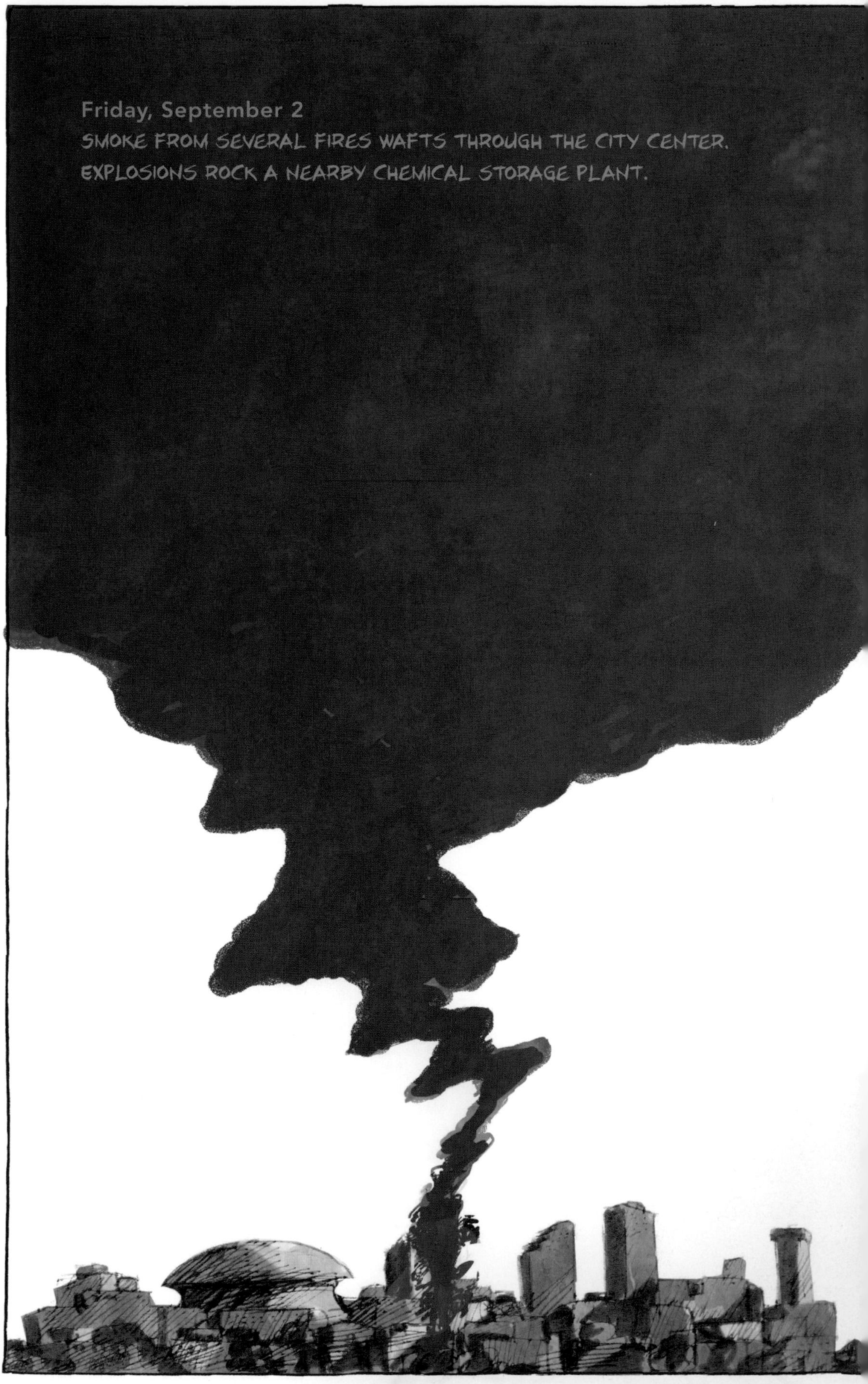
Friday, September 2
SMOKE FROM SEVERAL FIRES WAFTS THROUGH THE CITY CENTER.
EXPLOSIONS ROCK A NEARBY CHEMICAL STORAGE PLANT.

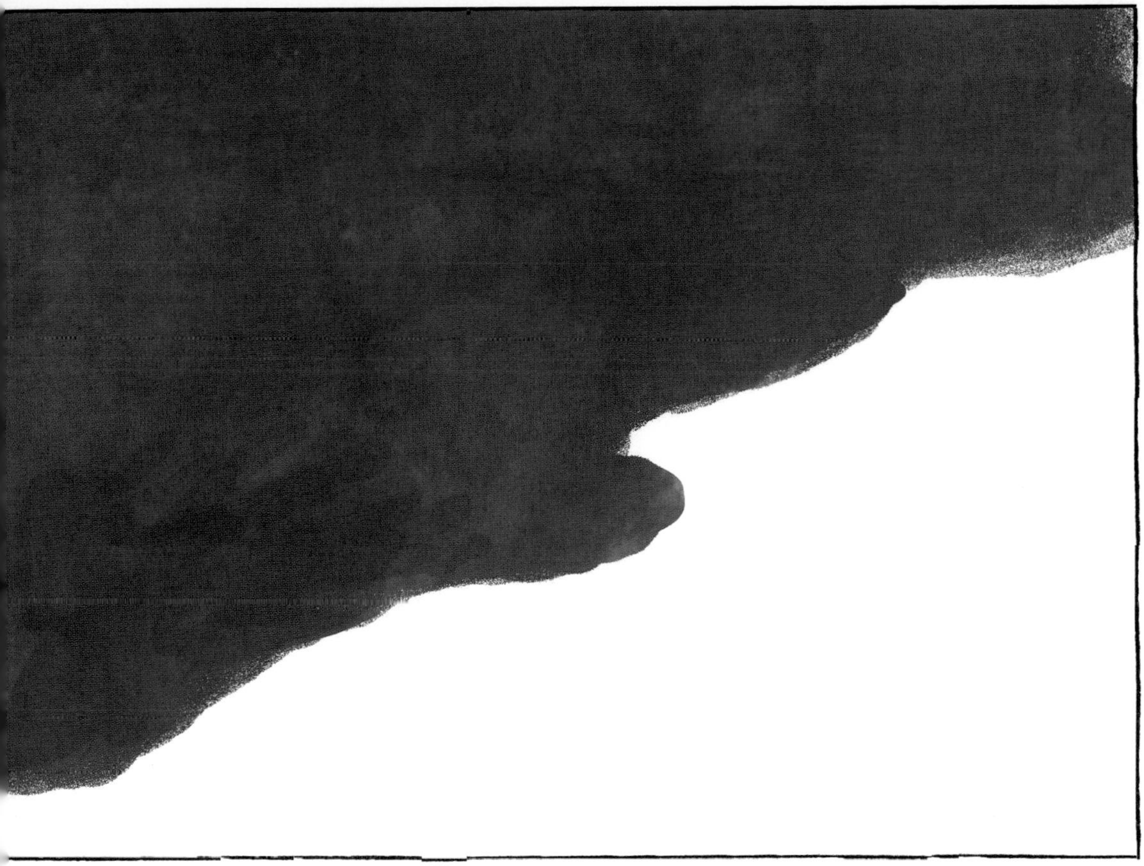

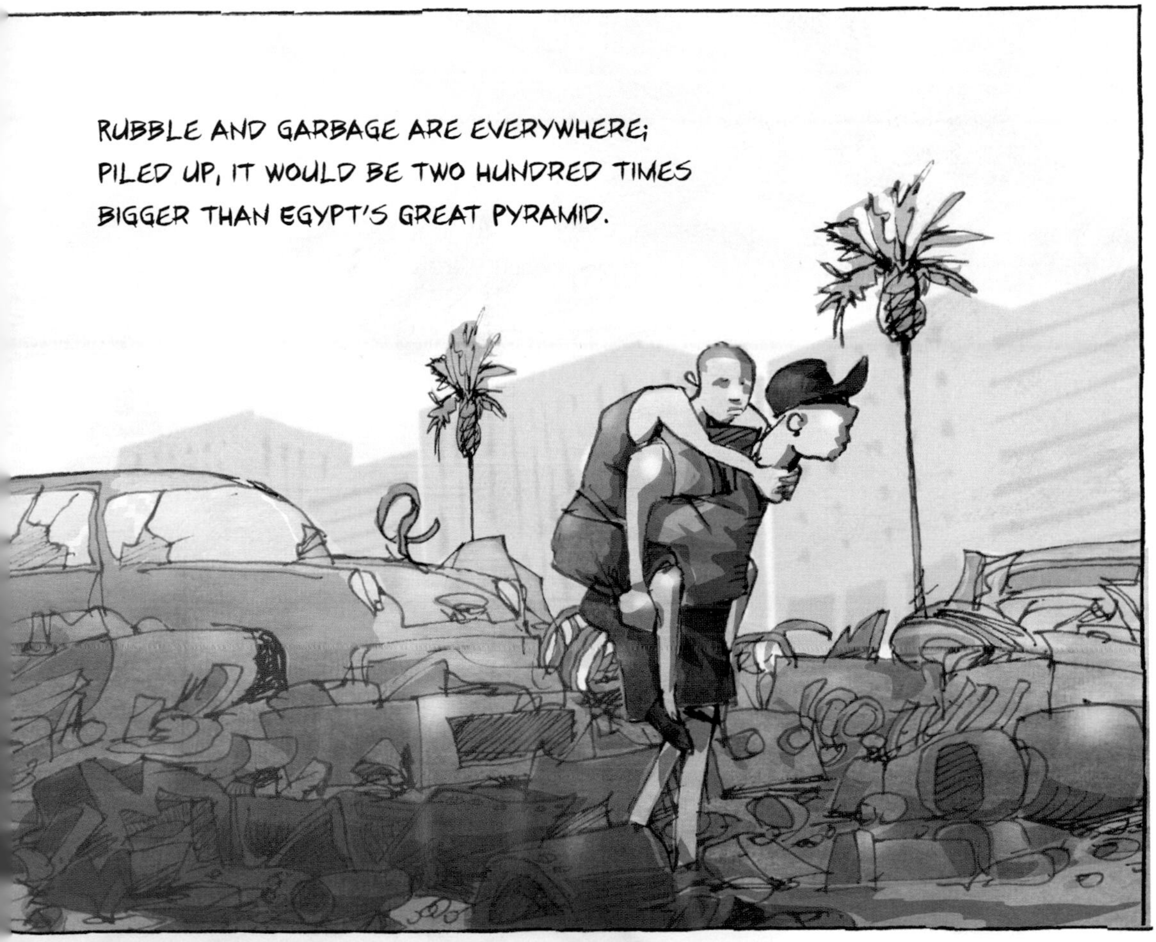
RUBBLE AND GARBAGE ARE EVERYWHERE; PILED UP, IT WOULD BE TWO HUNDRED TIMES BIGGER THAN EGYPT'S GREAT PYRAMID.

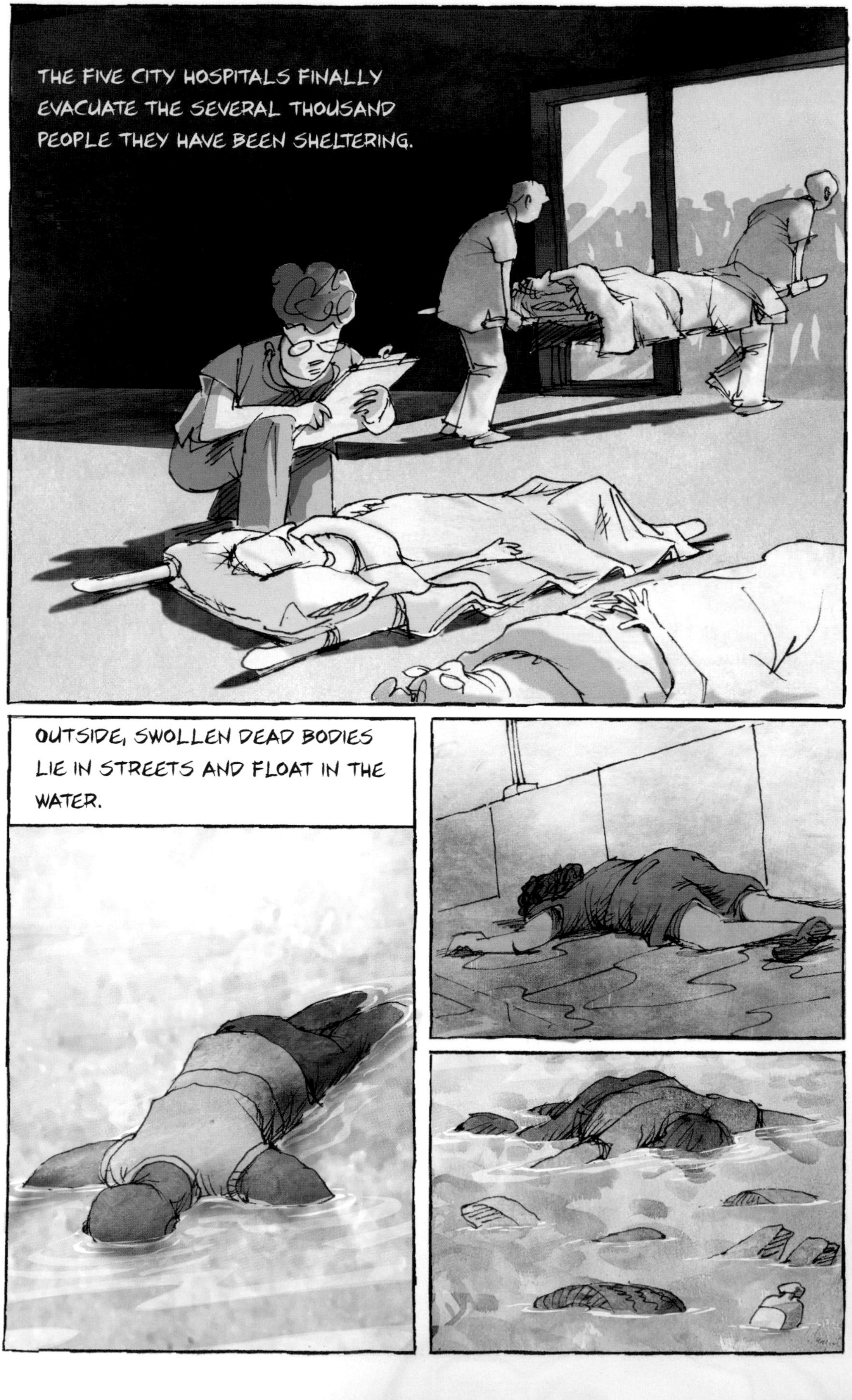

THE FIVE CITY HOSPITALS FINALLY EVACUATE THE SEVERAL THOUSAND PEOPLE THEY HAVE BEEN SHELTERING.

OUTSIDE, SWOLLEN DEAD BODIES LIE IN STREETS AND FLOAT IN THE WATER.

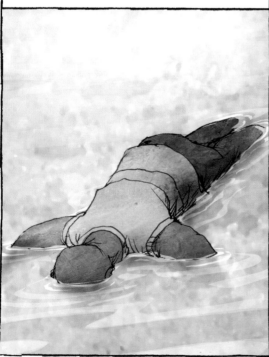

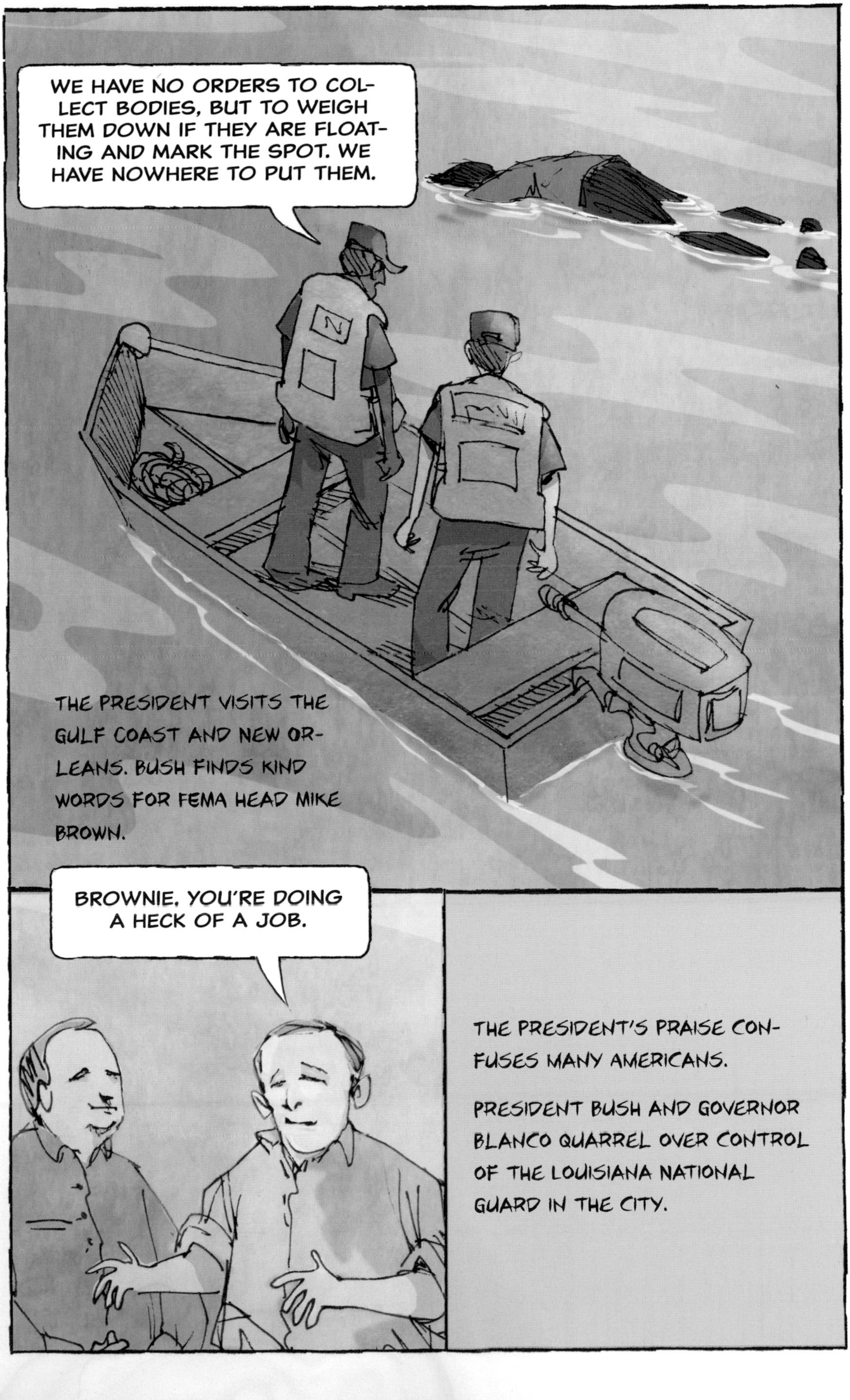
WE HAVE NO ORDERS TO COLLECT BODIES, BUT TO WEIGH THEM DOWN IF THEY ARE FLOATING AND MARK THE SPOT. WE HAVE NOWHERE TO PUT THEM.
THE PRESIDENT VISITS THE GULF COAST AND NEW ORLEANS. BUSH FINDS KIND WORDS FOR FEMA HEAD MIKE BROWN.
BROWNIE, YOU'RE DOING A HECK OF A JOB.
THE PRESIDENT'S PRAISE CONFUSES MANY AMERICANS.
PRESIDENT BUSH AND GOVERNOR BLANCO QUARREL OVER CONTROL OF THE LOUISIANA NATIONAL GUARD IN THE CITY.

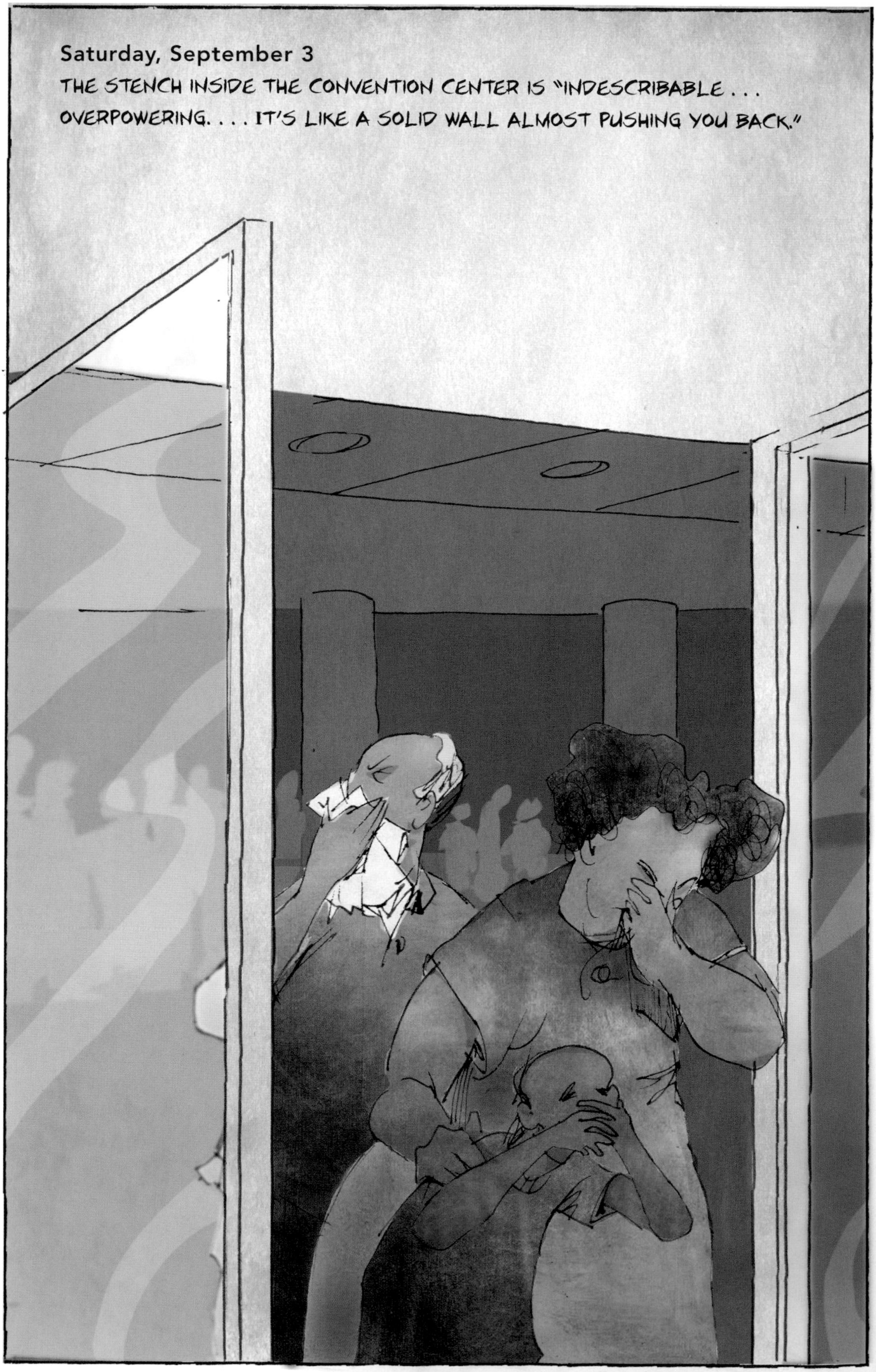
Saturday, September 3
THE STENCH INSIDE THE CONVENTION CENTER IS "INDESCRIBABLE . . .
OVERPOWERING. . . . IT'S LIKE A SOLID WALL ALMOST PUSHING YOU BACK."

HUNDREDS OF BUSES EVENTUALLY ARRIVE IN THE AFTERNOON. THE SURVIVORS ARE TAKEN TO SHELTERS ALL OVER. ONE OF THEM IS A SEVENTY-SEVEN-YEAR-OLD WOMAN WHO HAS SPENT FIVE DAYS AT THE CONVENTION CENTER. ASKED WHERE SHE IS BEING SENT, SHE SAYS, "ANYWHERE."

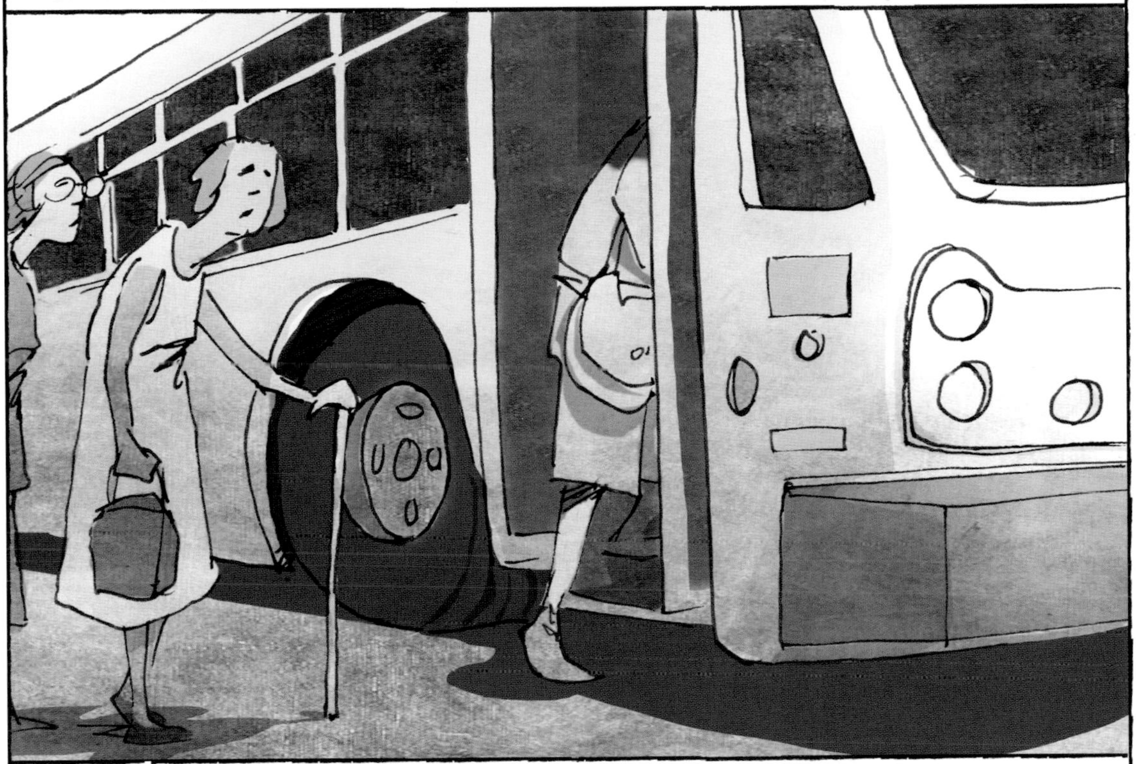

NATIONAL GUARD TROOPS FROM ALL OVER THE COUNTRY PATROL THE STREETS AND LIFT THE SPIRITS OF EVERYONE.

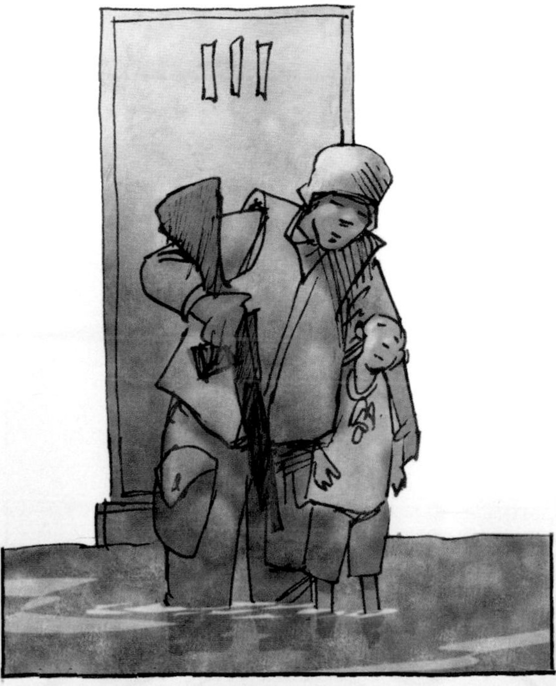

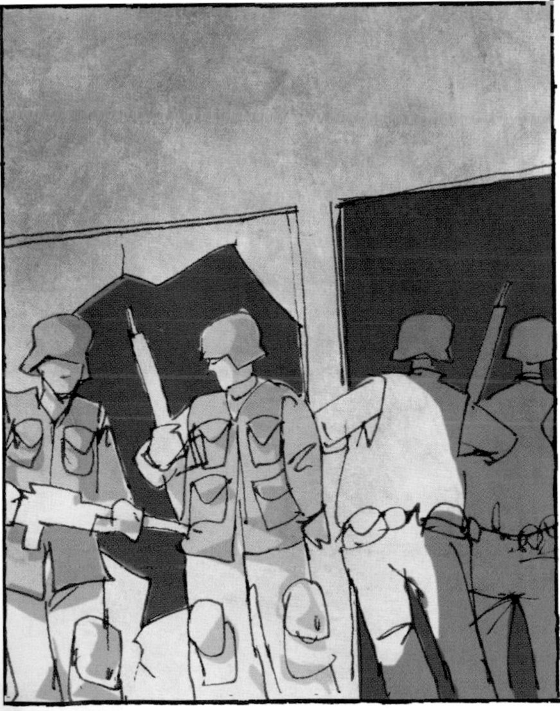

BUSES FINALLY ARRIVE AT THE SUPERDOME. SCORCHING ONE-HUNDRED-DEGREE HEAT ROASTS A LINE OF TEN THOUSAND EVACUEES AS THEY TRUDGE THROUGH KNEE-HIGH TRASH TO BOARD THEM. THEY ARE SO ANXIOUS TO LEAVE THAT SOME URINATE WHERE THEY STAND RATHER THAN RISK LOSING THEIR PLACE IN LINE BY LEAVING.

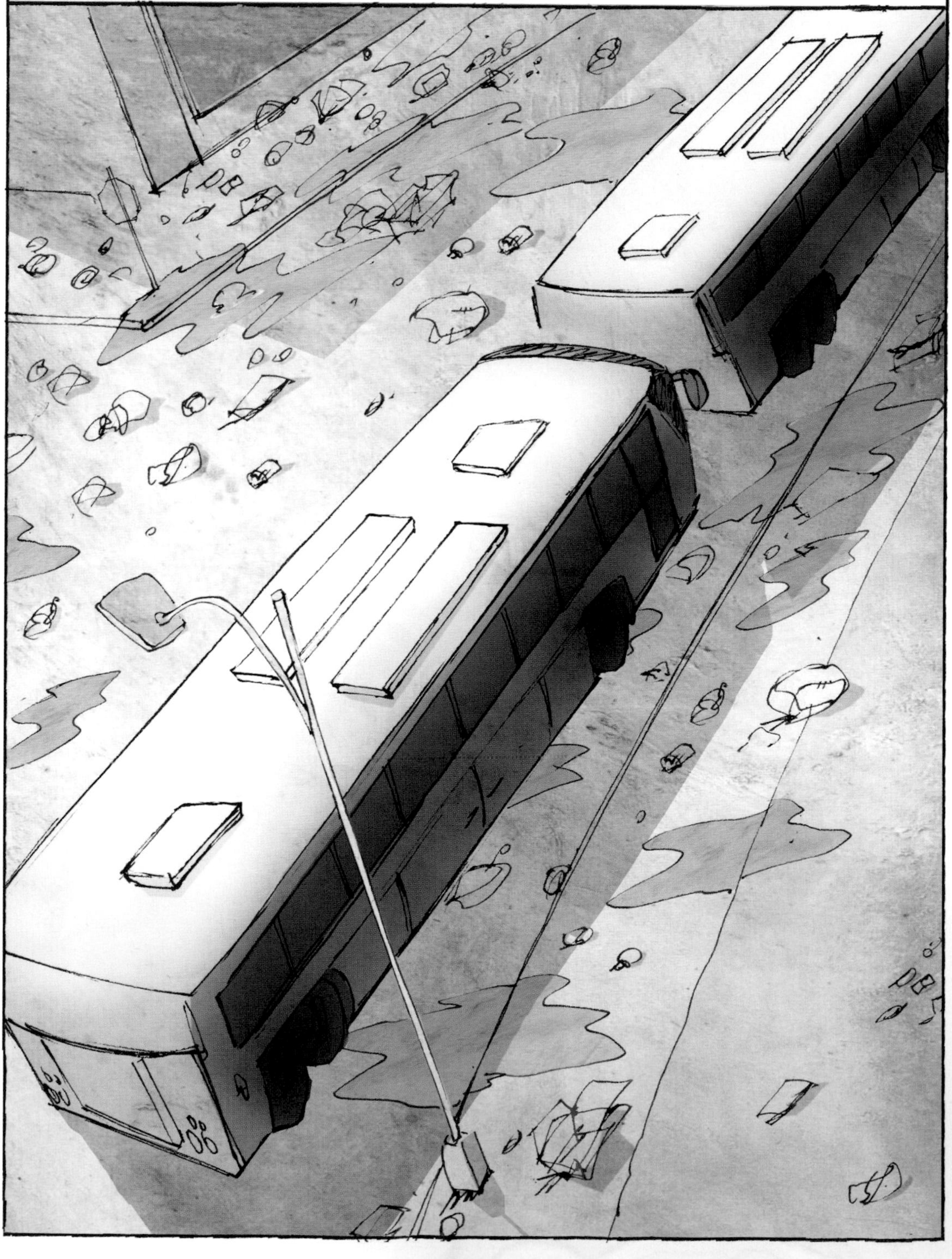

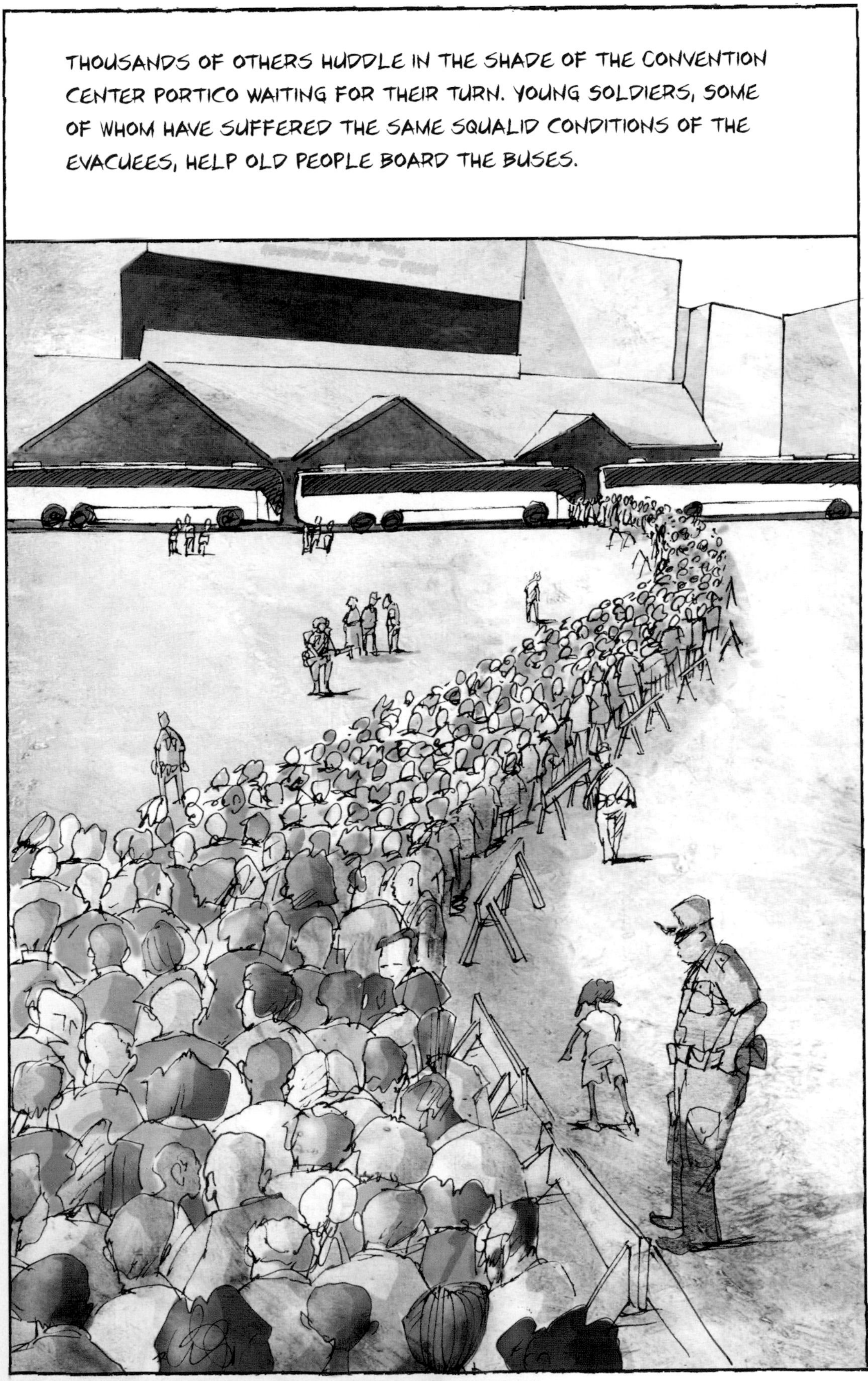
THOUSANDS OF OTHERS HUDDLE IN THE SHADE OF THE CONVENTION CENTER PORTICO WAITING FOR THEIR TURN. YOUNG SOLDIERS, SOME OF WHOM HAVE SUFFERED THE SAME SQUALID CONDITIONS OF THE EVACUEES, HELP OLD PEOPLE BOARD THE BUSES.

NEW ORLEANS IS LEFT MOSTLY TO SOL-
DIERS, DISASTER WORKERS . . . AND THE
DEAD. CORPSES DRIFT IN THE FLOODWATERS,
LIE IN STREET GUTTERS, AND REST AMID
RUBBLE, ON CEMENT PATIOS, AND AT THE
FEET OF OFFICE BUILDINGS. MANY ARE HID-
DEN IN THE HOUSES AND ATTICS WHERE THE
PEOPLE DIED.

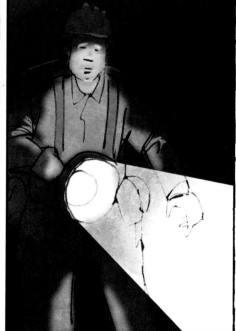

DISASTER TEAMS SEARCH THE
RUINS. SENSITIVE NOSES HELP
LOCATE HOUSES WITH DECAY-
ING DEAD PEOPLE OR ROTTING
ANIMALS. AFTERWARD, TEAMS
MARK INSPECTED PROPERTIES
WITH AN "X," NOTING THE RES-
CUE TEAM'S NAME, THE DATE
OF INSPECTION, HAZARDS TO
BE AVOIDED, AND THE NUMBER
OF DEAD WITHIN.

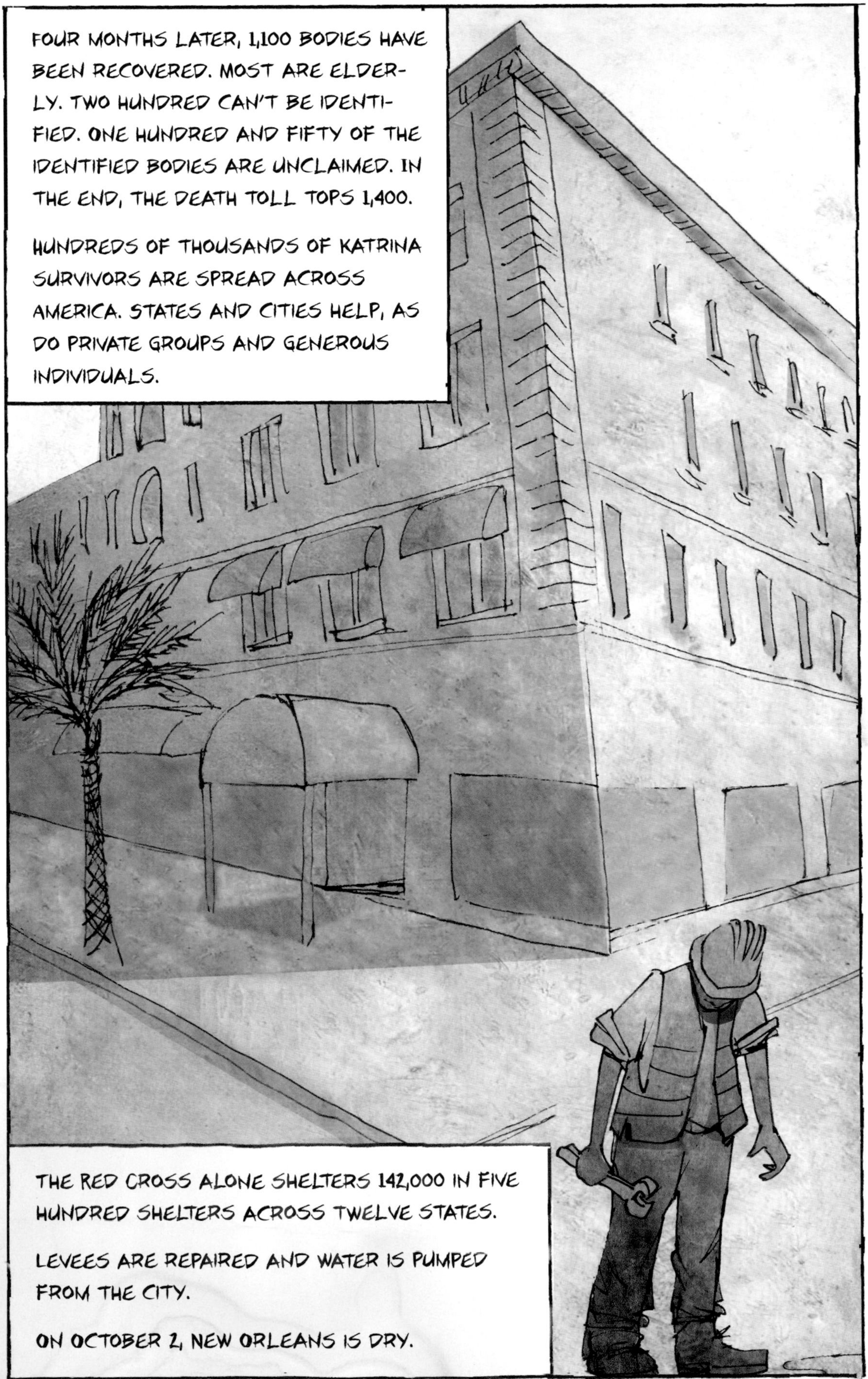
FOUR MONTHS LATER, 1,100 BODIES HAVE BEEN RECOVERED. MOST ARE ELDERLY. TWO HUNDRED CAN'T BE IDENTIFIED. ONE HUNDRED AND FIFTY OF THE IDENTIFIED BODIES ARE UNCLAIMED. IN THE END, THE DEATH TOLL TOPS 1,400.
HUNDREDS OF THOUSANDS OF KATRINA SURVIVORS ARE SPREAD ACROSS AMERICA. STATES AND CITIES HELP, AS DO PRIVATE GROUPS AND GENEROUS INDIVIDUALS.
THE RED CROSS ALONE SHELTERS 142,000 IN FIVE HUNDRED SHELTERS ACROSS TWELVE STATES.
LEVEES ARE REPAIRED AND WATER IS PUMPED FROM THE CITY.
ON OCTOBER 2, NEW ORLEANS IS DRY.

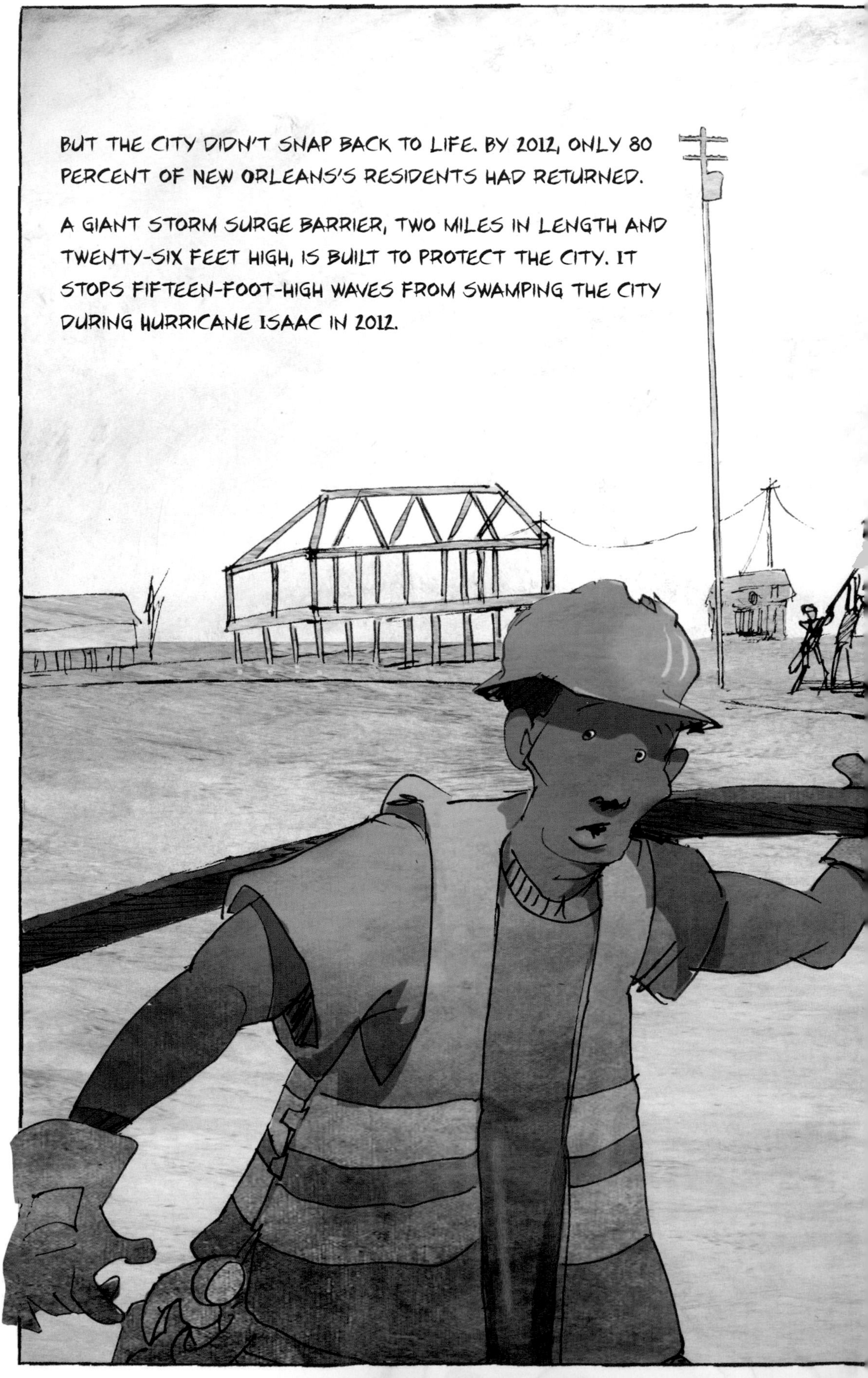
BUT THE CITY DIDN'T SNAP BACK TO LIFE. BY 2012, ONLY 80 PERCENT OF NEW ORLEANS'S RESIDENTS HAD RETURNED.
A GIANT STORM SURGE BARRIER, TWO MILES IN LENGTH AND TWENTY-SIX FEET HIGH, IS BUILT TO PROTECT THE CITY. IT STOPS FIFTEEN-FOOT-HIGH WAVES FROM SWAMPING THE CITY DURING HURRICANE ISAAC IN 2012.

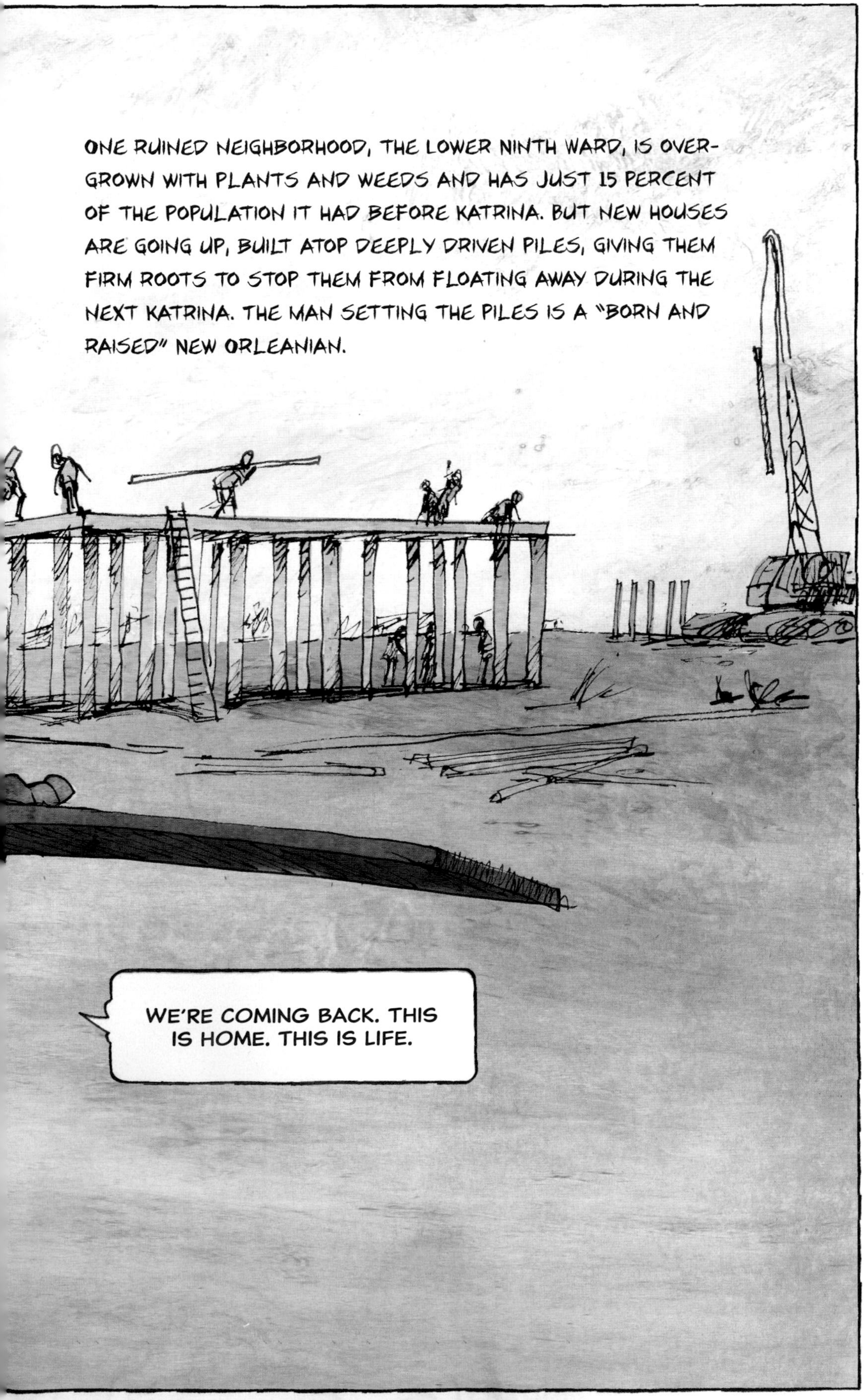
ONE RUINED NEIGHBORHOOD, THE LOWER NINTH WARD, IS OVERGROWN WITH PLANTS AND WEEDS AND HAS JUST 15 PERCENT OF THE POPULATION IT HAD BEFORE KATRINA. BUT NEW HOUSES ARE GOING UP, BUILT ATOP DEEPLY DRIVEN PILES, GIVING THEM FIRM ROOTS TO STOP THEM FROM FLOATING AWAY DURING THE NEXT KATRINA. THE MAN SETTING THE PILES IS A "BORN AND RAISED" NEW ORLEANIAN.
WE'RE COMING BACK. THIS IS HOME. THIS IS LIFE.

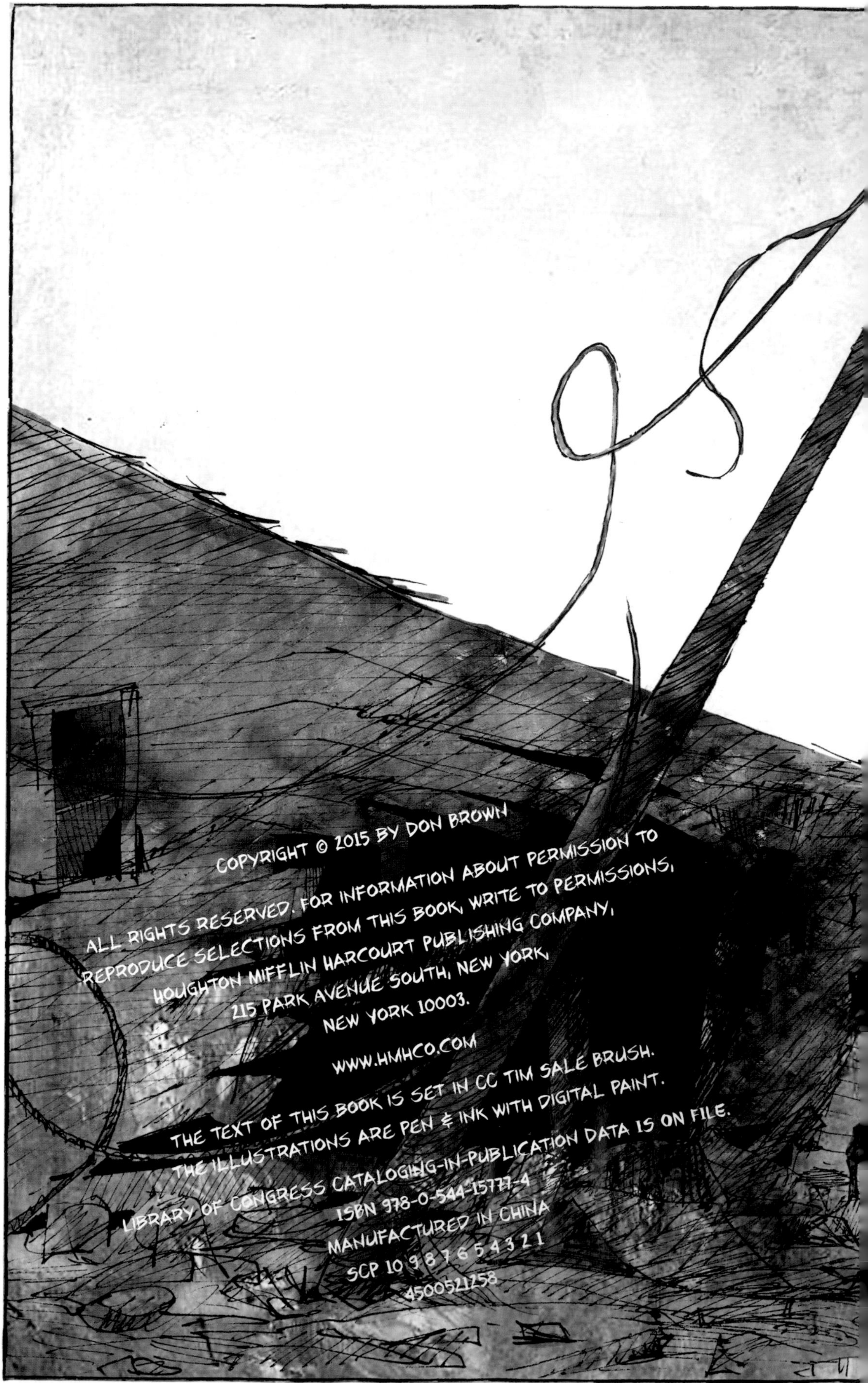

WWW.HMHCO.COM

THE TEXT OF THIS BOOK IS SET IN CC TIM SALE BRUSH.
THE ILLUSTRATIONS ARE PEN & INK WITH DIGITAL PAINT.
LIBRARY OF CONGRESS CATALOGING-IN-PUBLICATION DATA IS ON FILE.
ISBN 978-0-544-15777-4
MANUFACTURED IN CHINA
SCP 10 9 8 7 6 5 4 3 2 1
4500521258

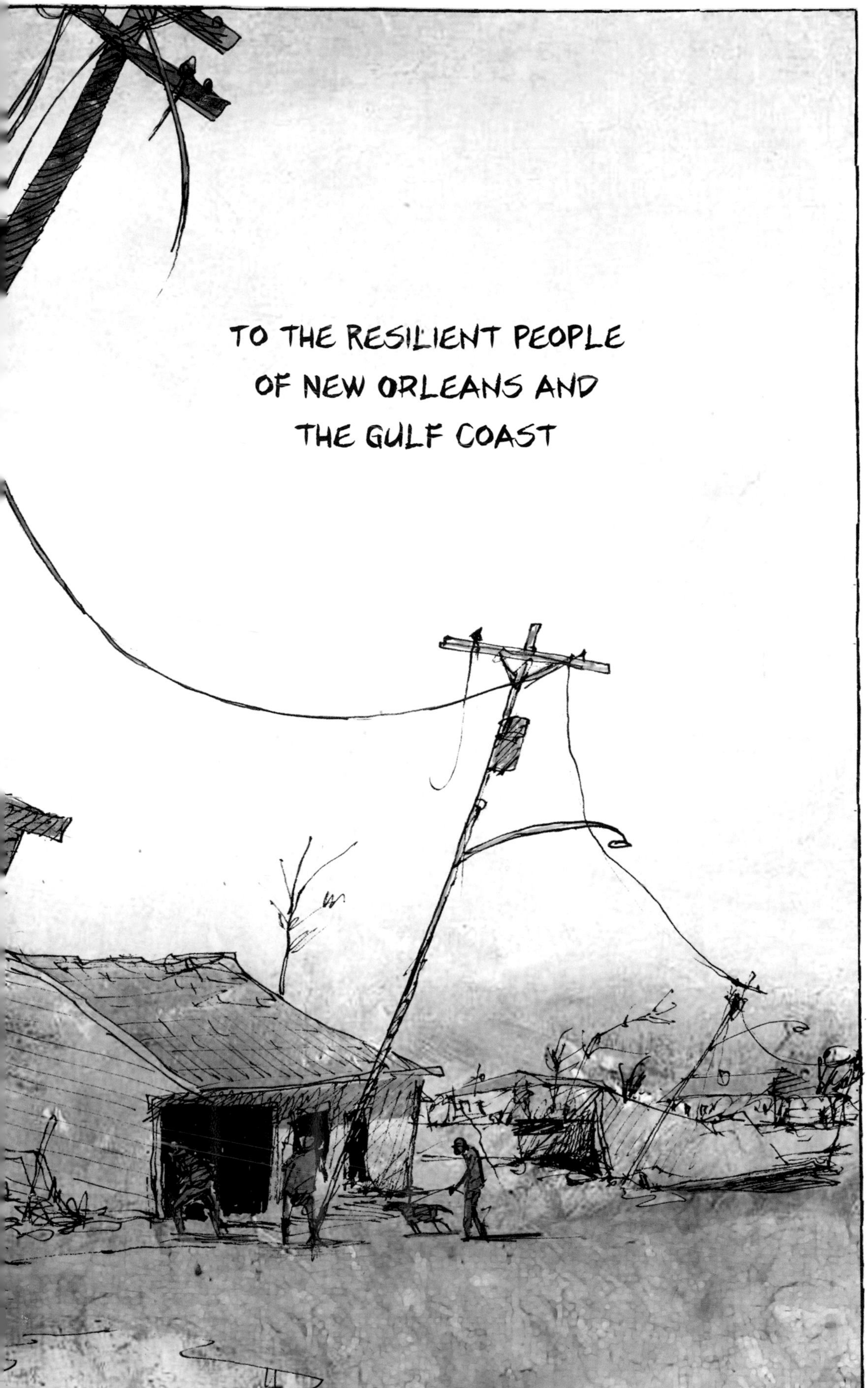
TO THE RESILIENT PEOPLE
OF NEW ORLEANS AND
THE GULF COAST

SOURCE NOTES

A swirl of unremarkable wind: Cooper and Block, 96.

From a smudge of foul weather: Cooper and Block.

Hurricane Katrina slices: Brinkley, 3.

Katrina careens: Hurricane Katrina Advisory Number 25; Brinkley, 17.

And it is swirling: Brinkley, 3.

Along with a major: Brinkley, 13.

"When I have a nightmare": Cooper and Block, 18.

On the morning of August 26: Brinkley, 79–80.

As it crosses the Gulf of Mexico: Hurricane Katrina Advisory Number 25.

When this bubble is coupled: Hurricane Katrina Advisory Number 23.

Sirens, bullhorns: Hurricane Katrina, 37.

People who are fortunate: Horne, 39.

But about 200,000: Cooper and Block, 122.

New Orleans's mayor, Ray Nagin, issues: Brinkley, 90.

"I'm just more comfortable": Thevenot and Torres.

"Come on then": Brinkley, 62.

But most who stay: Cooper and Block, 122; *Failure of Initiative,* 103, 111; Brinkley, 53.

Three hundred and sixty city buses: Brinkley, 90–91.

"We offered": Brinkley, 92.

The hurricane's strength: Failure of Initiative, 71.

At the last moment: Brinkley, 133.

Its eye sweeps: Ibid.

Two hundred and thirty-one people die: Failure of Initiative, 71; Mohr.

A drilling platform: Failure of Initiative, 71.

In New Orleans, ferocious winds: Horne, 44; Thomas.

The consequences: Horne, 63.

Water rolls: Horne, 77.

"I don't know": Cooper and Block, 126.

"It's gushing, gushing": Thevenot and Torres.

"Oh, baby, I don't think": Horne, 10.

In other attics: Thevenot and Torres.

A five-hundred-foot barge: Cooper and Block, 163.

A nearby oil refiner tank: Cooper and Block, 129.

The Army Corps of Engineers: Failure of Initiative, 89.

But Mayor Nagin: Hurricane Katrina, 90.

Although the roof is reportedly: Brinkley, 135.

The New Orleans Police Department: Brinkley, 117.

Some of the cops: Brinkley, 117.

Afterward, more than two hundred: Horne, 121.

Meanwhile, the Louisiana: Brinkley, 630.

By week's end: Brinkley, 297.

Over the next ten days: Brinkley, 213.

Hundreds of ordinary people: Horne, 66, 69.

It is not a shelter: Brinkley, 276; Cooper and Block, 176.

Fuel for its emergency generator: Failure of Initiative, 281.

But the people there: Brinkley, 631.

Shops and businesses: Philbin.

The mayhem encourages: Peristein and Thevenot; Horne.

Some gun-toting business owners: Thevenot, Spera, Russell, and MacCash.

"We need your help": Horne, 59–60.

"We've got equipment": Cooper and Block, 143.

Eighty percent of New Orleans: Horne, 84.

The dark is filled: MacCash and O'Byrne.

Water still washes: Shea, "Daylong Efforts."

Telephone poles lie: Lewis.

At first, the water: Horne, 74.

Now the water: Hurricane Katrina, 19; "Katrina's Public Health Risks."

Barely working communications: Cooper and Block, 172.

"We are completely": Shea, "Weariness, Danger."

Across the city: Horne, 76.

"This was the Big One": Cooper and Block, 160.

Waist-high water: Cooper and Block, 154.

She asks Brown: Cooper and Block, 163.

Electric pumps needed: Brinkley, 631.

"The sewers": Brinkley, 481.

A hospital worker: Hurricane Katrina, 87.

All manner of saved people: Lee, "Rescues Continue."

"I don't think they have a clue": Varney.

"I don't know where my baby is!": Witt and Fergus.

About five thousand children: Horne, 181.

"We are constantly": Cooper and Block, 172.

Lake Pontchartrain: Brinkley, 633.

In turn, the water: "Engineers Punching Holes."

Governor Blanco: Brinkley, 633.

New arrivals at the Superdome: Brinkley, 632.

FEMA promises: Cooper and Block, 184–86.

Meanwhile, three thousand victims: Hurricane Katrina, 43.

Rescue helicopters and boats: Failure of Initiative, 194; Brinkley, 405; Hurricane Katrina, 43, 113.

Rescuers report guns fired: Brinkley, 508.

A helicopter searches: Cooper and Block, 184–86.

"This is overwhelming." Cooper and Block, 190.

While heading back: Cooper and Block, 191.

Within days, Texas: Hurricane Katrina, 98–99.

A navy hospital: Cooper and Block, 187.

"I never stole": Horne, 81.

Mayor Nagin claims: Failure of Initiative, 249.

None of the rumors: Horne, 108, 109.

More than 15,000 people: Brinkley, 634.

Mayor Nagin is never: Failure of Initiative, 281.

"The smell was real bad": Williams.

"We are out here": Horne, 115.

"Help us!": Ibid.

The 25,000 people: Russell; Failure of Initiative, 80.

"Nagin should come speak": Russell.

About seven thousand people: Brinkley, 464; Failure of Initiative, 310.

"I don't want to be": Brinkley, 464.

The evacuees retreat: Kopp.

"It's like flying": Hurricane Katrina, 85.

Scores of sick: Witt with Fergus.
The floodwaters are now filthy: Brinkley, 407; *Hurricane Katrina,* 112.
Wading through it: Lewis; *Failure of Initiative,* 282.
Swallowing just a drop: Brinkley, 318.
On an open wound: "*Vibrio* Illnesses."
Just the smell: Brinkley, 407.
The threat of disease: NPR News Special Coverage.
Dogs stagger down: Horne, 123; *Hurricane Katrina,* 112.
Animal lovers: Brinkley, 516–18.
The newsman asks: Koppel.
Smoke from several fires: Hurricane Katrina, 45.
Rubble and garbage: Hurricane Katrina, 114.
"*We have no orders*"*:* Dinmore, "City of Rape."
"*Brownie, you're doing*"*:* Horne, 93.
President Bush and Governor Blanco: Brinkley, 636.
"*It's like a solid wall*"*:* NPR News Special Coverage.
One of them: Weekend Edition Sunday.
Hundreds of buses: Hurricane Katrina, 47.
National Guard troops: Brinkley, 564.
They are so anxious: Brinkley, 210.
Thousands of others: Williams.
Young soldiers: All Things Considered.
Disaster teams search: Brinkley, 406.
Afterward, teams mark: Moye; Lee, *When the Levees Broke.*
The Red Cross alone shelters: Hurricane Katrina, 100.
Levees are repaired: Hurricane Katrina, 114.
By 2012: United States Census Bureau.
One ruined neighborhood: Rich.
"*We're coming back*"*: Build It Bigger.*

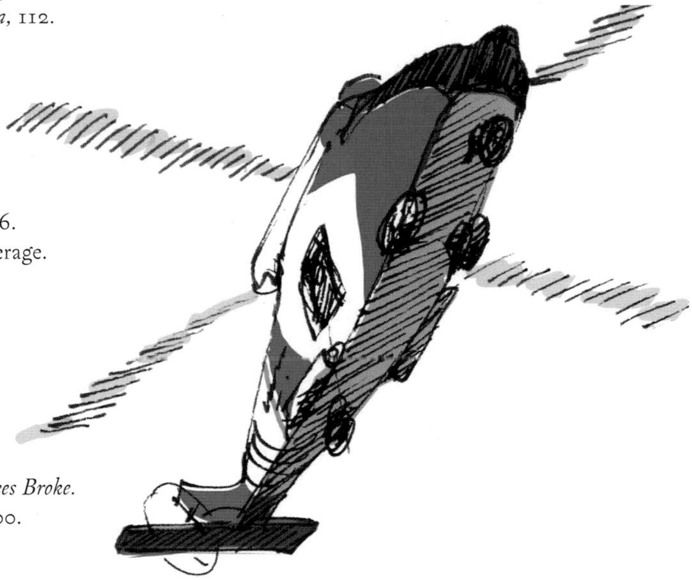

BIBLIOGRAPHY

All Things Considered. NPR. September 3, 2008.
Brinkley, Douglas. *The Great Deluge.* New York: Harper Perennial, 2007.
Build It Bigger. Science Channel. April 22, 2010.
"Chertoff: Katrina Scenario Did Not Exist." Cnn.com, September 5, 2005. (edition.cnn.com/2005/US/09/03/katrina.chertoff/index.html)
Cooper, Christopher, and Robert Block. *Disaster: Hurricane Katrina and the Failure of Homeland Security.* New York: Henry Holt and Company, 2006.
Dinmore, Guy. "City of Rape, Rumor, and Recrimination." *Financial Times* online, September 5, 2005. (guydinmore.wordpress.com/2005/09/05/city-of-rape-rumour-and-recrimination).
——. "Military Occupation Turns New Orleans into War Zone." *Financial Times* online, September 6, 2005. (www.ft.com/intl/cms/s/0/432369b2-1f0a-11da-94d5-00000e2511c8.html#axzz37lUTv8Ct).
"Engineers Punching Holes in Levee to Speed Draining." *New Orleans Times Picayune,* September 1, 2005, A1.
A Failure of Initiative: Final Report of the Select Bipartisan Committee to Investigate the Preparation for and Response to Hurricane Katrina. H. Rept 109-377. Washington, D.C.: U.S. Government Printing Office, 2006.
Horne, Jed. *Breach of Faith: Hurricane Katrina and the Near Death of a Great American City.* New York: Random House, 2008.
"Humanity Prevails in New Orleans." *All Things Considered.* NPR. September 3, 2005.
Hurricane Katrina: The Storm That Changed America. New York: Time Books, 2005.
Hurricane Katrina Advisory Number 23. Bulletin from the National Weather Service/National Hurricane Center, August 28, 2005. (www.nhc.noaa.gov/archive/2005/pub/al122005.public.023.shtml?)
Hurricane Katrina Advisory Number 25. Bulletin from the National Weather Service/National Hurricane Center, August 28, 2005. (www.nhc.noaa.gov/archive/2005/pub/al122005.public.025.shtml?)
"Identifying Katrina's Victims." Transcript of December 28, 2005, episode of *PBS NewsHour.* (www.pbs.org/newshour/bb/science/july-dec05/katrina_12-28.html)
"Katrina's Public Health Risks." Transcript of September 12, 2005, episode of *PBS NewsHour.* (www.pbs.org/newshour/bb/weather-july-dec05-dentzer_9-12)
Kopp, Carol. "The Bridge to Gretna: Why Did Police Block Desperate Refugees from New Orleans?" CBS News online. December 15, 2005.

Koppel, Ted. Interview with Michael Brown. *Nightline,* ABC, September 1, 2005.

Lee, Spike. *When the Levees Broke.* HBO, 2006.

Lee, Trymaine D. "Rescues Continue as City Hospitals Lose Generator Power." *New Orleans Times Picayune,* September 1, 2005, A2.

Lewis, Michael. "Wading Toward Home." *New York Times,* October 9, 2005.

MacCash, Doug, and James O'Byrne. "'We Lost Everything: Cars, Art, Furniture, Everything.'" *New Orleans Times Picayune,* August 30, 2005, A2.

MacQuarrie, Brian. "LA Governor Calls for More Troops as Violence Rises in New Orleans." *Boston Globe,* September 2, 2005, A1.

Martinez, Michael. "A Desperate SOS." *Chicago Tribune,* September 2, 2005, 1.1.

Mohr, Holbrook. "Katrina's Wind and Rain Hit Mississippi Coast Just as Hard." *New Orleans Times Picayune,* August 30, 2005, A12.

Moye, Dorothy. "Katrina + 5: An X-Code Exhibition." *Southern Spaces: An Interdisciplinary Journal about Regions, Places, and Cultures in the US South and Their Global Connections.* (www.southernspaces.org/2010/katrina-5-x-code-exhibition#section2)

NPR News Special Coverage. September 3, 2005.

Peristein, Mike, and Brian Thevenot. "Looters Leave Nothing Behind in Storm's Wake." *New Orleans Times Picayune,* August 31, 2005, A5.

Philbin, "Widespread Looting Hits Abandoned Businesses." *New Orleans Times Picayune,* August 30, 2005, A19.

Rich, Nathaniel. "Jungleland: The Lower Ninth Ward in New Orleans Gives New Meaning to 'Urban Growth.'" *New York Times Magazine,* March 21, 2012. (www.nytimes.com/2012/03/25/magazine/the-lower-ninth-ward-new-orleans.html?pagewanted=all&_r=0)

Russell, Gordon. "Refugees Find Dome an Intolerable Refuge." *New Orleans Times Picayune,* September 1, 2005, p. A5.

Shea, Dan. "Daylong Efforts to Repair Levee Fail." *New Orleans Times Picayune,* August 31, 2005, A1.

———. "Weariness, Danger, Death Take Hold in Drowned City." *New Orleans Times Picayune,* August 31, 2005, A2.

"The Storm." *Frontline* PBS, November 22, 2005.

Suggs, Ernie. "Most Came with Tales, Little Else." *Atlanta Journal-Constitution,* September 2, 2005, C2.

Thevenot, Brian, and Manuel Torres. "Hundreds Believed to Be Trapped in Their Attics." New Orleans Times Picayune, August 30, 2005, A7.

Thevenot, Brian, and Keith Spera, Gordon Russell, and Doug MacCash. "Old West Has Nothing on Katrina Aftermath." *New Orleans Times Picayune,* August 31, 2005, A7.

Thomas, Greg. "CBD Landmarks in Tatters; Poydras Littered with Debris." *New Orleans Times Picayune,* August 30, 2005, A8.

Varney, Jim. "Empty I-10 a Triage Center." *New Orleans Times Picayune,* August 31, 2005, A13.

"*Vibrio* Illnesses After Hurricane Katrina—Multiple States, August–September 2005." *Morbidity and Mortality Weekly Report* (Centers for Disease Control and Prevention) 54, no. 37 (2005): 928–31. (www.cdc.gov/mmwr/preview/mmwrhtml/mm5437a5.htm)

United States Census Bureau. State and County QuickFacts—New Orleans, Louisiana. (quickfacts.census.gov/qfd/states/22/2255000.html)

United States Department of Commerce. Service Assessment: Hurricane Katrina, August 23–31, 2005. (www.nws.noaa.gov/om/assessments/pdfs/Katrina.pdf)

Weekend Edition Sunday. NPR. September 4, 2005.

Williams, Mike. "Water, Fire, Thieves Make City a Waking Nightmare." *Atlanta Journal-Constitution,* September 3, 2005, A1.

Williams, Mike, and Ken Herman. "Help at Last: Federal Response Takes Flak as Bush Tours Region." *Atlanta Journal-Constitution,* September 3, 2005, A1.

Witt, Howard, and Michael Martinez. "Thousands Feared Dead in Lawless City." *Chicago Tribune,* September 1, 2005, 1.1.

Witt, Howard, with Mary Fergus. "A Sad, Slow Procession for Refugees." *Chicago Tribune,* September 1, 2005, 1.1.

SEP 1 4 2015